The Birdwatcher's Companion

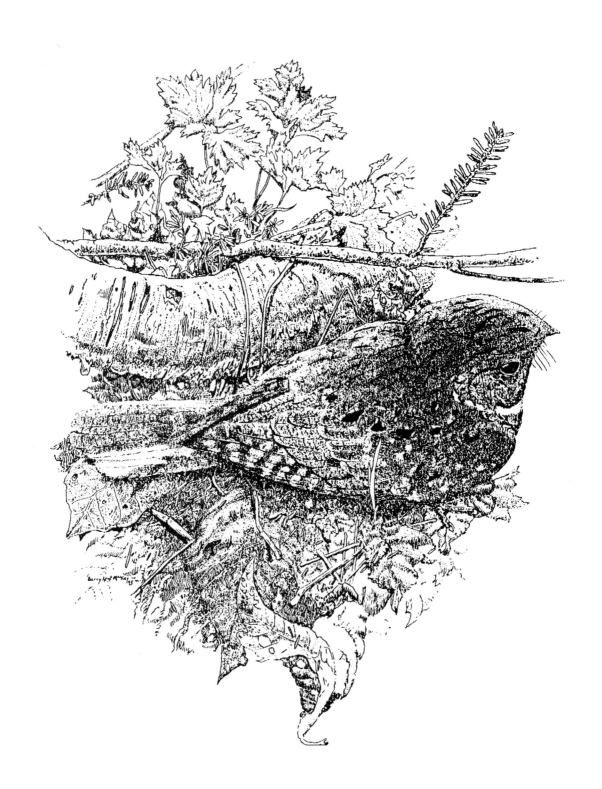

THE

BIRDWATCHER'S
COMPANION

BARRY KENT MacKAY

KEY PORTER·BOOKS

Dedicated to:
My friend, mentor and birding companion,
Dr. J. Murray Speirs

CANADIAN CATALOGUING IN PUBLICATION DATA

MacKay, Barry Kent, date
The birdwatcher's companion

ISBN 1-55013-467-1

1. Bird watching – Canada – Guidebooks.
2. Bird watching – United States – Guidebooks.
I. Title.
QL681.M33 1994   598'.0723471   C94-930042-X

Key Porter Books Limited
70 The Esplanade
Toronto, Ontario
M5E 1R2

Distributed in the United States of America by
National Book Network, Inc.
4720 Boston Way
Lanham, MD 20706

The publisher gratefully acknowledges the assistance of the Canada Council
and the Ontario Arts Council in the publication of this work.

Design: Scott Richardson
Typesetting: MacTrix DTP
Printed and bound in Canada

94 95 96 97 98 6 5 4 3 2 1

PAGE i:
WHITE-THROATED SPARROW

PAGE ii:
WHIP-POOR-WILL

OPPOSITE:
GRAY FLYCATCHER

C O N T E N T S

Introduction
1

I
MY CORNER OF THE CONTINENT
11

II
THE EAST COAST
59

III
THE SOUTH
91

IV
THE WEST
115

V
PRAIRIE AND POLAR BIRDING
167

Journal
185

Index
211

GREAT KISKADEE

INTRODUCTION

Like the character Merlin in T. H. White's tales about King Arthur, I sometimes feel I've led my life backward, or at least, I have done so with regard to my attitudes toward birding.

To be sure, I began young and in the usual way with the checklist of bird species to be found in my Peterson's *Field Guide to the Birds.* The checklist remained largely innocent of check marks for years. Would I *ever* see a prothonotary warbler, ruff, phainopepla, gyrfalcon or anhinga? Now those birds are checked off in my Peterson's guide, and in that respect the arrow of time has pointed me in the normal direction.

It is my attitude that has been backward, temporally speaking. As a child, my first interest in birds was predominantly scientific. Science was my obvious calling and birds were what I would ever-so-objectively study, spending my adulthood bent over trays of preserved bird specimens, writing and illustrating books about birds, and looking for birds in far and exotic places. I thus tried to start where it might have made more sense to end up.

While generally assuming my life would be spent as a collector and ornithologist, I was certain that I would be an artist in the tradition of the world's great bird illustrators: American Louis Agassiz Fuertes, dead long before my birth; the Canadian bird illustrator Major Allan Brooks, whose works were widely published and who died about the time of my birth; American ornithologist and bird artist George M. Sutton, who followed in the footsteps of Fuertes with his

exquisite watercolors and life studies; and British bird artist
D. M. Reid-Henry, whose works astounded me with their
fidelity to the birds he so wonderfully portrayed. Of particular
influence was Terence M. Shortt, whom I had the greatest
pleasure of knowing during his last decades, when he was the
finest of Canadian bird artists. The first time I met him, I was
so little that my feet dangled in the air as I sat on a chair in
his office. I visited him frequently, showing him my own
immature efforts at drawing birds and then watching in awe
as he took a pencil and, with a few deft strokes, showed me
what I had been doing wrong.

Roger Tory Peterson, more than any literary,
entertainment or sports celebrity, was one of my heroes and
role models. I also admired and envied the nature columnists
who wrote for the three newspapers in my city. Rachel
Carson became another of my heroes after I read her famous
book, *Silent Spring*. That volume explained with carefully
compiled documentation how we were methodically poisoning our environment, and for that reason alone, it was an
important part of my education. What most interested me
was not so much the book itself, however, as some of the
reaction to it. Carson came under intense, personal attack
from influential people with interests in the chemical and
pesticide industries. They could not defend themselves with
logic and reason but, instead, used their financial resources to
attack Carson personally, apparently in the belief that if they
could publicize something unsavory about her, they would
succeed in discrediting her findings. It was an early lesson in
environmental activism.

I hated school for keeping me indoors and tried to
fashion the basement at home into some kind of museum and
studio for the study of all that interested me, most of that being
birds and other animals. From my third year to my early teens,
except for a few years spent in Los Angeles, California, my
family lived in Toronto, Ontario. Most of my early birding
away from my immediate home turf was in or around Ajax

LONG-EARED OWL (NESTLING)

and Whitby, just east of Toronto, on the shores of Lake Ontario. My mother, Phyllis E. MacKay, was an early pioneer in what is now called wildlife rehabilitation, and wherever we lived as I was growing up, our home was filled with live birds of many species, as well as sketches, drawings and photographs of birds; dead birds and preserved specimens of birds; books about birds; and, very often, visitors knowledgeable about birds.

On one occasion, however, a non-birder friend of my parents was standing in our small living room, talking with considerable animation about something or other. "Watch the owl," my mother cautioned, nodding toward a motionless long-eared owl sitting on a corner of the television set. The man glanced at the bird and then went on talking and gesticulating. Again he was warned and again he ignored the warning. Suddenly the owl did what owls sometimes do when threatened; he spread his wings into a broad fan with his head weaving and bill clacking. The shocked friend, in his haste to move away, fell to the floor, his legs twisted around each other. The owl looked down at him, then calmly straightened up, closed his wings, fluffed his feathers and resumed his sleepy-eyed, motionless stance. Our visitor had assumed that the bird was a stuffed specimen and that the warnings were that he not knock it off its stand.

Another visitor was made ill by the sight of a whip-poor-will opening its mouth. Whip-poor-wills and related species have tiny beaks, but huge mouths that extend back below the eyes. Apparently, as she explained upon returning from the bathroom, she had thought that the bird's head had divided into two. The pink, veined mouth-lining had looked like the bird's internal anatomy, suddenly exposed in some grotesque gesture of self-destruction by the bird.

We had countless adventures rescuing birds, and I developed singular, if not marketable, skills as a catcher of hurt or injured individuals. My art also required specimens as models and my shrill cry to "Stop the car!" could unnerve anyone unwise enough to drive me anywhere near an avian roadkill.

I checked every beach for birds and became positively vulturine in my attention to marshes where hunters often left crippled ducks or other species to die in the cattails. I wasn't always as concerned about the freshness of such specimens as I should have been and once when I skinned some overripe gulls in our backyard, we had complaints about the smell from several houses away. Strange, unpleasant odors were a frequent annoyance to the rest of the family.

In the late 1950s, after my mother became a bird bander licensed by the federal government, my parents and I caught, banded and released tens of thousands of birds. Each one had a lightweight, numbered aluminum band placed around one tarsus (the lengthened part of the foot often called the "leg"). The species, their age and sex, and the time and place of the banding were recorded in a log, along with their weight, their condition of molt, the amount of fat they were carrying or anything else that could be determined from a brief, in-hand examination. Then the birds would be released. Most were never heard from again, but some would be found later. The information, based on their band numbers, was centrally recorded in Ottawa and Washington, D.C., as part of a huge database of statistical information about bird migration routes, distribution, hazards and longevity.

My mother has always loved birds and was my companion on many of my first birding expeditions. My father, Charles Davison (Dave) MacKay, died many years ago. I vividly recall how he had to overcome an innate fear of anything fluttery, while I had to outgrow an allergy to feathers. I'm not sure either of us was entirely successful in our respective endeavors.

My father put up with my interest in birds (and even shared it) but he had to endure that fear of anything small and fluttery, from moths caught to feed fledglings to small sparrows and finches that could trigger alarm by unexpectedly flying near to him. Once he decided to lay tiles on the stairs going downstairs. He spread the top landing with glue, then moved down a step, spread glue and moved down a step, and so on, to the basement, with the intent of then reversing the procedure and laying the tiles from the bottom step up. Unfortunately, when he reached the bottom step, one of my smaller birds was flying loose and poor Dad panicked and ran up the steps, through all the glue he had just put down.

In time my list of birds encountered grew to respectable proportions, but as that was happening, my attitudes were shifting. My love of trying to be logical revealed hypocrisy in many of my dealings with animals, and I slowly became involved with the so-called "animal rights" movement. I dislike the overused terms "animal rights" and "animal liberation" because of their connotations with extreme fundamentalism. I prefer to call myself an animal protectionist, seeing that as part of a continuum of social concern for others.

In the last twenty years I have significantly expanded my horizons and acquired new and cherished friends in the process. Some barely know a tanager from a teal, but they share the kind of respect for each that I think is ultimately essential if we are to at least slow current rates of environmental degradation and species extinction. If there is no other reason for constantly questioning the nature of our relationships with other species, it is the fact that we are currently experiencing the greatest rates of extinction since the loss of the dinosaurs, and humans are the prime cause of this horrendous and permanent loss of species.

The changes in my own activities were profound as I put away my guns and nets and changed my diet to vegetarianism. As a lifelong naturalist, however, I recognize the very naturalness of our consumptive and competitive behavior, and I am leery of the self-righteous dogmatism that characterizes extremists on both sides of controversies surrounding animal protection. While I don't expect all birders to share my depth of concern for the welfare of non-human species, I am heartened by their growing sense of responsibility toward birds.

Many of the things that birders, myself included, used to
do are now frowned upon. We no longer clear vegetation
from nests to allow better pictures to be taken; we don't
follow northern owls about, pointing telephoto cameras and
telescopes at them, driving them from perch to perch when
they should be resting or hunting; we don't swarm around
a nervous rarity, preventing it from eating or resting; we
don't rush at flocks of resting or feeding shorebirds to force
them to flight so we may look for identifying wing and
lower back patterns; we don't continuously play territorial
songs in the habitat of a nesting rarity to entice it into view
or provoke an interesting reaction; and we don't drag ropes
across fields in order to flush ground-nesting meadowlarks,
upland sandpipers and other species. And if we do indulge
in such activities, we risk censure from more progressive
and concerned birders.

After a hiatus of several years spent working full time
and overtime on behalf of animal protection, I find myself
again enjoying the pleasures of painting and drawing birds,
writing about them and simply birding, the latter often done
on the run during travels for other reasons. Seeing a new
species of bird in its native habitat remains one of my greatest
thrills, and that thrill, impossible to explain or quantify, has
remained a constant through my life. I now find less pleasure
in the science of ornithology as an end in itself, less interest in
the collection of long lists of birds seen and more interest in
the kind of contemplation that, I suspect, first leads most
people to start birding.

The title of a book by George M. Sutton, *Mexican
Birds: First Impressions*, appealed to me in my childhood, as
did the text of the book and Sutton's beautiful illustrations.
First impressions are the strongest and sometimes they are the
most valid. Most of what follows primarily deals with my
first impressions of some of the countless wonderful birding
localities to be found in North America.

I cannot answer the question, frequently asked of me,

of how I first became interested in birds. From earliest childhood the interest was simply there. As a person who shares that interest, I hope you will take advantage of the opportunity provided at the back of this book to record the birds and other wildlife you see, along with your first or any other impressions of your experiences afield.

TOPOGRAPHY OF BIRDS

1	Tongue	16	Primary coverts	31	Knee
2	Upper Mandible	17	Flank	32	Shin ("Thigh")
3	Lores	18	Tibia	33	Talon (Claw)
4	Eye	19	Heel	34	"Ear" Tuft
5	Crown	20	Tarsus ("Leg")	35	Forehead or Forecrown
6	Eye Stripe (Supercilliary)	21	Toes	36	Facial Disk
7	Ear Covert (Auricular)	22	Belly	37	Gorget
8	Nape	23	Greater Wing Coverts	38	Beak or Bill
9	Upper Back	24	Middle Wing Coverts	39	Cere
10	Scapulars	25	Breast	40	Nostril
11	Secondaries	26	Lesser Wing Coverts	41	Orbital Ring
12	Primaries	27	Bend of Wing (Wrist)	42	Lower Back
13	Tail Feathers (Retrices)	28	Throat	43	Rump
14	Upper Tail Coverts	29	Chin	44	Alulua ("Bastard Wing")
15	Under Tail Coverts	30	Lower Mandible		

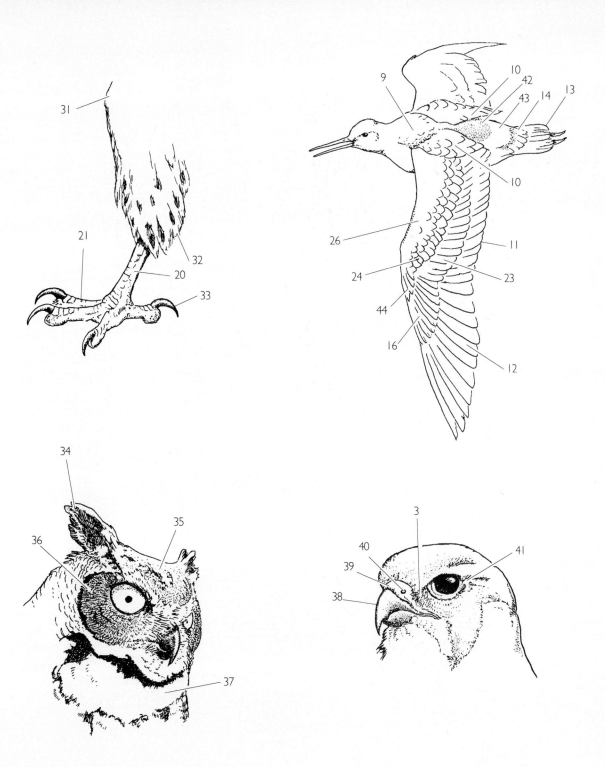

SAW-WHET OWL

I
MY CORNER OF
THE CONTINENT

P O I N T P E L E E

It's heresy for a birder to say so, I know, but for me mornings have often been the downside of birding. Early morning is the time a birder is supposed to be afield because that's when birds are most active. Mind you, I enjoy being up with, or even a little before, the sun; it's just that I seldom enjoy the process of getting up early and must do so, at times, with steely resolve.

One spring in the 1950s I arrived at Point Pelee with my parents late at night. The next morning, I tumbled out of bed, pulled on my clothes without indicating that I had even seen anyone (according to subsequent claims by my parents) and shuffled off into the early morning splendor of low, glowing sun, newly unfolding leaves, dew and birdsong. It was my first morning ever at Point Pelee, where my parents had rented a motel room in the days when it was possible to do so inside the park. I was probably nine or ten years of age and the keenest of birders. Breakfast could wait.

As I was nearly sleepwalking, I doubt that I noticed many birds at first as I began making my way through an old orchard and toward the woods beyond. But then I pushed my way through a dripping hedgerow and nearly stepped on a red fox. The fox twisted about, looked at me through pupils rimmed in amber and, possibly deciding I was too big to be eaten and too little to be feared, turned around slowly and continued on his way. It was the best view of a wild fox I had ever experienced and brought me fully awake to a day of birding adventure.

SUMMER TANAGER

VISITING POINT PELEE

Point Pelee National Park is just south of the town of Leamington, Ontario. Most birders go there in early May, although September is the second-best month for migrant birds. While there may be enough in the park to keep birders happy, often experienced birders will also look for birds in the onion fields and Hillman (Stein's) Marsh, just outside the park, or in nearby Rondeau Provincial Park. Many local motels cater to naturalists, and in May and September it's advisable to book accommodation in advance.

LIFE BIRD

A life bird, or lifer, is a bird species encountered and identified for the first time. It is added to the birder's life list. Birders impose a variety of rules governing what qualifies as a life bird, but in general it must be a free-living, wild bird that has not originally escaped from captivity. Some birders don't count those species of birds heard but not seen; some birders don't count species of birds seen but identified by someone else. Not all birders maintain life lists, but even some of us who have no such list still count the finding of a lifer as a major thrill of birding.

Point Pelee is like that; although the park is famous for its birds, it is a place to expect the unexpected from nature. And that is what the best birding, which ought to have a better name, is really about – the enjoyment of birds, along with other wildlife and the surrounding environment.

Point Pelee, Ontario, is the southernmost projection of mainland Canada. From the air it can be seen as the tip of a funnel where the land tapers, from north to south, to a sandy point thrusting into the southern end of Lake Erie. It's easy to see why southbound migrant birds tend to concentrate at the bottom of the funnel each autumn. There they can feed and rest before spilling out across the water, continuing south.

If northbound migrants cross the lake at its southern end, or follow the shoreline from the St. Clair River, they will arrive at Pelee. And while the point has always attracted large numbers of avian migrants, the exhaustive deforestation of southwestern Ontario has left the wooded areas of Point Pelee National Park as an oasis for flycatchers, jays, nuthatches, creepers, wrens, catbirds, thrashers, thrushes, gnatcatchers, kinglets, waxwings, vireos, warblers, tanagers and other woodland species. They can be found there on the best birding days each spring and fall, sometimes in spectacular numbers of both species and individuals. This is a place, unlike most on the continent, where daily counts of well over a hundred species are almost routine during the height of the migration. More than three hundred species have been recorded in the park, and of special interest to many birders, a disproportionate number of rarities have been seen at Pelee. Even when things are bad they can be good. I remember "slow" days when relatively few species were seen, but there would still be an impressive rarity or two, or perhaps large numbers of a few species, such as migrant sharp-shinned hawks in the fall.

The point is at the same latitude as northern California. It's home to such southern fauna and flora as five-lined skinks, prickly pear cacti and tulip trees. Flowering dogwoods bloom there, and if you are very lucky, you may encounter a chuck-will's-widow, red-bellied woodpecker or Bell's vireo perched among them. The assembly of plant and animal species that constituted the vast Carolinian forests of eastern North America reached their northern limits in this region, where they were systematically destroyed in the nineteenth century to be replaced by geometric patterns of farmland. All that remains of the original forests are a few remnants to be found in Point Pelee, nearby Rondeau Provincial Park and a few other sites in southwestern Ontario. The surrounding land-scape is pancake flat, highly cultivated and well-drained farm-land, with remnant patches of second growth woods here and there, like spots of green ink splattered on a checkerboard.

It may partly be a self-perpetuating function of the numbers of birders who visit Pelee that it has been known to host such an awesome variety of rare birds. The more birders there are the less likelihood of a rarity escaping detection. Northern gannet, white ibis, white-fronted goose, fulvous whistling duck, cinnamon teal, American swallow-tailed kite, Mississippi kite, Swainson's hawk, gyrfalcon, long-tailed jaeger, black skimmer, thick-billed murre, lesser nighthawk, rufous hummingbird, Lewis' woodpecker, sage thrasher, Townsend's solitaire, Virginia's warbler, black-throated gray warbler, lark bunting, Cassin's sparrow – a partial list of rarities from the region reads like a grab bag of North American bird species representing all parts of the continent.

With so many people going to Pelee now, things have to be more carefully regulated than when I was a youngster. We banded birds there, stringing mist nets through the grapevine entanglements at the point and making ourselves entirely unpopular by chasing what others had come to see into our nets. Bird banders were eventually banned, and quite rightly, although I cannot deny the fondness of my childhood memories of catching birds there, including my first Bewick's wren. How delicate the woodsy shades of brown were in the small bird; how fine and fragile the darker pencil tracings

BIRDING ETHICS

While there will always be "boorish birders," more and more people are remembering their manners and respecting others. Do not enter private property without permission. Always leave gates as you found them. Respect wild vegetation, lawns, gardens, crops and livestock. Respect the birds themselves and respect other birders' access to good viewing areas by taking turns. (I remember my frustration, as a child, at not being able to see past a cluster of adults gathered in front of a boreal chickadee, and thus having to wait another decade to see the species.) Sometimes frictions occur between birders and photographers when both have a legitimate "claim" on the bird. Few places have a better designed infrastructure to assist birders than Point Pelee, but respect for others is always a necessary component to produce maximum enjoyment for everyone.

BLACK-THROATED BLUE WARBLER

were on its wings and tail, the latter with corners of parchment white. How privileged I felt to hold and sketch so perfect a being.

At Pelee I first saw the golden flash of a prothonotary warbler. My first summer tanager, my best look at a Henslow's sparrow, my first discovery of a red-throated loon and many other first or best sightings have all happened at Pelee. There were times when the twigs and branches swarmed with multitudes of highly colored migrant songbirds. The colors to be found in the feathers of a scarlet tanager, a yellow warbler, a red-headed woodpecker, an indigo bunting or a northern oriole were supernatural in their intensity. Here was my first tufted titmouse, blue-gray gnatcatcher and orchard oriole, all species whose names conjured southern places I then had yet to visit.

Although I spent a lot of time catching and handling birds, I'd also go off in pursuit of them, going from shoreline to hedgerow and from swamp to marsh. Sometimes we'd drive to ponds and sewage settling ponds near the park, particularly in response to reports of a flock of lesser golden plovers or a sighting of a Eurasian wigeon or a great egret.

There is always debate among birders about the virtues of staying in one likely place and the virtues of going off in active search of birds. Pelee is home of the "Big Sit," an inactive activity involving nothing more than sitting in one place and letting the birds come to the birder. It is probably one of the best places I know to do this, and I've always argued that taking up a quiet post in a good habitat is an excellent way to see birds. However, being of a restless nature, I'm one of those who usually keeps moving. It's important to stay on trails to avoid damaging foliage, but away from such intensely used habitats as Pelee, I like to get off the trail. This does not always produce the best birding. On the contrary, the best birding is usually at the edge, not the middle, of habitat. There's more to birding than birds, though, and such penetrations often reveal ecological surprises and a different sense of the area.

In the fall I've stood in one place near the tip of Point Pelee and tried to calculate the numbers of blue jays dropping down into the trees in flock after flock. I estimated that one flock contained about five thousand birds, and it was only one of many such flocks that day. Walking through the old woods and abandoned orchards of the park, I've been thrilled by the dashing boldness of the sharp-shinned hawks as they pursue flickers, thrushes or other songbirds. Waterfowl, seabirds straying inland, shorebirds, field birds and marsh birds all find habitat in or near Point Pelee.

Birders came to Pelee from all corners of the continent, and still do, although some old-timers can be heard to complain that there are not as many birds to be seen there as there used to be. I seldom go there now, not since the day I decided there were more birders than birds and the mild phobia I've always had about crowds clicked in. I like to bird alone, with one or two companions (canine or human) or with a very small group.

Or maybe I rarely visit Pelee because I don't want to face the possibility that numerous studies are right – there are many fewer songbirds than there were when I was young. So many factors enter into such considerations that it is hard to be sure. Possibly more birds go elsewhere, or maybe our earliest memories are our fondest ones and can't be matched by the reality of the present.

I envy every neophyte birder going there for the first time on those special May mornings when a warm front has passed through. The birds are suddenly present in numbers beyond anything that could have been anticipated. Another black-throated blue warbler, white-eyed vireo or rose-breasted grosbeak is spotted. Then the word spreads among the birders that a blue grosbeak has shown up in Tilden's Woods – and have you seen the laughing gull down at the point, next to where the willet was the day before?

FINDING THE RARE ONES

A rare bird may occur virtually anywhere. The experienced birder carefully examines all birds in a flock of gulls, shorebirds, waterfowl or other species; tries to check out all habitats in an area; tracks down all unfamiliar bird calls; and knows what to expect and what might possibly occur in each place visited.

The more birders visit the site, the more likelihood that rarities will be found. Also, the more attractive a site is to birds, the more likelihood that rarities will occur there. Point Pelee scores exceptionally high in both categories. It's hard to imagine that a rarity could spend much time there during the height of the migration and not be found. Given the number of birders, the bulletin board where sightings are posted and the knowledgeable park naturalists on hand to assist birders, it's a good place to easily discover what's around.

L O N G   P O I N T

It was late at night and fiercely cold, with a few days left until October. To our right the gale forced a pounding surf against the beach. We could see nothing but what was illuminated in the headlights of our four-wheel-drive vehicle as we made our way along the beach. The sand ahead was breached by a black, snaking curl of water. With dunes and marshes to the left, we had no choice but to either challenge the shallow water, and hope to get through, or turn back. With adolescent bravado I was all for continuing.

But the water-soaked engine died on the other side. Don Baldwin, then a preparator of bird specimens for the ornithology department of Toronto's Royal Ontario Museum, was driving. I was his only passenger. We were now stranded. "What," asked Don, "do you know about engines?"

"Nothing," I replied. Don told me to get the flashlight, and after much fumbling in the dark I found it, only to discover it didn't work.

It turned out that Don knew enough about engines to be able to dry the right parts. He was forced to work by feel as there was no trace of light. The driving rain made it difficult for him to keep the rag he was using dry. The engine finally coughed to life, and we continued our long drive out to the tip of Long Point, Ontario.

Long Point projects many miles into Lake Erie, its contours changing from year to year from the eroding effects of wave action. From the air it appears as a long, vaguely

TUNDRA SWAN

scimitar-shaped sand-spit extending from the middle of Lake Erie's northwestern shore, with the cutting edge facing more or less south, in the form of a long, empty beach. In the waters surrounding the tip, milky-buff swirls of sandy sediment and barely submerged shoals are also often visible from an airplane window, particularly on a sunny day following heavy weather.

As we drove along the beach, our vehicle was the only human manifestation in the raging storm. After several eye-straining hours, occasionally seeing little flocks of sanderlings bleached white by the glare of our headlights as they ran up the shore in front of us or flashed into flight and were gone, we finally saw ghost-colored beams of light carving through the driving rain in the sky ahead. They came from the light-house at the end of the point. At about the same time, a ray of light shot up from behind the seat. A final jar had caused the flashlight to come on, now that we didn't need it.

We parked and walked over to the lightkeeper's residence. Inside, in bright, warm, coffee-scented comfort, we relaxed while the lightkeeper told us of the huge wreck that had happened the night before. He was talking not about a shipwreck, many of which have occurred in the treacherous shoals for which the area is infamous, but a different kind of wreck. "Come on," he said. "I'll show you."

He took us to another building. One of the two things that I remember most was how the night was filled with noise – the high-pitched peeping of unseen birds, the creaking branches, the painfully moaning foghorn, the shrieking wind, hissing sand and pounding surf. The other element of that night I remember most was the large number of stinkbugs. These flat, green insects, which looked like tiny, animated escutcheons, were everywhere, clinging to surfaces in numbers greater than I have seen before or since.

We entered the building and there, in mounded piles on the smooth concrete floor, were what we had come for: two thousand dead birds killed hitting the lighthouse the

SONG SPARROW

previous night. They were mostly songbirds, all of them picked up by the lighthouse keeper as a favor to the Ontario Bird Banders' Association. The association had recently set up what was to become the Long Point Bird Observatory, the continent's oldest such facility for ongoing field studies of birds. It then consisted of a simple cottage near the lighthouse.

The birds were to be used by the Royal Ontario Museum. Tabulations of species and number, weight, age and sex ratios would help scientists learn more about birds and migration hazards. In fact, Don Baldwin has since written technical papers on this subject.

At that time we knew that light emanating from tall structures would often attract nocturnal bird migrants, particularly on an overcast night. Stormy weather also forces some night migrants down into lower altitudes, where they risk hitting tall structures. However, this kill had happened on a starry night, as sometimes happens, although I don't think anyone has discovered yet why it does. Usually on a clear night birds will fly high, as if drawn toward the stars. The safest nights are when there is a clear sky and full moon. One thing is certain: light attracts most nocturnal migrants apart from waterfowl and shorebirds, and even they are occasionally encountered in nocturnal bird kills, or wrecks, as the English call them.

Unfortunately, birds will sometimes begin to migrate on a fair night when conditions seem perfect, only to encounter the dangers of bad weather hours after they start out. Such natural hazards alone can take fearful tolls. There are records from Long Point of millions of variably colored and patterned feathers washing up on the beach after a bad storm.

As my mother and I had been monitoring bird kills at a TV broadcasting tower near our home, I was pleased to have the opportunity to accompany Don to Long Point. The same night of that particular kill, some six hundred birds had been killed or injured hitting the broadcasting tower. My parents and I retrieved those birds and then called Don, who was

LONG POINT BIRDING

Late March and early April are the best times to see large numbers of waterfowl in the Long Point area. However, great flocks of tundra swans are less frequent now than in past decades; the birds disperse over a broader front in southwestern Ontario or favor the marshes of Lake St. Clair. Although much of this spectacular spit of beach, dune, woods and marsh is difficult for the average birder to access, the causeway extending from the base of the point out through the marshes on either side of the road (where there is a National Wildlife Area) to the main concentration of cottages is a good place for birding. Past the cottages is Long Point Provincial Park. Anywhere on the Point where there are ponds, marshes or stands of trees can provide good birding opportunities, and don't forget to check the beach and the expanse of Lake Erie. You might also want to visit Turkey Point, Backus Mill Conservation Area and other nearby sites with good bird habitat.

studying the problem by determining species and numbers of birds involved in such kills and the conditions under which these events occurred.

In the many years we did this work, a large number of the birds we found were still alive. Some were so badly injured they had to be euthanized, but others could be saved and released and they were our priority. Indeed, other benefits or studies aside, we engaged in this work to save injured birds and to try to convince management authorities of tall, illuminated structures to reduce lighting. Once the dead birds were tabulated, I would preserve them as specimens I could use in my artwork. (I had a federal permit to do this.) Others were donated to the museum.

Don and I spent the night in the bird bander's shack with only a thin wall between our heads and the fury of the storm. Sleep was constantly broken by the noise of the wind and the interminable chirping of birds, and once or twice by the screams of some animal, perhaps a rabbit, in distress. Once I blundered out into the night to see if I could find the source of the distressed sounds, but I could see nothing although I sensed the presence of small birds all around.

Our return journey was in daylight. As we drove the long way back along the point, we saw thousands of birds trying to cope with the strong winds. In the area of the cottages at the base of the point, we found thousands more white-throated sparrows, ovenbirds, red-eyed vireos, nuthatches, song sparrows and many other species huddled on window ledges, in wood piles and under buildings, seeking respite from the wind. Many of the birds were drenched and no doubt thousands of them perished as a result of being soaked by rain and chilled by wind. We were helpless to defend them against the fury of the elements.

Although that night was the first time I had been to the tip of Long Point, it wasn't my first visit to the area. That happened a number of years earlier. My parents and I went down to see the whistling swans, an adventure I enjoyed with

NOCTURNAL MIGRANTS

Most of the smaller, mainly insect-eating songbirds that nest in the temperate latitudes annually migrate to warmer climes. Many species migrate at night. They leave at dusk, normally on empty stomachs to reduce weight and fly all night. Because they lose a significant percentage of their starting weight through the night, in the morning they usually land and commence feeding. They may spend days, or even weeks, possibly with some daytime migratory movement, before again making an overnight flight on the next stage of a journey, which, depending on the species, may take them well into the tropics.

The same species that are nocturnal migrants in the fall are also night migrants in the spring. Spring migrations tend to be more compressed in time and involve fewer numbers, attrition having taken its toll.

childish enthusiasm. The whistling swan, now officially known as the tundra swan, was a species I had never seen.

Early spring weather and bird sightings at Long Point are both unpredictable, but I had the good fortune of first visiting the point on a beautiful, sunny morning when the earlier stages of bird migration were in full progress. First experiences can be the most intense in childhood and on that spring day I had many encounters with new avian species. As I have since seen so many beginning birders do, I fumbled with my field guide or asked questions of the experienced birders who lined the causeway, to determine what it was we were watching. I peered through borrowed telescopes and enthused over the crisp plumage of a drake goldeneye or the elegant perfection of a pair of ring-necked ducks or the fine patterning of a greater yellowlegs. After a long, gray winter, spring was suddenly a wonderfully explosive presence amid the woods, fields, marshes and bays of Long Point.

WHITE-THROATED SPARROW

Canvasbacks flew low over the water, their sharply sloping profiles distinct, their wings smaller than I thought they'd be. The speed and the dashing form of these hardy ducks greatly appealed to me. I've encountered canvasbacks countless times since and usually when I see them I think of those first canvasbacks, flying in long strings low over the water, their wings a throbbing blur. For me the species personifies wildness. The canvasback has suffered from habitat destruction and overhunting and I seldom now encounter large numbers of them in one place.

The great marshes of Long Point were saved by a private hunting club, formed in the previous century. Were it not for the hunters, the habitat would have been lost to the industry and agriculture that dominates the surrounding countryside, a fate suffered by much of the marshland in the lower Great Lakes region.

I have spent the better part of my life in opposing sport hunting, of which I consider waterfowling to be one of the cruelest manifestations. However, to deny that hunters have had, or in some instances continue to have, positive roles in protecting animals overall is to deny reality. On the other hand, to deny that the Long Point hunters have dumped many tons of toxic lead into the wetlands, wounded who knows how many thousands of birds or justified killing waterfowl in the name of sport is also to deny reality.

Those concerns were for the future. As a boy I lacked much knowledge about such things, content just to enjoy the vibrancy of the life around me. Oddly, two of the bird species I best remember from that memorable first visit are two of the most common species found throughout most of North America.

The first, the mourning doves, I remember for their gentle cooing at dawn. It was a softer version of the familiar sound of city pigeons, throaty and deeper at the beginning, and then rising to a higher pitch at the end. The lower neck and upper breast of the males swelled and then they bowed, cooing and partly spreading their wings and tails, as if enduring considerable effort to impress their nearby mates. If the female doves were impressed, they managed not to show it. The fawn-colored birds perched in the tops of towering elms and mature maples across the road from the small hotel where we had arrived the night before. Mourning doves are beautiful birds of graceful form and subtle color and, in those days, were strongly migratory in southern Ontario. Since then, they have become far more common, and far less migratory, so that it is hard for me to imagine that I once thought of their cooing as a particularly apt symbol of early spring.

The other bird species that impressed me is even more common. Red-winged blackbirds were everywhere. As we stood on the causeway, they arrived in flocks from across the lake, seeming to express great jubilation as they swept into the black willows and cattail marshes, singing their coarsely unmusical songs. As a boy I eschewed anthropomorphism, but that day I had to think that the birds were expressing joy at having successfully flown across Lake Erie.

What also impressed me about the red-wings was their coloring. In the spring sun, the black of their plumage was a darkly glowing blue, while the red of their epaulets glowed brilliantly scarlet as if illuminated from within. Those two colors were set off by the narrow buff band formed by their middle wing coverts. They were so vibrantly beautiful that I continued to stop and stare at them, no doubt to the amusement of older, seasoned birders.

The tundra swans were the main attraction, and while we saw and heard many, it was not until we drove over to nearby Turkey Point that we encountered the main flock. Three thousand birds, according to one estimate, were spread out over marshes and flooded fields below us as we stood on higher ground by the edge of the road. They seemed so transient, these snow-colored creatures of the Arctic. They make only a brief appearance each spring on their way from the Atlantic coast marshes to their tundra breeding grounds.

One year we stayed in a hotel filled with birders at the very base of the point, within view of the marshes, and awoke to the calling of multitudes of swans. Their calls are hauntingly beautiful. Such natural alarms, from the song of white-throated sparrows in the north woods to the yelling of mealy parrots in the lowland jungle of Costa Rica, are the only alarms I ever look forward to in the morning.

There is special joy for many of us in seeing groups of animals in large numbers. The fabled ungulate herds of Africa are a tourist attraction, as would be the bison herds of the plains had we not wiped them out. The tundra swans at Long Point gave me my first look at a huge number of animals in one place at one time.

When most people think "swans," they think of the orange-beaked, curve-necked mute swan of parks, zoos and estates, which is now an established feral species in parts of eastern North America, but native to Europe. I feel privileged to be able to see, each spring, so truly wild and native a species as the tundra swan, and sometimes in numbers that suggest

SWANS

Ontario is one of a growing number of places in eastern and midwestern North America where there is an effort underway to establish trumpeter swans, our largest swan species, in the wild. The trumpeter is somewhat bigger than the tundra swan and lacks the yellow spot in front of the eye usually found in the tundra. It also has a wine-colored "gape" mark on its beak, although it's usually only visible, if at all, at very close range. Unlike both tundras and trumpeters, the mute swan has an orange beak with a black knob at the base. Mutes usually carry their necks gracefully curved for longer periods than do the other two species, and the males often furl their back feathers into sail-like fans.

the wealth of life that once was common to this continent and this planet.

Each spring, birders try to guess when the best time to see the swans at Long Point might be. Sometimes the snow lies deep, the inshore water is frozen and the swans are few and far away. Other times it is warm, the garter snakes are out of hibernation, the chorus frogs are singing at night and most of the swans have gone on. However, it is always interesting, and with every visit I bring away from Long Point a collection of snapshot memories: a white-tailed deer bounding over thin ice, falling through, scrambling out and continuing on into the protection of the cattails and thickets of red osier; a mink roaming the snow-rimmed shore of a melt pond nervously watched by a single bufflehead in the middle; flocks of oldsquaw vanishing into a snowy squall; greater yellowlegs circling overhead, crying plaintively; woodcock calling over moon-touched alders on a cold, clear evening; and most of all, the numerous waterfowl that make Long Point one of the best birding areas in my corner of the continent.

STAGING

During migration it is sometimes possible to find large concentrations of one or a few bird species in areas where there is prime supportive habitat. Such a place is sometimes called a "staging" area. These locations, where a flock can replenish itself before commencing the next stage in its migration, are essential to the well-being of migrating birds.

GREATER YELLOWLEGS

PRESQU'ILE PROVINCIAL PARK

The first pale hints of dawn were nearly two hours away. I was in my early teens and enthusiastic about being at the south end of the long, wide beach that faces west, down the length of Lake Ontario.

It was late August. The shallow water was soup-warm. To reach it we had waded through thick, crusted gray mats of dead algae, which stunk richly and were covered with small flies. The spines of dead sticklebacks stabbed our bare feet. The algae and the multitudes of small invertebrates it hosted attracted thousands of shorebirds, whose plaintive piping and peeping filled the night. When we had driven onto the upper beach, we had seen the birds flashing by in the beams of our car headlights, the first hint of the excitement to come.

Working against the clock, we began placing mist nets. These nets, about five feet (1.5 m) tall and thirty feet (9 m) long, were suspended between sets of interlocking aluminum poles. The mesh was like that of a hair net, fine to the point of being invisible under most conditions. They could catch birds unharmed.

We placed the nets at right angles to the shoreline, as the nocturnal shorebirds tended to fly parallel to the beach. Each net or grouping of nets was called a set. Some sets were placed in angled doglegs, in the theory that the birds might see one net and swerve into the other one. Other sets were placed in rows of two or three nets, extending nearly sixty or ninety feet (18 or 27 m) into the bay. They were staggered so we could pass between them but birds would be less likely to do the same. The water was shallow a long way out, and the rippled sand bottom was a firm base for the poles. The place seemed almost designed to facilitate the capture of shorebirds.

Sandpipers were being caught from the time our first two or three nets were in place. I looked at the first sandpiper I held, seeing by the glow of a flashlight's beam a wonderful little creature with a straight beak, dark eyes and rubbery black feet. The long, pointed wings were so beautifully proportioned and angular that they reminded me of the wings of swallows, although with the inner tertial feathers elongated and the undersurfaces more deeply concave. The bird's slightly oily plumage was quite dense and firm, so unlike the softer feathering of the songbirds I was more accustomed to holding. Its skin was black and stretched tautly over golden fat. Spreading the bird's toes I could see the partial webbing that gives the species its name – semipalmated sandpiper. They were the most common species we encountered that day, as they usually are during the first half of the fall migration at Presqu'ile.

My parents were as new at this as I, but there were a few more experienced shorebird banders in our small group. Tasks were assigned and then changed so we could take turns doing different things; some urged the birds in the direction of the net; others took birds from nets or carried them up to where the cars were parked. There the measuring, weighing, banding and recording of data took place, followed by the release of the birds.

The darkness slowly dissolved as we worked, walking from one set of nets to the next, removing the birds and placing them in wooden boxes or cloth bags. We had to be careful, as some birds would become badly entangled. Occasionally it became necessary to cut strands of the nets in order to free the birds without too much stress, one person working on the bird, the other holding the flashlight.

As daylight took command, we began to see more and more birds on the beach wearing the bands we had placed on their feet. We recaptured a few, keeping them just long enough to make sure the numbers on the bands corresponded with the series we were using. We always hoped we might catch a bird banded in some distant place (as would be determined much later after the number had been mailed to the government and a reply received), but we never did.

SEMIPALMATED SANDPIPER

While we were doing all this in the interest of science, it was also an opportunity to handle and examine minutely each new species. I could study the pale feather edgings of the inner flight feathers, the delicate markings of the back plumage and the fine details of the markings of the face or breast of this or that species. We caught lesser yellowlegs and short-billed dowitchers, semipalmated plovers, some plump red knots, exquisite least sandpipers and many sanderlings.

Sometimes we netted rarer species, like the Baird's sandpiper, with its distinctively marked back markings, or the pectoral sandpiper, with its sharply defined breast pattern. The bigger black-bellied plovers continually managed to elude us, as did the graceful Bonaparte's gulls patrolling the shallows bordering the beach. Killdeers also seemed to avoid the nets, although we did catch one or two, plus a few spotted sandpipers in their crisp fall plumages. We captured a stilt sandpiper and a white-rumped sandpiper, greater yellowlegs and, most spectacular of all, a beautiful common snipe. On later visits, ruddy turnstones and dunlin were among the species added to our list of birds banded.

There were times when most of a flock would hit a net, dragging it down with the weight of so many birds. When that happened, we would have to run to grab handfuls of netting and support the birds above the water until more help arrived. We didn't always make it, and there were some drowning casualties. I was of mixed opinion about those, on the one hand regretting the loss of the birds, but on the other hand knowing that I now had specimens that I could preserve for use as artists' models and for the scientific research I thought I would one day conduct.

There is actually a tide in Lake Ontario, albeit one of only a few inches. This, too, managed to put the birds we were catching at risk, because the water rose a few inches higher than the bottom strands of the nets and sometimes sandpipers were caught in the lower parts of the net. They would drown if not immediately rescued. Losses overall, however, were light. While it has been more than two decades since I've thought of subjecting animals to such stresses or since my faith in science could be used to justify such endeavors, within the context of my attitudes at the time, we were careful.

From that morning on, I have first and foremost thought of Presqu'ile in terms of shorebirds. Since then I've been to places where there are equal or superior shorebirding opportunities, but few, if any, that have as many shorebirds in conjunction with as many other good wildlife viewing possibilities.

It's only a few miles from the entrance to Presqu'ile, which is just south of Causeway Marsh, to the tip, where there is an historic lighthouse. The lighthouse keeper's residence had been remade into a museum, open during the summer months. I worked there one year as head naturalist. I was in my early twenties and in charge of a couple of younger staff members. It was a good job to the degree that it gave me the opportunity to explore the park and to teach campers about nature through the park's interpretation program. On the other hand, struggling with the government bureaucracy and office politics, I often felt terribly out of place.

Early each morning I used to ride a decrepit bicycle from the staff quarters along the paved road through the woods to the museum/visitor center. There were hazards. Nestling songbirds defecate their feces in gelatinous sacs, which the parent birds carry away to be dropped where they won't draw attention to the nest. There seems to be an instinctive drive to drop the fecal sacs into water. This makes sense as otherwise the presence of the droppings might betray the location of the nest to predators. Unfortunately, instinct doesn't

BIRDING AT PRESQU'ILE

Much of Presqu'ile's charm lies in the variety of habitats to be found in a relatively small area. Outside the entrance is a causeway overlooking extensive cattail marshes. After entering the park, the visitor can choose between the dunes and marshes on the east side of the road or the extensive beach on the left. The south end of the beach is usually best for birding, especially in late summer. Although the islands are out of bounds in the nesting season, breeding gulls, terns, black-crowned night herons, double-crested cormorants and other species can be seen from Owen Point. The wooded areas at the eastern end of the park, including the area near the park museum and visitor's center, are excellent for warblers and other migrants, spring and fall. King eiders, harlequin ducks and, on the rocky south shore, purple sandpipers are regional rarities to be looked for in the park late in the fall or in the winter.

differentiate between streams and ponds, on the one hand, and swimming pools and roads that sort of look like streams, on the other. Thus the road was well splattered. The challenge, over which I had little control, was to arrive at work with my clothing unsoiled.

But I enjoyed those early morning bike rides as they brought me into contact with strutting woodcock, ruffed grouse with their tails fanned, shy white-tailed deer and an occasional whip-poor-will or pileated woodpecker. The songs and calls of ovenbirds, wood thrushes, red-eyed vireos, scarlet tanagers, rose-breasted grosbeaks, great crested flycatchers and other woodland species accompanied me.

Our regularly scheduled nature walks were always held at 2:00 p.m, when animals were little in evidence, as that was park policy. However, the staff naturalists and some of the most enthusiastic campers knew that this was one of the worst times to see wildlife. Therefore we held some of our own walks in the early mornings to give campers a better opportunity to see the park's wildlife.

I didn't yet know my way around when I was ordered to take a pre-camping-season group of Scouts and their families on the Indian Point Nature Trail. We convened in the parking lot amid the great dunes that parallel the beach. Tall, broad cottonwoods are the dominant trees in the area, and junipers and some white cedars and grapevines also grow there. One of the most common plants is poison ivy, and as this was May, the leaves were fresh and oily. Most people have strong allergies to the oil, an allergy that can develop any time in life and cause a painful rash that, when scratched, can spread to other parts of the body.

My job was partly to help people learn to identify fauna and flora, and I began by teaching this group to identify poison ivy. It was abundant. There were complaints that park staff should "do something" about it. With no time to explain why poison ivy was less of a hazard than the herbicides that would be used to destroy it and anyway was something that belonged there, I told the worriers that I'd take care of it, leaving them to think I'd report the vegetation so it might be sprayed. In fact, I had been told to report poison ivy for that very reason. I managed to put off filling out the reports until the fall, when it was too late. I saw no reason to dump herbicides on something so easy to avoid.

We made our way through the dunes, the kids dancing and twisting with squeals and laughter as they competed with each other in running down the steep, sandy slopes without touching the poison ivy. Some older brothers and sisters and their parents were more awkward and not quite so amused by the need to twist and turn or even jump over clumps of trail-encroaching vegetation.

Once through the dunes and the poison ivy, we reached the edge of the marsh. There was a floating boardwalk extending over a patch of water to a "finger," which was the name given to parallel strips of sand and gravel bars and their mantles of vegetation that extended into the marsh. I pontificated briefly about the area's geology and then decided to test the boardwalk. It bobbed a little under my weight, but remained well above water as I made it to the other end and stepped onto the finger.

"Seems safe," I said, calling back to the group on the opposite shore. "Come on across."

I walked a little way down the finger, to allow room for the more than two dozen people to follow. I assumed they would do so a few at a time. When I heard screams, shouts and laughter, I turned to see the boardwalk and most of the group on it slowly sink into the chilly water. People splashed off in both directions as they sank up to their knees. The youngsters didn't seem too upset at the soaking, but some adults were plainly not pleased with my leadership skills and started to say so.

"Look," I said, abruptly changing the subject. "A least bittern!"

A small bird, one of the first least bitterns I had ever

seen, flopped out over the marsh beneath a darkening, over-cast sky. Least bitterns are seldom encountered as they usually remain hidden in marsh vegetation. With their golden-buff and brown tones, they are quite attractive. No one seemed interested.

We continued, me pointing to a catbird here, a song sparrow there and stopping to identify a brown thrasher's song. Dense red-osier dogwood and alders began to close in on us. When we reached a fork in the path, I realized that it would have been better had I explored this trail earlier, as my employment manual had directed. I wasn't certain which way to go.

The sky was now ominously dark. To thousands of mosquitoes we were a providentially appearing cluster of refueling stations. People were slapping at the ubiquitous insects. I had sprayed myself with insect repellent at the car but had not brought any, a mistake I have never repeated when taking people on nature walks in mosquito season.

Suddenly I spotted a garter snake amid the freshly growing jewelweed at my feet. I caught the animal, thinking that it might cheer grumbling people to have a good, close look at so beautiful a reptile. The snake's head had been hidden in leaves and grass, but after I picked up the wriggling animal, I saw that it was in the process of swallowing a small leopard frog.

Had I known the snake was so preoccupied I would have left it alone, however, since I now held the snake, the hind part of a frog's body jutting from its mouth, I opportunistically decided to discuss predator and prey relationships. A couple of adults expressed unreasoned fear of snakes, ignoring my reassurances that garter snakes are harmless. Their reaction was not so bad as that of the little girl who found herself staring at the partly eaten frog inches from her eyes. I quickly let the snake go and tried to distract the child by directing her attention to the delicate growth of jewelweed at her feet. She regurgitated her lunch into the delicate growth of jewelweed. Her brother rolled his eyes as if to question what would you expect from a younger sister, but her mother was angry at me for upsetting the children. Actually only her daughter was upset; most of the others were sorry that I had so abruptly released the snake, whose dining habits they found to be "gross."

A short while later, I realized I had made a wrong guess in choosing directions. We were now in a dead-end entanglement of dogwoods and alders. Someone wondered aloud why a park naturalist wouldn't have had the brains to know where he was going. I desperately prattled on about the interesting successional stages in vegetation growth we could see as we made our way back to the fork where I had made the wrong turn.

The delay was unfortunate because it kept us from reaching the cars in the parking lot before the rain started to fall, a drenching downpour, which saw all of us running through the sand dunes toward the parking lot, me yelling at people to watch out for the poison ivy.

The Indian Point Nature Trail and the short, sinking boardwalk have been replaced by a truly magnificent, self-guiding boardwalk extending well out into the marsh. Marsh wrens can be seen from it in late spring through summer, energetically singing their explosive songs as they hold head and tails at sharp angles and cling to cattails almost within arm's length of viewers. Moorhens, waterfowl, pied-billed grebes, black terns and numerous other species, depending upon luck and the season, await birders who stroll the boardwalk.

Presqu'ile is sort of boot shaped, with the heel in the southwest corner and the toe at the southeast corner. Extending, like a spur, from the heel is Owen Point. It points at a spit of sand that comes and goes from year to year and has been known as Sandpiper Island. Past that is low-lying Gull Island.

Sometimes it is possible to wade from Owen Point to Gull Island, or it would be, except that in the summer the islands are a bird sanctuary where trespassing is generally prohibited. Past Gull Island there is a deep channel and then High

Bluff Island, which is the largest of the islands and the only one that rises to a substantial height and supports small wood-lots and meadows.

At the time I was park naturalist, Gull Island hosted what was probably one of the world's largest nesting colonies of common terns. Walking past the colony was like walking through a three-dimensional nature film, with thousands of terns filling the sky, screaming and diving at intruders. Since then, year by year, the ring-billed and herring gulls have taken over, as common terns experienced population declines throughout the Great Lakes and elsewhere in the world.

Black-crowned night herons, Caspian terns and even cattle egrets have nested on Presqu'ile's islands. Double-crested cormorants currently nest there, on the eastern end, quite visible from Owen Point.

The year I worked at the park I assisted Doug Meeking, the federal government's waterfowl bander, in live-trapping, banding and releasing ducks out on the islands, par-ticularly Gull Island, where we had the most success. It was late summer. Doug placed corn in the shallows around the shoreline, than set out walk-in traps. The ducks, many of them in summer molts rendering them flightless, would follow trails of dried corn into the traps and then not know how to get out. That was the theory, although some ducks did seem adept at reversing themselves and finding the entrance.

We caught and banded blue-winged teal, northern pintails, mallards and American black ducks. Gadwall were present and we tried to capture other ducks at night from a motorboat, using a powerful light to transfix them, and then scooping them up with a large fish-landing net. Because it was too stressful on the birds and not very productive, we soon stopped this method of capture, but not before we managed to get our boat propeller entangled in more than one fishnet that crisscrossed the shallow bay, just under the surface. The nets were of dubious legality, and so were our knife-wielding efforts to free the propeller.

SEMIPALMATED PLOVER

One stormy day our traps were full. Darkness would be upon us long before we could process the birds. We decided to try to take the ducks back to the staff house. We carried the ducks in three cages that consisted of wooden slats on the bottom, and soft, fishnet mesh above. Doug took the boat and all that it would carry, including two of the duck-filled cages, while I carried the third one.

When I reached Sandpiper Island, it was awash with waves slamming in from both sides. The trick was to wade through the middle, not allowing the waves to push me into deeper water and treacherous currents on either side of the submerged spit. The deeper the water, the less grip on sand and shingle I had with my running shoes, and the harder it was to maintain balance. I wore only a T-shirt and shorts, and the weather had turned cold, with the chilled water of the lake to my right spilling into the warmer water of the shallow bay.

I would lean into each surge of water hitting me from the left or the right, although often the surges would simultaneously hit me from both sides, clapping together over my head and leaving me sputtering and fighting to hold the cage. The last few feet I had to swim, pushing the cage ahead of me. The park chaplain, there to conduct religious services for campers, had been told that I'd be bringing in the last of the ducks and was on hand to help when I finally dragged myself ashore looking, as he put it, like a drowned rat.

Later that night we released the ducks into empty closets and two of the bedrooms of the staff house – mine and Doug's. I shared my room with another naturalist, who took in his stride the fact that he had to push his way through waddling wild ducks to get to the bathroom in the night. Other staff members were not as nonchalant about the black ducks, mallards, blue-winged teal and northern pintails, all finally banded and released by late the next morning.

The woman who came in to cook for us was only mildly annoyed about the ducks. Nor had she cared about the turtle in my linen drawer or the jumping mouse I had rescued from a drenching rain and cared for in my bathtub. But she had threatened a boycott when she learned I had also been helping a scientist catch, tag and release bats. Before our cook agreed to return to the kitchen and hungry colleagues stopped scowling at Doug and me, we had to make solemn oaths that no bats, nor snakes, would enter the house.

Each spring Presqu'ile attracts thousands of human visitors on specially designated waterfowl-viewing weekends. There are viewing stations with blinds and telescopes set in place and naturalists on hand to assist in identifying the ducks. Presqu'ile is one of the best places to see redheads, which seem particularly attracted to Presqu'ile Bay, spring and fall, and even breed there. Offshore waters are attractive to brant and all three species of scoter, which may appear in huge numbers.

Although less famous than Point Pelee, after making allowances for the number of birding visitors, I think Presqu'ile produces more rarities than does Pelee. Such completely unexpected species as the Mongolian plover, band-tailed pigeon and sulphur-bellied flycatcher have been seen there and have been international attractions. Anyone visiting Presqu'ile can check the log of bird sightings posted daily to discover what's around.

Apart from unpredictable rarities, in the early spring ducks are a major attraction, although American woodcock and various woodland species are also to be found. The May migration can be spectacular and on those special days when a "wave" of migrants descends, Presqu'ile is a birder's hot spot. I remember one glorious May day when there was an unusually large number of red-headed woodpeckers in the park, along with such beautifully plumaged birds as scarlet tanagers, rose-breasted grosbeaks, northern orioles and numerous warblers. All the pretty bird pictures of my childhood books had come to life and filled the park.

While shorebirds are fewer in spring than fall, the third week in May is a good time to look for flocks of whimbrel.

MERLIN MISSES

Merlins are swift-flying little falcons that normally eat birds taken in hot pursuit. However, studies seem to indicate that merlins miss far more often than they connect in their dashing attacks on flying prey. Maybe, but I sometimes wonder if what is scored a "miss" is actually a form of entertainment. Certainly merlins cause quite a stir when they rapidly fly up the length of a beach, scattering sandpipers in all directions. Sometimes they don't seem to be trying to make a capture, but rather, they give the appearance of exulting in their own flying skills and their effect on the shorebirds. I've seen merlins chase monarch butterflies, which birds find unpalatable. They could easily catch the insects, but seem more interested in simply using the butterflies as focal points for their flying skills.

Spring is also the time to see such species as the ruddy turnstone, red knot, sanderling and dunlin in their brightly colored spring plumages.

In the late fall, dunlin are, but for the odd straggler of another species and the few purple sandpipers or sanderlings that may winter there, the last of the shorebirds at Presqu'ile.

After the swimmers have left for the season, Presqu'ile's long sand beach provides a wide-open sweep for merlins. The dashing little falcons seem to delight in flying full speed up its length, their swift passage marked by swirling flocks of shorebirds. I've watched merlins as they seem to play with monarch butterflies, chasing the erratic insects in the air, grabbing at them, but not actually catching them, perhaps knowing that the monarch is ill-tasting. The butterflies themselves, which can number in the thousands during the fall, are a major attraction to naturalists and photographers.

No other place more than an hour's drive from where I live draws me more often to bird than Presqu'ile Provincial Park.

WATERFOWL VIEWING WEEKENDS

In early spring Presqu'ile attracts thousands of visitors to two consecutive special waterfowl viewing weekends, when blinds are available along Bayshore Drive, overlooking Presqu'ile Bay. This is an excellent spot to see redheads, goldeneyes, both scaup species, ring-necked ducks and other waterfowl sporting their finest breeding plumages. The open lake may host loons and mergansers, and sometimes there are gatherings of thousands of white-winged scoters offshore.

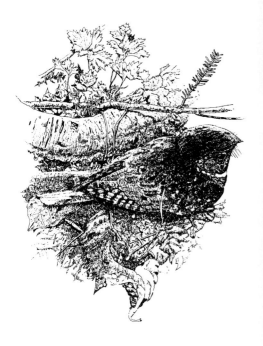

WHIP-POOR-WILL

THE CORNER, THE CUT, THE WOODS AND THE FLATS

Birders call the marsh at the foot of Duffin Creek, Ajax, just east of Toronto, the Corner Marsh. That's because one of the better birding outlooks is a corner where the east-west road turns sharply south, to end at Lake Ontario.

On the northwest shoulder of the marsh is a right-of-way for Church Street, extending south of where the road comes to a dead end. When I was a kid that right-of-way consisted of an extensive hedgerow of red-osier dogwoods and tangled wild grapevines infringing upon a track that petered out in thickets bordering Corner Marsh. It was through the densest vegetation that we wielded machetes to carve paths, or cuts, at right angles to the hedgerow. We set mist nets in the cuts to catch birds. The thicker the vegetation, the more likely it was that the birds would not see the nets. The birds we caught were banded and released. This site eventually became my mother's banding station and we called it the Cut.

Almost every spring and fall afternoon, weather permitting, my mother would pick me up after school and we'd go to the Cut to band birds. Dad, our boxer dog Taaya, and even some of the native birds being cared for by my mother would join us on weekends, when we'd arrive early in the morning. On summer afternoons at the Cut I would take breaks from catching birds to catch grasshoppers to feed some of the birds in our care, each of whom was in a separate cage. Zuma, the kestrel; Danny, the bluebird; and Misty, the mockingbird, all learned to anticipate a grasshopper treat when they saw me with the insect net.

When few birds were being caught I would sometimes take the time to do some homework, always my lowest priority. We would drive partway down the right-of-way and park. The ground around our car became a home away from home, with the dog, the caged birds, school books, banding equipment, picnic lunches, blankets and extra clothing scattered about. Other bird banders often joined my mother on weekends and helped create the stuff of fond memories.

The Woods is located on the eastern edge of Corner Marsh, on a rather shallow and irregular bluff, about a five- or six-minute drive from the Cut. It used to be surrounded by fields and hedgerows. On some maps the Woods is called MacKay's Woods, the name given to it by surveyors who, also being birders, knew how much time my family spent there.

At the Woods we sometimes would catch, band and release dozens of birds in a single day. On one such day at the Woods, the count reached over one hundred and fifty birds, of which over one hundred were white-crowned sparrows.

By recapturing banded birds, we established that some of the yellow warblers and song sparrows that nested in the Cut returned to do so again in following years. But virtually every migrant bird we caught, banded and released – including hundreds of white-throated, white-crowned, Savannah and song sparrows; ovenbirds; bay-breasted, chestnut-sided and other warblers; both kinds of kinglet; Swainson's, hermit and other thrushes; chickadees and creepers – were never heard from again.

If a bird we had banded was found in another location and its band number reported to the appropriate office in Washington, D.C., or Ottawa with the date and place where it was found, that information was relayed to us. We heard about some of the non-songbird species we banded and some wintering species of songbirds, such as evening grosbeaks, or common breeding species of songbirds, such as grackles, after these reports were filed. But returns were extremely rare for

BIRD COUNTS

Often it can be difficult to determine if downward population trends in bird species are real or perceived. Habitat that seems more birdless than it used to be may have matured to a point where it is less attractive to the birds in question. Because migration routes can change, records showing a decline in a species of migrant bird at a given location may reflect a shift in distribution, not an actual decline in numbers. In part or all of their ranges, some species' numbers seem to go down quickly and for little or no obvious reason. Often conservationists can only be sure which bird species are in actual decline through exhaustive efforts at maintaining breeding bird censuses and habitat requirement evaluations throughout a significant part of the species' range and over a long period of time.

migrant or passage songbirds, in contrast to raptors and water-fowl and such colony nesting species as terns, gulls and herons.

Some thought low returns were better than no returns and if people were willing to band migrant songbirds, it was worth doing. Others believed low returns meant banding efforts had to be increased to enhance statistical probabilities that returns would also increase. Still others claimed banding migrant songbirds should only be done in conjunction with well-planned research projects, which often involved extra handling of the birds. And there were those who decided migrant songbirds should never be banded.

There is no absolutely right opinion. Personally, the greatest value I received was nothing so grand as scientific discovery. As a budding bird artist and birder, I learned more about the finer details of birds' appearances than I could any other way. That's not a justification for the imposition on the birds, as minimal as we could make it, but it is fact.

GREEN-BACKED HERON (FLEDGLING)

There are growing numbers of terribly intense birders who can cite multitudes of fine details useful to separate a species, or an age and sex class within a species, from something extremely similar. But many birders still only learn basic distinguishing field marks. In terms of actual birdwatching, I think I fit between those two extremes. For example, I don't share some birders' difficulty in telling Swainson's from gray-cheeked thrushes or in telling a fall-plumaged blackpoll warbler from a corresponding bay-breasted, all being species I've handled in large numbers. On the other hand, some of the oddly plumaged wintering gulls or Pacific seabirds that other birders deftly pick out of the flock can leave me a bit bewildered, and I've never impressed anyone but neophytes with my ability to identify the songs and call notes of warblers.

Birders bird wherever there are birds to be seen. We will be the only ones among thousands of pedestrians to notice the nighthawks above bustling city street corners or to observe the Wilson's warbler gleaning insects from an ornamental hedge as we attend an outdoor wedding reception.

And so while we were banding at Ajax, and in between sessions of banding, we also birded.

Black terns, more common in those days than now, nested at the Corner Marsh in a fairly large colony. I could never tire of their graceful forms. Great blue herons would begin to congregate there in August and at times we could see dozens with one sweep of the binoculars.

One day in the Woods I encountered a whip-poor-will as it flew up from the leaf-cluttered woodland floor in front of me. It is a natural reflection of the nature of humans and whip-poor-wills that the former hear far more of the latter than they ever see. Until that moment the only whip-poor-wills I had ever found were spotted by their ruby eyeshine as they sat on the side of rural roads at night. They would perch there between forays into the night sky, where they would fly with their mouths open, swallowing any insects that bumbled into the birds' gaping maws. The whip-poor-will is intricately patterned in the same woodsy colors as the dead leaves, twigs and lichens on the ground or on tree limbs. By day it generally sits motionless. Unless you pass close enough to flush it, the whip-poor-will is simply too well camouflaged to be easily spotted.

Another day, however, as I walked through the Woods, I thought I saw the eye of a whip-poor-will, on the ground, some yards away. How often do we tend to see what we want to see? A classic birders' version of this phenomenon is the tale of a chuck-will's-widow at Point Pelee. This large relative of the whip-poor-will is a great rarity at Pelee. Hour after hour, the story goes, birders came to look at one perched on a limb, dutifully record it on their lists and depart, until one person went closer and discovered that the "chuck-will's-widow" was actually only a knot in a branch.

I was in luck, though. Once I had that whip-poor-will's eye in focus I stared hard and was rewarded by the sight of the bird itself, quietly sitting in its natural habitat. I counted that sighting a major accomplishment.

IS IT A WADER OR A SHOREBIRD?

In North America, we tend to use the term *shorebird* to describe sandpipers, plovers and allied bird families. Most of these species do occur along shores, particularly during migration, although some, such as the American woodcock and the upland sandpiper, do not. In other English-speaking parts of the world, these birds are called waders. Most do wade, at least at times, although some do so sparingly or never. To confuse the situation a little more, in North America the term *waders*, or *wading birds*, is often applied to larger, long-legged species such as herons, storks and ibises, while elsewhere the term *shorebird* may be applied to any species that occurs regularly in seaside habitat. International travel is breaking down these distinctions, and the terms *shorebirds* and *waders* are becoming interchangeable in the minds of most birders.

COMMON YELLOWTHROAT

It was in the Woods, as well, where I first found a great horned owl on my own. I had been told where to look for them by adult birders, but this time I actually found one by myself. The bird was so huge, with great yellow eyes, that it seemed impossible that it would be hard to find, and yet its woodsy brown plumage with dark splotches and fine mottlings caused it to blend into the intricate filigree of twigs and branches, high in a white pine. Indeed, even after seeing the bird, I had trouble finding it again when I looked away for just a moment or when I approached the bird from a different angle. Thereafter I infrequently flushed one or the other of the pair of great horned owls that nested each year in the Woods and counted it great luck to again locate a bird before it gave itself away by taking flight.

The Woods provided me with some of my first good views of pileated woodpeckers. These crow-sized woodpeckers are spectacular, their black plumage contrasting with bold, white wing flashes and white streaks on the heads and necks, all set off by flaming red crests. In spite of their often brash behavior, loud call, large size and bright markings, in Ontario (the northern end of their natural breeding range), pileateds can be remarkably shy and difficult to see. But that makes good sightings all the more memorable. My first close encounter with one of these impressive birds held me spellbound on a glorious fall day as the bird noisily and methodically chipped great flakes of wood from a tree trunk near where I stood.

From the low bluff at the back of the Woods I could look down on a rather hidden patch of water in Corner Marsh. That's where I saw my first Wilson's phalaropes, as they swam in tight little circles in shallow water, their needle bills delicately probing at tiny organisms.

Whether we were banding or birding, the best thing about the Woods was its outright attractiveness to migrant birds. Woods, marsh, hedgerows and open fields all came together there to provide wonderful habitat for a multitude of bird species. Now the fields and hedgerows are gone and a subdivision presses hard against the truncated edges of the Woods. The birding joys I experienced there as a youngster cannot be repeated.

Worse, from a birder's perspective, was the fate of the Flats. This area of fields and hedgerows sloping down to the shore of Lake Ontario had been a secret military installation during the Second World War. Earthen ramparts, which (I was told) had once been missile launching ramps, were still apparent. They faced the lake. Obviously if missiles had been launched, the projectiles had been lightly fueled or unarmed. After all, a neutral country and eventual ally was just over the horizon!

In the late fall, through the winter and into early spring, the Flats could be bleak, but at such times they were the best place to take visiting birders to look for short-eared owls, rough-legged hawks and snowy owls. Northern shrikes hunted there, perching jauntily alone on the tops of leafless ash trees as they waited for prey to come into view. Red-tailed hawks and northern harriers were common.

My first Lapland longspurs were with a flock of snow buntings and horned larks on the Flats. Snow buntings frequently stopped there, and so, some winters, did common redpolls, among whom we would look (sometimes successfully) for the much rarer hoary redpolls. All of these birds impressed me with how round, firm and perfectly patterned they were, as they calmly went about the business of gleaning seeds from the sere, brown weeds that thrust above the snow. The late bird artist Allan Brooks was sometimes criticized for making his birds too plump, but he was a master at creating winter skies and lighting. The rounded and beautifully patterned snow buntings, redpolls, horned larks and longspurs he painted looked just like these fine birds I so enjoyed viewing.

From the bluffs overlooking the lake we could sometimes see red-necked grebes in flocks scattered upon the dull, gray surface of the lake during cold weather. Mostly they were

FINDING RAPTORS

Some raptorial species, such as shrikes and hawks, hunt by day, while most owls hunt by night. However, snowy owls and northern hawk-owls are frequently active in daylight, particularly during overcast weather, and short-eared owls also sometimes hunt at this time.

When wind conditions are appropriate, American kestrels and rough-legged hawks can hover over one place, scanning the fields below for prey. But others, such as red-tailed hawks, soar on thermals and rarely hover. Shrikes often sit on the tops of telephone poles and other perches with a wide view of open spaces, while kestrels seem to prefer telephone wires. Northern harriers fly low over fields, marshes and hedgerows with the intention of taking prey by surprise. Sharp-shinned hawks, northern goshawks and Cooper's hawks, on the other hand, fly through wooded or park-like areas, gardens and hedgerows in active pursuit of prey.

in gray winter plumages, although some individuals sported touches of the reddish neck plumage that gives the species its name.

One bleak winter day, the shingle beach below the low bluffs produced my first purple sandpiper. The rounded, plump little bird seemed oblivious to either winter cold or me, allowing me to approach within a few yards.

Now the Flats are gone, completely covered by a residential community. And the swampy woods to the south of Bailey Road, where I used to watch migrating flocks of rusty blackbirds, where I went in winter to find long-eared owls and where American woodcocks and common snipes performed mating rituals, were bulldozed a few years ago, their place taken by a plain of dried landfill that presumably awaits what we call "development." The little marsh across the road from there, where black terns once nested, has filled in with purple loosestrife.

I seldom visit the Cut anymore, as development in the entire area leaves me depressed. I prefer to remember it as it used to be.

Not all of the memories are good ones. Once my father's ability to overcome his inherent fear of anything that fluttered faltered badly just as he was about to grab a nighthawk from a net, and the bird got away. The species is a close relative of the whip-poor-will and I desperately wanted to hold one in my hands and examine it closely. I was upset but I need not have worried; in the years ahead many nighthawks were to pass through my hands.

There was the time when my mother's thumb was banged in a car door, bandaged and then severely bitten by the only northern shrike we ever captured. The bird would not let go of Mom and she would not let go of the bird. I learned a lot about hidden corners of my mother's vocabulary that day. I did, however, enjoy the close, in-hand look at the shrike, its soft plumage a wonderful blend of black, white and gray.

A happier memory for my mother was the migrant

WINTERING RAPTORS

In northern latitudes, voles and other small rodents are the main prey of wintering hawks, owls and shrikes. Since these prey species often eat seeds in the winter, predators tend to frequent fields and other open areas where there is an abundance of seeding grasses and weeds. Birds attracted to feeders can also become a source of food for some of the more agile birds of prey.

black-capped chickadee who lit on her shoulder, having arrived from the north woods unaware that people were something to fear. One extraordinary autumn we experienced a huge flight of boreal chickadees. They were everywhere, although usually they are a great rarity so far south.

I remember Mother, nervous of snakes, working furiously to free a female red-winged blackbird from the bottom strands of a net that had unintentionally been placed over a garter snake hibernaculum. The snakes were wide awake and seemed to be hungry for a blackbird-sized meal.

They weren't the only predators in the area. We had to constantly patrol the Cut to reach the birds in the net before the northern harriers found them. Once, to my surprise, I flushed a harrier from an adult wood duck he was eating and presumably had killed.

I recall the hunters trudging up from the marsh carrying the bloodied remains of tiny teal, not knowing or caring what species they had shot. I remember having shotgun pellets whistle through the branches overhead, disturbing both us and a flock of robins.

One fall day, years ago, I stood on an overlook, viewing a marsh that seemed empty of nearly all life. A northern harrier began to glide low over the marsh and I watched closely, concerned because I knew there would be hunters hidden in blinds. They were inclined to shoot protected species.

Suddenly a blue-winged teal spurted out from the base of a clump of cattails where it had been hiding. There was a barrage of gunfire, more than a dozen shots, as hunters reared up from several blinds and poured concentrated fire at the hapless bird. I left as the hunters began to argue over who should take home the tiny body.

Once hunting was banned, Corner Marsh became an excellent spot to bird in the fall, and remains so until this day. Perhaps my single favorite birding moment at the Marsh came on a glorious fall morning when I managed to have a Forster's tern, an American white pelican and a marbled godwit all in

CHICKADEES AND TITMOUSES

In North America, the terms *chickadee* and *titmouse* are used for the small birds of the *Parus* genus. Those with black, brown or dark gray caps and black bib markings, but no crests, are called chickadees (the name sounding a little like the typical *chi-ka-deee-deee-deee* call of several species), while those with crests are called titmouses. The one exception is an Asian species, the Siberian tit, which is also found in Alaska and the Yukon; it used to be known in North America as the gray-headed chickadee. The pretty little bridled titmouse of the southern United States and Mexico has the black bib and cap of a chickadee and the crest of a titmouse. There are three titmouses and seven chickadees native to North America.

my binoculars' field of vision at the same time. It was as if a large prairie slough had been transported a thousand miles east.

Better known birding locations exist near Ajax. They include Cranberry Marsh, a few miles further east at Whitby, where I saw my first Eurasian wigeon, with its distinctively buff-colored forehead, my first little gull as it fluttered over the marsh, showing the dark wing linings that characterize the species, and many other "firsts," and where I still go birding quite regularly. Thickson's Woods, near Oshawa, is another location of local fame among birders, complete with trails and a book recording the day's sightings. The woods is managed by a dedicated group of birders who saved it from the ax.

Although the rivermouth marshes east of Toronto have been degraded in my lifetime, most (including Oshawa's Second Marsh) have been more or less saved, often only after prolonged effort by dedicated conservationists. A typical day's birding for me still begins at Frenchman's Bay, to the west of Corner Marsh and ends, many miles to the east at Corner Marsh, near Oshawa. At each stop along the way I encounter old friends – both birds and birders.

BIRDING AT THE SPIT, JUNGLE, ISLANDS AND GAPS

CHIMNEY SWIFT

Every birder has one or more home bases, thus one or more ecosystems supporting an avifauna of particular familiarity. For me, home has meant somewhere in or near Toronto. Like any city I've ever been in, from London, England, to Kota Kinabalu, Borneo, Toronto has places to go birding. In fact, it is fairly typical of the better cities in the world for birders to live in or visit.

The first and most important birding location for the earliest years of my childhood was my own back garden. It was a small yard in a raw subdivision, but fast-growing trees were planted, and in a few years we had formed something of an arboreal oasis in our neighborhood.

One exciting day, sometime in the early 1950s, we saw over ninety species during the height of spring migration. That's an unbelievable total for a small suburban garden, although it did include such overhead migrants as a turkey vulture (rarer then than now), some swallows and chimney swifts. It also included some unexpected birds, particularly a blue-winged warbler, seen before the species had been added to the official Toronto checklist. That was the first time I had ever found a species not on the checklist for the region I was in and at the time I think I might have used the experience to define the word *thrilling*.

The blue-winged warbler is bright yellow with a thin, black mask pattern through the eye and blue-gray wingbars. I was the only one in my family to see him and I reported the sighting to James L. Baillie, writer of the bird-watching column in the *Toronto Telegram* and associate curator of ornithology at the Royal Ontario Museum. Without some independent documentation, in the form of either the bird's body or a good photograph, a sighting by a young boy, however enthusiastic, was not acceptable. But I knew what I had seen. I had viewed the elegant little bird clearly, at close range through binoculars, with every field mark and feature plainly visible. It was my first blue-winged warbler.

The cemetery behind the houses across the street was a fruitful birding ground when I was able to avoid grumpy care-takers who, it was rumored, were not incapable of burying alive any kid they caught in their domain. I would duck behind tombstones, trying to get close to birds. It was a fine place for ring-necked pheasants, and my first look at a male, his plumage blazing with burnished glory in the sunlight, left me ecstatic with the pleasure of the experience.

Another childhood birding habitat was the open garbage dump at the bottom of our dead-end street. I went there to find such highly urbanized wildlife as Norway rats, raccoons and starlings. As an adult, no wilderness experience has touched me more than my first discovery in this uninviting setting of newly hatched spotted sandpipers. What exquisite little creatures, all fluff and minute detail, vibrating with life and innocent determination.

Small urban garbage dumps are a thing of the past in the Toronto area. Now, like all birders, I make regular trips to sewage settling lagoons in search of the shorebirds attracted to such putrid places, and I visit open landfills, as garbage dumps are currently called, in search of gulls. Others may express dismay at the swirling masses of gray and white gulls that characterize landfill sites, but within those swarms there might be a lesser black-backed gull, an Iceland gull, a Thayer's gull or perhaps a glaucous.

I'm old enough to remember Toronto's Ashbridge's Bay, at the

PLANTING YOUR GARDEN FOR THE BIRDS

Gardens can provide birds with both food and shelter. Ideal food plants are those that produce berries or other small fruit. These include mulberry, mountain ash, raspberries, elderberry, wild cherries, dogwoods and wild grapes. Apple and other orchard trees provide food in winter if some of the fruit is allowed to remain on the trees or on the ground when it falls. Willows are attractive to insects, which, in turn, may attract warblers, vireos and other insectivorous migrants. Often food and shelter can be found in the same species, such as Virginia creeper, barberry, spicebush, dogwoods, hawthorns, junipers, red cedar, privets, wild grapes, bayberry, flowering crab apple and multiflora rose.

Some birding gardeners like to leave a wild section in their gardens where plants are allowed to develop in thick, weedy tangles that attract some of the shyer species of wildlife. Others like to feature native flora, although care should be taken not to acquire stock from rare, threatened or endangered wild plant communities.

mouth of the Don River, before the magnificent marsh that existed there was destroyed. I've been told that the marsh was once home to the world's largest concentration of the rare "Cory's bittern." Cory's bittern is a dark-toned color phase, or morph, of the least bittern. It is so distinctive, with the buff coloring of the typical bird replaced by dark chestnut, that it was once thought to be a separate species. In the late nineteenth century, Ontario and Florida were the population centers for this rare morph.

The marsh also hosted a large colony of black terns, plus rails and other marsh birds and wildlife. Like the passenger pigeons that used to migrate up the Don Valley in sky-darkening numbers, they too are forever part of the history of the city.

Loss of the marsh and the subsequent dumping of landfill to produce what is officially known as the East Toronto Landfill and Tommy Thompson Park, but what almost everyone calls the Leslie Street Spit, resulted in a trade-off. One type of habitat was lost, another gained.

I'd rather have the marsh, to be sure. However, the Spit has given naturalists a living laboratory of plant and animal succession. From the primitive horsetails that are among the first plants to colonize bare mud, to woodlots of poplars, sumach and box alders, ever-increasing numbers of plant species colonize the Spit without conscious human assistance. They, in turn, have altered ecological parameters to increase species diversity among animals, from microscopic organisms to foxes, raccoons and nesting colonies of birds.

Hour after hour, day after day, year after year, dump trucks have been carrying what everyone hopes is clean, non-toxic landfill out onto the Spit, extending it ever further into Lake Ontario like a great, deformed claw. Once there was a theoretical economic purpose to the exercise; the Spit was somehow supposed to alter currents in a way that would enhance the quality of the harbor for international shipping via the St. Lawrence Seaway. Anticipated increases in

UNSAVORY LOCATIONS

Near most communities there are garbage dumps, landfill sites and sewage treatment plants. Whatever they may lack in aesthetic appeal, such places attract certain species of birds. Gulls, crows, ravens and other scavengers visit dumps and landfills, as do birds of prey if rats or other rodents are present. Sewage treatment facilities often have settling ponds that attract large numbers of shorebirds. These facilities may or may not be open to the public and are often in out-of-the-way places. Travelers to new areas can contact local naturalist or birding groups to determine where sewage settling ponds are located and if they can be visited.

international shipping never happened.

Meanwhile, many Torontonians fell in love with the Spit as an urban wilderness for strollers, bikers, joggers, photographers, boaters and birders. To some extent, the boaters have been at odds with most of the others, wanting marinas and supportive infrastructures, including automobile access, in place. The current situation is something of a compromise, with many areas given over to the boaters. Further development is slated for some of the fields near the base of the spit, which are good habitat for wintering finches, raptors and other wildlife.

Still, the Spit does have a significant part of its land area protected as "wilderness" and for most of its length automobile traffic on weekends and holidays is generally restricted to a public bus sponsored by the Metropolitan Toronto and Region Conservation Authority, plus the odd service vehicle. All day the bus drives up and down the single, long road extending from the parking lot at the base to the automatic lighthouse at the tip, about six miles (9.6 km) from the foot of Leslie Street. The vehicle picks up footsore passengers along the way. Weekdays the Spit is closed to the public and trucks endlessly rumble up and down its length.

At one time the Spit hosted one of the world's largest gull colonies. In 1985, approximately forty-seven thousand ring-billed gulls, plus smaller numbers of herring gulls, nested on the barren ground. Like many populations of various gull species worldwide, the Great Lakes' population of ring-billed gulls had greatly increased as a function of growing amounts of food: garbage, die-offs of alewives and other non-native fish, and some agricultural practices. Out on the Spit, the growing competitive pressures led to changes in ring-billed gull behavior; the birds began perching in trees and bushes, a new behavior for the species.

The huge assembly of birds in the colony fascinated me, although some birders were indifferent to such a common species. It was certainly too much for city politicians, particularly each August when inexperienced, recently fledged ring-bills flocked throughout the city. Their grabbing of food spilling from unclosed bulk garbage containers, outdoor eating establishments, and antiquated storm and sanitary sewer systems resulted in complaints from voters.

Blaming gulls for degraded lake water quality also became a popular political pastime. In fact, the lowest coliform pollution counts were detected closest to the gull colony and the highest, beach-closing counts occurred after heavy rains forced the mingling of effluent from sanitary sewers with the flow of storm sewers. Nevertheless, the political "solution" was to begin a gull-control program. The methods, using chasing techniques and egg destruction, are more or less humane.

Indeed, some politicians argued it was more humane than doing nothing at all. Many young birds were starving before population controls were instigated, they claimed. However, gulls have always produced numbers greater than the environment can sustain; that's what gulls do. While the solution in this case was better than the poison "sandwiches" that have been served different gull species in other countries, I can't help but wonder if reducing the gulls' food base of various kinds of human waste might not have been the best solution.

Before the gull-control program began, I had a birding experience of the kind I would have dreamed of as a child. I took Roger Tory Peterson to visit and photograph the gull colony. America's most famous and influential birder was in town at my invitation to help defend the gulls and, by extension, the natural qualities of the Leslie Street Spit. At the time, there was a strong move from agriculturists and others to have the ring-billed gull's official protection under the Migratory Birds Convention Treaty revoked. The federal environment minister seemed to have little sympathy for environmental concerns, and I was worried that she might capitulate to the gull-haters. Peterson was obviously delighted, not only with

EVENING GROSBEAK

the opportunity to help protect gulls and enjoy a new birding experience, but also with the Spit itself. He kept asking me if Torontonians appreciated what they had.

Gull-control programs may have led to black-crowned night herons abandoning a colony on Toronto Island, perhaps because the disturbance caused by workers removing gull eggs from the ground below their nests was too great for the herons, causing them to move away. But their colony on the Spit is currently thriving. It is as well protected as is reasonable, given its proximity to the city. The Spit's vegetative cover has, in places, passed through successional stages to a simple form of woodlot, a significant change from its origins as a windswept wasteland of mud and gravel.

The increase in ring-bills and other aggressive, predatory gull species in other parts of the world could well be a contributing factor to an international decline in common terns. The Canadian Wildlife Service has experimented with anchored barges covered with sand to bring back the common terns, who have not only been displaced by gulls, but have also lost prime nesting habitat through increases in vegetation. The barges, placed just offshore at the Spit, simulate the early, successional stages of a newly emerged sand bar, a classic nesting site for terns but not ring-billed or herring gulls. It's working, with terns successfully nesting on the barges.

For several years I conducted Christmas bird counts on the Leslie Street Spit with other birders. We almost always saw a few species not encountered by bird counters elsewhere in the city that day. It was a good place to look for snowy, saw-whet and short-eared owls, snow buntings, rough-legged hawks and northern shrikes. On one Christmas bird count, we found a dark phase gyrfalcon at the sewage filtration plant near the base of the Spit.

The Spit provides excellent shorebird habitats, as well as lake waters that sometimes host a few red-throated loons, king eiders, harlequin ducks and often large numbers of common mergansers, red-breasted mergansers, white-winged scoters,

ARTIFICIAL NEST SITES

The idea of using sand-covered barges to attract common terns is quite new. A similar idea has been used for the common loon. Its nest sites have been disturbed as the wilderness woodland lakeshores it prefers for nesting become ever more "developed." Raccoons, which are effective loon-nest predators, have increased their numbers in cottage areas in response to the growing availability of garbage. To counteract both problems, loon conservationists have successfully experimented with floating rafts as loon nest sites. The rafts have a ramp for easy access from the water and a layer of soil and vegetation to provide cover and security. Although they can swim, raccoons are far less likely to bother nests that are on these small islands than ones on shore.

greater scaup, oldsquaws, Canada geese and mallards. Red-necked and horned grebes, plus such seafowl as jaegers, northern gannets and black-legged kittiwakes, have been found by birders looking out over the lake from the end of the Spit.

RED-NECKED GREBE

The Spit's reputation for attracting sharp-tailed, LeConte's and other rare sparrows and field birds may not survive planned development of the landward end of the headland. The shallow, transitory melt ponds at the base of the Spit are also probably soon going to be lost to proposed development. For now they are a good place for spring birding in search of snipe and other shorebirds, some presenting themselves at close range as they strut about in high breeding plumage.

Toronto birders have several other favorite birding spots. One area extending west from the base of the Spit, through Cherry Beach to the gap that separates the mainland from the east end of Toronto Island, used to be called the Jungle by birders. The term referred as much to the hobo colony, or "jungle," that thrived there in the Great Depression as to the thick entanglements of scrubby vegetation that attracted so many birds, especially saw-whet owls. During autumn migration, saw-whets tend to follow the northern edge of Lake Ontario and roost by day in suitable habitat, occasionally in substantial numbers.

The chunky little owls were attracted to the Jungle's thickets of willows and alders. Saw-whets appear in similar thickets still to be found on Toronto Island and now to be found on the Leslie Street Spit. Although the Jungle has been partly eliminated, the place still provides good birding opportunities, particularly in winter. The Martin Goodman bike and hiking trail passes this site.

The Toronto Islands embrace the southern end of Toronto Bay, forming the perfect place to stand and take pictures of the skyscraping architecture of the city's downtown core, as any buyer of Toronto postcards and calendars knows. The islands are also a good place to go birding, particularly in fall, winter and spring. Their towering black and weeping willows host a variety of migrant songbirds and there are some "natural" areas at the west end of the island complex that form an ecological oasis well worth visiting. The Toronto Islands are easily reached by frequently scheduled ferries from the docks at the foot of Bay Street.

The first time I visited the Toronto Islands, as one of a group of schoolchildren on a field trip in May, I was delighted by the numbers of migrant red-headed woodpeckers we encountered. The other youngsters were more keen than I on games or picnics, but I wandered around with my eyes on the trees overhead, finding it hard to believe that something so beautiful as the boldly black and white patterned woodpeckers with their glowing red heads could be ignored by so many of the people who were enjoying the Islands that fine spring day.

In winter, the Eastern Gap and the Western Gap, as the two channels bracketing the Islands are called, are excellent places to watch oldsquaws in full flight. Torontonians have been known to take their oldsquaws for granted. Many a visiting birder, though, has been thrilled to see impressive numbers of the dashingly handsome ducks at such close range when taken to the Eastern Gap or when leaning over the rail of a ferry churning through ice and water on the approximately ten- to fifteen-minute trip to the Islands.

The Islands can be good places to look for the three merganser species, the three scoter species, the king eider and the harlequin duck. Purple sandpipers, snow buntings and snowy owls are other possibilities during the bleak winter months. Sometimes rafts of greater scaup can be seen offshore from the Islands' lakeward edge or anywhere along Toronto's waterfront, particularly to the west, where it opens into a long series of public parks.

Humber Bay Park, well to the west, is another landfill park that is attractive to birds, particularly wintering waterfowl. Even beaver have lived there, once animal protectionists convinced local politicians and park managers that the large

IT DOESN'T LOOK LIKE ITS PICTURE

Birds and other animals are not stamped out of molds. There can be considerable variations in size, color and pattern within a species. Often there are differences between birds in adult plumage and those in immature plumages, between breeding and non-breeding plumages and between the sexes. Racial variations may also occur.

Some species, such as the eastern screech-owl, may appear in one of two distinctive color phases (or morphs). Dark pigmentation, called melanism, can occur in many species, particularly raptors. Even within the same race, age, morph and sex classification, there can be variations in markings and color, and further variations imposed by the condition of the plumage. Feathers may be stained or worn. Some species, such as the European starling, change quite dramatically through the process of feather wear. For others such changes can be subtle. In the end, there is no "typical" appearance for any given species, which adds to the challenge of bird identification.

BUFFLEHEAD

rodents would not chop down every valuable shade tree in the park. People's habit of feeding Canada geese, mallards, black ducks and (usually unwillingly) ring-billed gulls tends to give wary migrants a sense of security, I suspect. The park's contours provide small bays where birders can often enjoy close views of greater and lesser scaup, common (and the odd Barrow's) goldeneye, oldsquaws, redheads and other diving ducks. In spring and fall, some migrant shorebirds and herons may appear along the edges of these sheltered bays.

Just north of the waterfront, in the city's west end, is High Park, site of many organized and impromptu birding expeditions. At the southwest corner of the park is Grenadier Pond. People feed mallards, black ducks, mute swans and Canada geese there in the winter. Although less likely to take handouts, almost invariably gadwalls, northern shovelers, buffleheads and other waterfowl that might otherwise be found in warmer climes can also be found there. (Gadwalls have taken to Toronto in a big way. They tend to winter in the city, safe from the rigors of migration.) When the ice forms across most of the pond, the waterfowl congregate in the lower, southwest corner, where their concentrated activity keeps the water open. At such times normally shy species may be near enough to facilitate photography and close viewing opportunities.

Toronto is also blessed with a series of broad ravines running down to the lake in a more or less north to south axis and numerous parks and well-treed cemeteries. In addition to these locales, there are always surprises, such as the small, outdoor alcove of a building in the core of the city where a barred owl spent many weeks roosting, or Old City Hall, where a red-tailed hawk hunted the pigeons that rested on the window ledges. The raptor's abrupt appearance gliding past an upper floor window prompted many an office worker to excitedly call me to report a "huge eagle."

Other places I visit provide me with brief snapshots of what is there, without reference to the past. A lifetime of looking has allowed me to note changes in Toronto's bird populations, many of them positive. The mourning dove was not as common as it is today, and the species seldom wintered. Now it is one of the most common of our birds at any time of year.

The house finch has gone from being unknown in eastern North America (prior to its accidental introduction into New York State in the 1940s) to being a common urban bird throughout much of temperate eastern North America. I once drove several hours, from Toronto to Niagara-on-the-Lake, in the hope of seeing one. It is now one of the commonest species in my neighborhood.

Canada geese, like ring-billed gulls, have undergone population increases of such magnitude that they have been the subject of complaints. These grazing fowl love lawns, of which Toronto has many. The ancestors of the city's Canadas were put there years ago by a zoo official, the late Norm Scollard, who might have been concerned about the severe decline of the large race of the Canada goose in the early and middle part of this century. Or at least, that's the usual theory.

In fact, Canada geese increase rapidly when not perse-cuted and when provided with proper habitat, such as lawns and adjacent waterways. Whether or not any Canadas had ever been "planted," I suspect the outcome would have been the same. Visitors are sometimes pleased that they can see wild geese from city streets. Locals trying to find a clean place to put a picnic blanket in a park are sometimes less pleased.

Red-tailed hawks and American kestrels regularly patrol the Don Valley Parkway, the city's main north-south traffic artery. Late migrant common loons call from the lake each spring, prompting the odd non-birder to call and claim that he or she could have sworn they heard a loon, just like the ones they hear up north, but of course that's impossible, isn't it?

It's just recently that double-crested cormorants have started to nest on the Leslie Street Spit. They have become an increasingly common component of Toronto's avifauna, even

CHANGING MIGRATORY HABITS

Human endeavors are contributing to dramatic changes in the migratory habits of some species.

In recent years, there have been serious declines in several Canada goose populations, particularly those from James Bay and the Hudson Bay lowlands. These mimic the declines of past decades when overhunting had a devastating effect on these birds. On the other hand, the numbers of Canadas have reached high levels in some urban areas, where the birds enjoy grazing on grass lawns in parks, golf courses and other open areas. Geese that migrate face being shot; those that stay in urban areas are more likely to survive.

In the West, the mourning dove population appears stable, but significantly below the twenty-eight-year average, particularly in the central part of the range. However, in areas such as southern Ontario and Michigan, where there is no dove hunting and food is provided by feeders and agriculture, not only are mourning doves reaching record numbers, but they have become non-migratory.

showing up on inland water impoundments, such as Milne Park, Markham, a few blocks from my present home.

Great blue, green-backed and black-crowned night herons disperse throughout the city, each summer, wherever there are marshes, streams, ponds or wide rivers. Killdeer nest on playing fields and school grounds throughout the city, while common nighthawks lay their eggs on the bare gravel of flat rooftops. Chimney swifts nest in abandoned chimneys or roost in such places during migration. And purple martins take advantage of the martin houses provided on Toronto Island.

In his wonderful book, *Flashing Wings*, Richard M. Saunders wrote of April 14, 1935, following a prolonged cold spell: "Today was a great day. Songs were filling the sunlit air in . . . [High] Park and along Grenadier Pond – red-wings, song sparrows, juncoes [sic], golden-crowned kinglets, grackles, robins. And everywhere were brilliant males chasing each other, chasing females, fighting, singing. The spring sap is flowing strong now!"

The enthusiasm of the birder afield on such a glorious day remains the same, but it is shared now by dozens of birders afield in Toronto for every one there might have been when Dick Saunders wrote his book.

FOREST EDGES

Because forest-edge conditions tend to have a greater variety of vegetation than deep forest or open fields, they accommodate a greater variety of birds than does the deep forest. This is why birders are often advised to concentrate birding on the edge of habitat — anywhere two ecosystems come together. But some species of birds are very dependent on deep-forest conditions, particularly as it is only in this habitat that they can usually avoid the parasitical attention of brown-headed cowbirds. The wood thrush, for example, is definitely a bird of the deep, Carolinian forest of eastern North America. Unfortunately, only remnants of these forests survive and some conservationists fear the wood thrush may be facing extinction early in the next century.

GREAT CORMORANT

II
THE EAST COAST

EARLIEST AND LATEST IMPRESSIONS

NORTHERN GANNET

Standing braced against the motion of the deck, I felt like the figurehead of an eighteenth-century sailing vessel, facing into whatever the weather offered, unflinching. Except occasionally I did flinch when a scattering of chill, salt water slapped against my face.

We were taking the car ferry across the Bay of Fundy, from Saint John harbor, New Brunswick, to the port of Digby, Nova Scotia. It was in the mid 1960s and I was in my late teens, enjoying my first experience with pelagic birding, the term given for birding done far from shore. Although I had crossed Lake Ontario by boat, for me, then and now, pelagic birding requires salt water. Among all the passengers on board, only my mother, who would sometimes join me for awhile before the cold drove her back inside, knew that there was something to be seen other than gray waves, gray skies and dreary gray fog.

To reach New Brunswick, we had followed the St. Lawrence River. Once downstream from Montreal, tides and marine organisms start to appear, and below Quebec City, the river rapidly becomes salty.

Although we never saw any, a dwindling resident population of a few hundred belugas, or white whales, live in the river. We have since learned that they are the most toxically contaminated animals on the planet. The poisons they ingest in their food come not only from the effluent of Quebec's paper mills and aluminum smelters, which discharge waste contaminants into major tributaries, but also from the "Golden Horseshoe" of industry that brackets the lower Great Lakes.

At that time, though, the environment seemed remarkably pristine. All along the south shore we encountered picture-postcard-pretty fishing villages and small towns dominated by towering churches and inhabited by unfailingly courteous people. Although the people we met might not have understood why we wanted to observe birds, they were willing to assist us and to tolerate our fumbling efforts to communicate in French.

Great black-backed gulls and double-crested cormorants were among the first birds we saw that we felt we could primarily associate with salt water. Both species have since increased dramatically in the Great Lakes. But the real excitement came when we encountered our first true seabirds, black guillemots. They nested in crevices in the cliff faces overlooking the Gulf of St. Lawrence. We could look down on them as they rapidly flew in and out, their shadows following the shifting contours of the milky green, foam-marbled sea below.

Black guillemots, which are the size of medium-small ducks, are sooty black in color, with bright red feet and large white wing patches. As we watched, they often swam close to shore, calling with thin, high whistles that didn't seem to match their appearance. It may be that such calls are easily heard against low rumblings of surf and sea, an explanation that has been given for the piercing calls of bird species that live along noisy creeks and rapids.

The guillemots frequently displayed their bright red mouth linings. All true seabirds are feathered in shades of black, white, gray, brown or rust. Some subtle rose, peach or golden washes appear on the white plumage of a few species and some iridescent blue or green reflections appear on the black plumage of a few others. Touches of tanager-bright color – bright pink, red, blue, orange or yellow – are relegated to non-feathered areas, including feet, beaks, carbuncles, eyes, orbital rings, lores, pouches or, as in the case of the black guillemot, mouth linings.

Guillemots are members of the seabird family that includes puffins, auks, dovekies, murres and murrelets. Collectively they are known as alcids. These were the first alcids that we had ever seen. Also present was another bird we associated with salt water, the common eider. It is usually portrayed by artists and photographers in the striking black and white piebald coloring of the adult male in breeding plumage, but these bulky ducks, some of them flightless in their summer molts, were the dark, mottled brown of the non-breeding male, female and immature plumages.

Our excitement at viewing seabirds did not keep us from also enjoying the beautiful black spruce, white birch and poplar boreal woods and forests that dominated unfarmed or unpopulated uplands. On the Gaspé Peninsula, we took time away from the sea to observe black-backed woodpeckers; olive-sided, least and yellow-bellied flycatchers; gray jays; common ravens; brown creepers; boreal chickadees; Swainson's, gray-cheeked and hermit thrushes; several warbler species; Lincoln's sparrows; dark-eyed juncos; rusty blackbirds; pine and evening grosbeaks; and white-winged crossbills.

After we reached Percé, on the easternmost face of the Peninsula, the seas were too rough to make the visit that was to be the birding highlight of the trip. For the next couple of days we waited for the windy weather to abate. When we were not driving inland to look for forest birds, we puddled about observing marine life at low tide beneath the towering edifice of Percé Rock. This huge rock, with its soaring pinnacle on the landward end and see-through sea cave at the far end, is one of Canada's best-known and most photographed natural landmarks.

But the place we most wanted to visit was Bonaventure Island. From the moment we came around a bend in the road and saw the town of Percé, the rock and the distant island, we were in a state of high expectation. Out over the expanse of

BROWN CREEPER

COMPETITION AMONG SEABIRDS

Many seabirds species are forced to compete for nesting sites in colonies restricted to islands and headlands. Here large numbers of nest territories may be found in relatively small areas, each the size one nesting bird can successfully defend. Obviously such sites provide minimum space and no food. Seabirds may need to wander far out to sea in search of fish or other marine organisms in enough abundance to satisfy the energy demands of the hunt. When the birds consume more energy in searching for fish than the fish provide, starvation will occur. Although seabirds usually hunt fish species smaller than those of commercial value, that is not always the case; severe depletion of such fish as the capelin can have devastating effects on the seabirds of a region. Particular vulnerability exists during the nesting season, when nest site location limits the distance the birds can go in search of prey.

ocean, dappled by sun and cloud shadow, flew gannets, the first of their species we had ever seen. They glistened white against the gray patterns of sea and sky, their wing tips jet black. One of the world's largest and most famous breeding colonies of northern gannets lay offshore, on Bonaventure Island, if only we could get there.

Small boats take tourists past Bonaventure's sea cliffs, where gannets and other birds nest in great numbers. The boats land on the island, weather permitting. For two days, the weather did not permit. On the third and last day we could spend at Percé, the gods winked and it was announced that if any of the captains thought it safe, the tour boats could sail. However, it was doubtful if they could put us ashore on the island, and anyone prone to sea sickness was advised to stay ashore.

A converted fishing boat, the *Sea Parrot*, was the only tour boat whose captain was willing to set out that day. Once we were well away from shore and birds started to appear, I gallantly offered to stand so there would be more bench space for the other tourists, or so I said. The boat's guide objected, citing rules about everyone being seated, but when he saw that the huge swell and up and down motion of the boat did not bother me, he relented. I really wasn't being courteous; by standing I could enjoy a better view of the birds.

Black guillemots flew past us or swam in the heaving seas close by. Great cormorants, northern gannets and great black-backed and herring gulls were all easily identified. For a few moments I puzzled over a gull with a black half collar. There were so many they must be common, but what were they? Suddenly I realized that they must be black-legged kittiwakes, although not birds in the adult plumages so often illustrated in bird books. They were immature birds. My bird books didn't emphasize the dark collar as a field mark, and for a moment I had only been thinking in terms of the adult plumage. This was August and many young birds were fully fledged and on their own.

The mainland was soon hidden by high waves and mist, and as we circled the island, I became disoriented. However, what appeared to be the landward side of the island was sloped, while the seaward side ended abruptly in huge cliffs, giant mounds of fallen rock, soaring headlands and deep coves visible through shifting white veils of sea spray. The cliffs, which were predominantly an oxidized red, had been sculpted by natural forces into intricate shapes and surfaces inlaid with millions of pebbles and stones of all sizes. They were also the nesting grounds of hundreds of thousands of birds.

Most common were the black-legged kittiwakes, their white breasts gleaming from huge numbers of seaweed nests precariously clinging to the tiniest of prominences. The birds would swirl out from the cliffs in great masses, in testimony to the life-sustaining abundance of marine fauna in the cold seas.

Kittiwakes circled and called, hovered and swept by in great curves, milling like snowflakes but never colliding. The goose-sized gannets were much more direct in flight, lacking the gulls' maneuverability. While the gulls would flutter to the sea's surface, the gannets would dive from high above, folding their wings back and arrowing downward to slice into the waters.

A few razorbills and common murres could also be spotted on the cliffs. Others were swimming in the sea. These black and white alcids were so crisply patterned and so cleanly perfect that they were distinctly nautical in appearance. Unfortunately, most of the alcids, including all of the puffins, had left for the season.

The connections between my eyes and mind seemed to overload at times, as I found myself focusing from detail to panorama and from individuals to moving masses, all against enormous rock backdrops. Individual birds would somehow become multitudes within a twinkling white galaxy. The constant movement seemed orchestrated, but with a wild and alien intent.

The captain brought the boat in as close to the exploding surf at the base of the cliffs as he felt was prudent, aware that there were two birders aboard whose interest was at fever pitch. Once past the cliffs, he even decided that he would attempt a landing. My feelings about this were mixed. I certainly wanted to set foot on an island I had dreamt about visiting since early childhood, but I was also interested in avoiding a shipwreck. Mom simply thought it was too dangerous. So did most of the other passengers, but not the captain.

We docked, or rather, the captain did. A mooring rope was thrown to a man on the jetty just as a woman from Maine was saying, "I really don't think we should be doing this."

From the landing we had the option of walking overland to the site of the gannet colony or being carried on a wagon pulled by horses. We looked at the rugged, uphill trail of red mud, then at the heavy wagon filled with people and decided that we could not, in good conscience, add our combined weight to the horses' burden. For us, as well as the poor horses, it was a good choice. On foot we could more closely examine the intricacies of the stunted spruce and the rough turf of the windswept forest. We admired ancient, gnarled trees that were colored in somber tones and festooned with hanging mosses and ragged clumps of lichens.

Pine grosbeaks, the males bright pink and soft gray, the females burnished amber and gray, perched and called from the tops of small spruces. Juncos flitted from bush to shrub. Gray jays cocked their heads and looked at us with innocent curiosity tempered by a trace of the mischievous.

We finally reached the end of the trail and the gannet colony. Most of the gannets were far beyond reach of visitors. As gannet colonies grow, first occupying the inaccessible cliff-ledge nest sites, they eventually spill over the top onto flat tableland. Here, at one corner of this immense gathering, cords strung from post to post delineated paths the tourists were asked to stay on as they viewed the gannets. Birds close to the path were apparently quite conditioned to people and

COMMON MURRE

served to provide close-up detail. In the distance we could see the masses of birds and sense the great size of the colony.

We viewed many of the ritualized ceremonies for which gannets are famous. In his book, *The Gannet*, seabird biologist Bryan Nelson describes gannet behavior at the colony: "Territorial behavior comprises *fighting* and the various forms of *ritualized threat: flying-in with calling* and *bowing* . . . Sexual, pair-bonding and pair maintaining behavior comprise sexual *advertising* (male); *prospecting* (female); *nape-biting* (male); *facing-away* (female); *copulation with biting* (male); *mutual fencing* (greeting) and *mutual preening* . . . Activities functional in making a nest and caring for egg and chick are: *gathering nest material; nest building; nest digging; incubation; brooding* and *feeding the chick* . . . Body-care activities form another major group, comprising *bathing, preening, oiling, headshaking* (sideways and rotary), *defecating* and *thermo-regulating*." Each italicized phrase defines an activity or combination of activities. Most of those activities are evident in a gannet colony at any one time in a panorama of constant motion.

Of all these displays, fighting is the most spectacular. Disputes are usually between two birds, but as the combatants move into other nesting territories in their struggle with each other, neighbors may join the fray. The birds jab at each other with their beaks, or grab at necks, wings, tails or whatever is in reach. Much of this aggressive behavior has evolved in response to strong competition for limited nesting sites placed in close proximity.

Some of the chicks were still predominantly covered in dense, white down, while others were well feathered in the dark plumage of early maturity. It takes several years to attain the full adult plumage, and some of the flying birds were showing mixtures of both.

The nature trails were well arranged so that it was possible to look across dramatic chasms and down opposing cliff faces to the churning sea, far below. On those cliffs we saw a few common murres and razorbills, or razor-billed auks, as

DROPPING IN ON NEIGHBORS

When wind blows against the face of a cliff, it has nowhere to go but up. Cliff-nesting birds, such as the northern gannet, take advantage of these updrafts when they launch themselves into flight. Landing can be a far more awkward procedure. All four toes of the gannet are joined by webbing, which, along with the surface of the wings and tail, provides a braking mechanism for the landing bird. Still, it's often a clumsy activity that can promote much disgruntled reaction from neighboring birds as they disentangle themselves from the new arrival who has literally dropped in on them.

they were called at that time on this side of the Atlantic.

It was mid-summer, and too late in the season to encounter either Leach's storm-petrels or Atlantic puffins. Earlier in the year, the nocturnal storm-petrels had nested in huge numbers in burrows and crevices in the shaggy turf. So had puffins, albeit in much smaller numbers. I reached into each burrow or small crevice I passed, hoping to feel the sharp bite of a puffin's huge, razor-edged beak or the more gentle nip of a storm-petrel. No such luck. I did find the dried wings of Leach's storm-petrels, still attached to the bones of the shoulder girdle. The sooty brown wing feathers had the slightly oily feel and distinctive musk smell of storm-petrels. I've kept them to this day.

After leaving Percé, we drove down into New Brunswick, enjoying the bleak scenery of the northern shore, adding to our list of birds seen, and visiting Moncton, Fredericton and Saint John. It was at Saint John that we boarded the ferry for a cruise across the Bay of Fundy and my first true pelagic birding adventure.

Apart from the gulls and cormorants of Saint John harbor, the first seabirds I saw were greater shearwaters. With dark caps, small white rump patches and dirty smudges on their white bellies, they were quite distinctive. They were on their wintering grounds. Greater shearwaters breed only on remote islands in the South Atlantic, during the southern hemisphere's summer months.

Just as the books of my childhood said they would do, the shearwaters glided on stiff wings between the waves. At times, as they banked, it looked as though the lower wing tip was scratching the water's surface. Their mastery of flight was profound as they vanished in wave troughs and reappeared, engaged in a complex dance with the sea.

Twice I saw a sooty shearwater, dark all over except for its silvery wing linings. Once a Cory's shearwater flew by close enough for me to see the gentle blend of its medium-brown upperparts into the white underparts and the light color of the beak. This species breeds in the eastern Atlantic and Mediterranean.

There were sometimes several minutes when no living thing was in view. I'd think about moving inside, then suddenly a shearwater's bold form would appear off the bow and I would keep it in view through my binoculars until spray covered the lens or until the bird was swallowed up by mist and distance. Pelagic birding, I learned, was a matter of always looking. That's how I managed to see a few small flocks of red phalaropes, colored in the grays of non-breeding plumage.

In addition to four life birds recorded on a single crossing, the trip was wonderfully crowned by the appearance of a small pod of harbor porpoises encountered as we entered the outer reaches of Digby Harbor.

I've made several more trips down east since that first journey to the Atlantic region, including late winter visits to Prince Edward Island and the harp seal whelping grounds on the ice fields in the Gulf of St. Lawrence.

When Prince Edward Island is deep in snow, birding opportunities are limited, but there is pleasure to be had in touring the pristine winterscape when other tourists are absent. The great red cliffs along the island's northern edge are none the less scenic for the presence of snow and the absence of human swimmers on the beaches below, particularly when a bald eagle soars by low overhead. Barrow's goldeneyes can be found in open patches of water where rivers meet the sea, sometimes in the company of buffleheads, oldsquaws or greater scaup.

One of the greatest of birding pleasures to be had in Prince Edward Island in the winter is the spectacle of thousands of snow buntings swirling low overhead. Never had I seen so many as I did on the day I drove up to North Point, on the northeast corner of the island. I stopped and stared as the little white birds filled the air all around me. The white of their breasts reflected the gently contoured snow below, and against the tawny gray cloud cover of late afternoon, they seemed to glow. No written description can adequately convey the simple beauty of these small birds at such times. Although I have become a lover of tropical splendor and a connoisseur of steaming rain forests, in all of nature's designs, snow buntings in a Canadian winter remain a favorite source of delight.

The last time I saw the Canadian North Atlantic was in March, 1989. I was with animal protection colleagues in St. John's, Newfoundland, to protest the hunting of harp seals. After a media conference, I took the opportunity to steal away from the hotel and have lunch with a scientist I knew, who was studying the declines in populations of the harlequin duck, thick-billed murre and common eider.

As luck would have it, my trip coincided with a conference of seabird biologists at Memorial University. A pelagic trip was planned to the Witless Bay bird sanctuary the next day. Would I like to go?

Mention of Witless Bay brought back memories of a book I had received from my parents for my thirteenth birthday. The book was *The Birds of Newfoundland*, written by Harold S. Peters and Thomas D. Burleigh, both of the U.S. Fish and Wildlife Service, and illustrated by Roger Tory Peterson. How I used to pore over that book and its wonderful illustrations. One plate, particularly, came to mind. While most plates show generic backgrounds, Plate 16, illustrating the razorbill, common murre, Atlantic puffin and black guillemot, features an actual Newfoundland scene, with the birds in the foreground and an island in the background. The caption reads "All adult summer plumages at Witless Bay Islands." The map at the front of the book shows Witless Bay at the easternmost reach of this, the most eastern edge of North America.

I had given up much hope of birding before leaving home, but, as always, I had brought my binoculars, just in case. And so now, not too far out of St. John's, I found myself boarding a converted fishing vessel, as I had, two decades earlier, at Percé, Quebec.

THREATS TO SEABIRDS

When major oil spills occur, we often see news photos of dying seabirds covered in the oil residue. But while such destruction is dramatic, it is overshadowed by the much greater, if less well-documented, incremental effects of numerous small oil spills, including those caused by the illegal flushing of ballast and tanks at sea.

Fish nets, particularly the notorious drift nets, enmesh millions more seabirds each year. Drift nets, appropriately called "curtains of death" by environmentalists, are floating nets that may be many miles long. Fortunately, the United Nations has taken steps to make them illegal. However, lost commercial nets or net fragments made of long-lasting synthetic materials continue to catch and destroy birds and other marine life for decades.

Foxes, raccoons, rats, pigs, goats, stoats, cats, dogs and other predators or scavengers that are accidentally or intentionally placed onto remote islands can also be a serious threat to the survival of seabird nesting colonies.

Two boats went out. Among the scientists on our vessel was David Nettleship, well known for his seabird studies and an expert with whom I had conferred on seabird and fish population issues through the years, but had never met. This was an appropriate time and place to finally make his acquaintance.

The air was clear and frigid. There was a high swell on the sea, even as we left the harbor at Bay Bulls. We were hardly underway when we saw a small bird that excited me greatly. Only the size of a starling and colored black and white, it swam with cork-like buoyancy on the heaving surface of the sea. It was a dovekie, the Atlantic's smallest alcid and a species I had never before encountered.

The land was snow-covered and ice extended out from the more protected shorelines, but the black-legged kittiwakes were already nesting on the cliffs of the Witless Bay islands. Their seaweed nests seemed to be glued to impossibly perpendicular rock surfaces. On the famous Gull, Green and Great islands, the soaring rockscapes revealed tortured lines of strata and were often tilted on crazy angles. Wherever there was enough slope to the land for grass to grow, sunken, dark patches of bare earth, where generations of puffins had dug burrows, intersected white snow to form intricate patterns. There were no puffins present. We were two days earlier than the earliest date that the species had been known to appear in Witless Bay. Although alcids of other species had also not appeared yet, I was happy with the one good sighting of the dovekie.

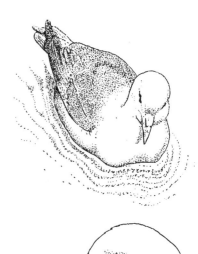

The kittiwakes put on an incredible show of numbers and massed formation flying, particularly when an adult bald eagle flew over the top of one of the islands, far overhead. All the kittiwakes erupted from the cliff faces in a living blizzard, its vortex the eagle.

One Iceland gull, identified by dozens of experienced eyes by noting how far the white wing tips projected past the tip of the tail, was perched on a seaside rock of cathedral proportions, just above the spray line. There were a few herring

NORTHERN FULMAR

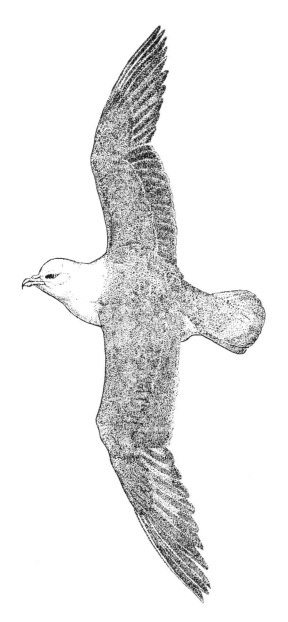

NORTHERN FULMAR

and great black-backed gulls about, as well. And amid teeming masses of white kittiwakes, we saw one common raven. The raven may be considered a bird of ill omen by some, and its numbers cause those kinds of people who are forever wanting to "control" wildlife to want to control them in northern communities, but for me the species is an indicator of wilderness. Usually where I have encountered ravens, I have encountered enjoyable interaction with wildlife in beautiful, natural settings.

The Canadian and marine biologists from around the world talked of the idiocy of Canadian government policy concerning the northwest Atlantic fishery. They knew then that the collapse in cod and other fish stocks that has since happened was going to occur, as did many fishermen and, presumably, politicians. But the scientists also knew that nothing would be done until it was too late. Such depressing talk was interrupted by shouts and pointing as this bird or that came into view. Most exciting for me were the fulmars, a superficially gull-like species of shearwater.

In its light color phase, the northern fulmar has a dove-gray mantle and white body, like a gull. A small smear of pigment on the plumage in front of each eye makes its dark eyes look even larger and darker than they really are. It has a somewhat more bull-headed look than gulls and tends to soar with greater skill, like other shearwaters. There is a dark phase, but we saw none that day.

Out over the ocean were lines of white birds with black wing tips: gannets. They were returning from more southern haunts and would soon be nesting on some remote island or headland. David Nettleship thought that gannets might once have nested in Witless Bay, but as is true of virtually all the prominent fauna of the Atlantic regions, their numbers have greatly declined since humans began "managing" fish stocks and other wildlife in the region. This decline is well, if depressingly, described in Farley Mowat's fine book, *Sea of Slaughter*. Certainly there are fewer common eiders than there once were, but we did see some, the last of the seabird species we encountered.

As we were about to leave, the powerful surf continued to erupt in spray-textured bursts against the massive rocks. The stage was set, and the first players were now arriving. The greater multitudes of seals and whales and seabirds were about to enter from the wings somewhere past the horizon. They would play out their respective roles as another spring and summer season unfolded. We had caught only the beginning of the first act.

GREAT BLACK-BACKED GULL

B R I E R I S L A N D

That first long drive my mother and I took heading east from Ontario ended at the home of Wickerson Lent, the light-keeper of Brier Island, Nova Scotia. It is an island that filled my dreams for many years.

Wickerson had been recommended to us by the well-known naturalist Robbie Tufts, whom we briefly visited at his home in Wolfville. Tufts was, I believe, in his early nineties, still fit, alert and active. He patiently answered our questions about local birding and told us tales of past adventures during a few wonderful hours spent in his wood-paneled den, the flames in his stone fireplace burning logs he had cut.

With a letter of introduction from Tufts firmly in hand, we started down the long peninsula of land called the Digby Neck. We had to cross the peninsula's two straits on small ferries, with the white foam breaking over the hood of our car. At the far end was Brier Island and West Light, the home of Wickerson, his wife Madeleine and their four children.

There is an awkwardness to suddenly becoming a stranger's houseguest. Mother wondered what Madeleine's Baptist sensibilities would do about the cigarettes in her purse or the bottle of rye in one of the suitcases. No matter. You don't have to be worldly to be understanding. Madeleine was used to hosting birders and, as a rich source of local gossip, judged no one too harshly. She loved to talk about Joshua Slocum, Brier Island's favorite son, who was the first man to sail alone around the world. However, the stories she told more often were about suicides, madness, mysterious deaths, drownings and other accidents. She liked to tell these tales on those nights when the fog was thick and the foghorn groaned loudly from the whistle house.

Madeleine had only once been out of Nova Scotia, and then only next door to New Brunswick. In fact, she had rarely been off this small island. When Russian trawlers and a massive factory ship appeared just offshore one evening, she mused, as she sat in her rocking chair, on the advisability of closing the front gate. Were the Russians not catching so many fish, they would, I suspect, have been more welcome, particularly if either birders or Baptists were among them.

Sometimes I accompanied Wickerson to attend the light, one of the last manually run lighthouses in the country. He would roll a cigarette, fire it up and talk about foreigners buying the cheap land. The future was pressing hard on Brier Island. Sometimes he'd talk about the past and the war years. He remembered the name and the number of the first American serviceman's body he had pulled from the surf when Axis U-boats prowled nearby. There were others, after that, whose names he did not recall. He showed me how fish was smoked and may have been disappointed that the smoked, uncooked fish sat uneasily in my stomach.

The woodstove in the house burned constantly. Apart from Madeleine's wonderful baking, nearly every kind of food was boiled. My mother and I made frequent trips to the woods in search of fresh blueberries to ease the monotony of boiled food. The tea, always simmering in its metal pot with tea bags thrown in from time to time, was powerful stuff.

Wickerson had a tough, lean, weathered look earned from years as a sailor and a fisherman. As a teenager, he had lost a leg in a hunting accident before the war, and he constantly wore out artificial legs on the rocky shoreline of Brier Island. Occasionally using his battered .410 shotgun as a cane, he tramped over the roughest terrain, sometimes falling but never complaining.

VISITING BRIER ISLAND

Brier Island is worth visiting at any time of year, but August and September may be the best times to see the maximum number of individual birds and different species. In August, the shorebird migration peaks and the songbird migration is getting underway. In September, there are still plenty of shorebirds to be seen and the songbird migration peaks. The raptor migration begins in September as well and continues into October. Rarities can occur at any time, but it's always worth visiting Brier Island or any other good birding location along the coast following a major storm. At such times, wind-blown strays of great rarity may put in an appearance.

Wickerson was, like myself at the time, licensed to kill birds for scientific purposes. He prided himself on his ability to find and collect birds new to the area, thereby leaving his mark on Nova Scotia's ornithological history. Brier Island's location on the southwestern tip of the province, where the Bay of Fundy meets the Atlantic Ocean, makes it the Point Pelee of the Maritimes.

The island was a blend of two ecosystems I wanted to know better – the coastal boreal woods and the shoreline. Wickerson and I tramped the beaches, coves, rocky outcroppings and spruce bogs. Among the thousands of questions I fired at him as we walked was whether there were Lincoln's sparrows or sharks in the neighborhood.

Wickerson paused for a moment at my enthusiastic juxtaposition of totally unrelated species and then said, "Yes."

"Yes?"

"Yes. We have both sharks and Lincoln's sparrows."

Our first visit only lasted a few days, but the next year we returned for a prolonged stay in late August. The diversity of habitats and the freedom to move about without the inconvenience of true wilderness were major attractions.

On one side of the island there stood giant black basalt columns, encrusted with lichen above the tide line and white barnacles below. It was a good place to sit in the sun and daydream, while watching the great breakers of the Atlantic burst against the rock. Just offshore, eiders and great cormorants flew low over the churning white foam. The adult male eiders were starting to develop some of the white-and-black pattern of their winter plumage, although most were females and young, colored dark brown like the rocks and the seaweed. On the rocky beaches and in tide pools, masses of algae of various types formed endless swirling patterns, which I loved to sketch and photograph.

The Bay of Fundy has the world's highest tides and the shoreline was constantly changing. At low tides, large numbers of shorebirds gathered on the exposed mudflats of shallow

GOLDEN PLOVERS

There are three species of golden plover. The one most likely to be seen in North America is the lesser (or American) golden plover (*Pluvialis dominica*). It has the largest bill and longest wing of the trio. A little smaller, trimmer and brighter of color is the Pacific golden plover (*P. fulva*). It is found in Asia, although a small number breed in Alaska. This species was formerly considered a race of the lesser golden plover. The largest and most heavyset of the goldens is the greater (or Eurasian) golden plover (*P. apricaria*). Its stripe over the eye tends to be less well-marked than the stripe on the other two. Although native to Europe and Asia, it shows up fairly regularly in Newfoundland in spring, when its white flank stripe is an aid to identification.

coves and bays. Red knots, now in the gray plumage of autumn, were present in flocks, each bird with the bland, gentle expression characteristic of the species. Some ruddy turnstones still sported the red of breeding plumage, as they probed about among rocks and seaweed; others were brown. Short-billed dowitchers, sanderlings, semipalmated sandpipers, black-bellied plovers, common snipe, Baird's sandpipers, greater yellowlegs and many other familiar species were common in greater numbers than I had previously known.

The pea fields on the high center of the island were a good place to look for lesser golden plovers. They were in molt, each bird distinctive from the others in the combination of bright breeding plumage and the less colorful feathers of winter.

Although the two trips were planned to coincide with the shorebird migration, we also encountered migrant song-birds. Wickerson gave me a dead yellow warbler, a northern waterthrush and some specimens of other warblers that had struck the lighthouse a few weeks earlier, in late July or early August. Such migratory species as ruby-crowned kinglets and yellow-rumped warblers – usually associated with late fall back home in the Toronto area – nested on Brier Island. Non-migratory boreal chickadees and gray jays seemed appropriate to the northern feel of the island's spruce and poplar bogs.

As in the best birding locations, there was always that wonderful sense of not quite knowing what was going to be seen next. Once a northern mockingbird showed up in the tiny community of Westport, at the far end of the island from the light. Another time it might be a red-throated loon at sea or gannets in the distance.

The only life bird I recall from Brier Island was a Swainson's hawk, a western species that had been recorded on the island before. It perched in plain view on top of a tele-phone pole while I compared its dark breast, lighter belly and the lightly barred pattern of its tail with the picture in my field guide. Sharp-shinned hawks and kestrels were both

YELLOW-RUMPED WARBLER

BROAD-WINGED HAWK

extremely abundant. Northern harriers would glide low over open areas, their wings held in a shallow "V." Merlins were also common. The bold flight of these little falcons would scatter the sandpipers.

Broad-winged hawks perched on nearly every telephone post on the island and up and down Long Island and Digby Neck. Back home I had seen them by the hundreds, even the thousands, but usually as they circled far overhead. Here they were relatively tame and perched close enough to be carefully examined through our binoculars.

One bitterly cold, star-spangled night I stood in front of the Lents' house and listened to the deep whooshing exhalation of a great whale, probably a finback, just offshore. It was my first encounter with any kind of whale. The next afternoon, Wickerson took me out in his dory to a protected cove just behind the house. He pulled up his lobster traps from the bottom to show me not only the lobsters, but also the crabs, sea urchins and other marine fauna that made their way into the traps. When I pulled off a remarkable wing shot, dropping a green-winged teal in mid-flight, Wickerson grinned his approval and said he'd make a hunter of me yet. But he was wrong.

I dreamed so often of Brier Island because, I think, it represented an ultimate sort of freedom. It was glorious to be in a wonderfully diverse natural setting, to sample it, to take home parts of it and to try to reproduce the essence of the place afterward as a writer and artist. At one time I had thought of buying a house and spending summers there, but integral to my memories of Brier Island is Wickerson Lent and his family. Madeleine is dead; the family has moved away; Wickerson has retired and moved off the island. Brier Island belongs to a different, younger me and a time when things were simpler and when I had yet to travel widely and see other wonderful places. But I still remember it and recommend it as a top birding site in the Maritimes.

OUT OF BOSTON

SOOTY SHEARWATER

The eighty-six-foot (26 m) long *Virginia C-II* was designed to take tourists out into the Atlantic to look at whales, but I was on board in May, 1984, to look for birds, as well. As the boat slid out of its moorings and started to cross Boston Bay, a tour guide talked about the surrounding landmarks, dating from the American Revolution. Less because of my Loyalist ancestors (including Benedict Arnold) and more because of my interest as a birder, I paid little attention, focusing, instead, on local avifauna.

I watched the buoyant grace of delicate Bonaparte's gulls with delight. Sharply patterned in gray, black and white, they wore the black hoods of their breeding plumage. Great black-backed gulls patrolled the harbor, along with the smaller herring gulls and still smaller ring-billed gulls. They were joined by common terns, whose colloquial name, sea swallow, evokes their elegant form and flying skill.

Both great and double-crested cormorants were on hand. The white bellies of the immature greats helped distinguish them from the double-crested cormorants with their more solidly brown underparts. But there was an overall darker, heavier look to the adult greats, quite evident during this opportunity to compare the two species. (Such a distinction, based more on overall impression than specific features, is known among birders as the "jizz" of the bird.) With their sinuous necks and green eyes, cormorants have a vaguely reptilian look. Their appearance, combined with their voracious appetite for fish, earn cormorants a degree of notoriety. They have always been one of my favorite subjects to draw or paint.

Soon we reached open water, the headlands slipping down below the horizon behind us. Most of the people settled on chairs and benches, knowing it would be a couple of hours before we reached Stellwagen Bank, where, with luck, the whales would be waiting. I stayed at the railing in the hope of seeing seabirds, but except for lines of northern gannets, I had little luck.

Once, however, a single sooty shearwater glided by, its distinctive silvery wing linings catching the sun as it searched for small fish, crustaceans and cephalopods. The bird was likely from the Falklands, or perhaps Tierra del Fuego, deep in the high latitudes of the southern hemisphere, where sooty shearwaters nest, beginning in October. Found in both hemispheres, the sooty shearwaters of the Atlantic tend to migrate north off South and North American coastlines before curving east, toward Europe, where they are usually seen late in the northern summer. From there they continue south, off the coasts of Europe and Africa, before finally swinging back toward the bottom end of South America. Most sooties are found in the Pacific region, and worldwide the species is millions strong. In New Zealand, about 250,000 are legally killed and marketed as food each year.

To keep us interested while we were still an hour from our destination, the shipboard naturalist handed out an excellent whale and dolphin identification chart. He talked to us over the loudspeaker, imparting many facts about whales, expertly heightening our anticipation.

Although the sun was hot and the sky clear, the wind was cold. Those of us who stayed on deck tried to keep as much of our anatomy as possible in the sun. The sea was choppy. Some people were obviously becoming bored and a couple became seasick, leaning over the railing, not necessarily heeding the captain's friendly advice to do so on the leeward side of the boat. Crew members carried buckets on ropes with which they pulled water from the sea to be dashed onto

JIZZ AND FIELD MARKS

The term *jizz* was coined by British birders. The bird's jizz is the blend of often subtle aspects of form, shape, proportion, behavior and attitude that allow it to be identified, sometimes at a glance, even when the most obvious identifying characteristics of color and pattern may not be apparent.

Field marks are those characteristics of color and pattern (and sometimes structure) that serve to distinguish a species from other similar species. Field marks are not necessarily a bird's most obvious features, since the most obvious feature of its color and pattern may be shared by other species. For example, the red of a scarlet tanager is the first thing you see, but it is not a field mark, because the hepatic tanager, summer tanager, northern cardinal and vermilion flycatcher are also bright red. But the combination of an all-red body with black wings and tail constitutes a field mark.

the sloping decks to clean away products of poorly aimed regurgitation.

Suddenly, in the distance, we could see the exhaled breath of our first whale. Everyone was quickly alert.

A fin-topped back briefly curved up through the waves, not much, but enough to identify the species as a humpback whale. We came closer, and the captain cut the engine of the boat to idle. Some of the great humpbacks came extremely close alongside. They did so on their own; never did our captain pursue them. Some individual whales chose to stay well back, but others seemed curious, or interested, or perhaps just cooperative. People laughed and pointed and held children above the rail. Cameras clicked furiously.

Huge snouts erupted out of the sea, paused at the apex and then slowly slid back down below the surface. From the side of the boat we could look down on the whales as they glided by just below the surface. Their huge tail flukes thrust straight up out of the water when they began their dives.

The whales attracted us, but what attracted the whales was an abundance of sand lances, slender little fish that congregate at Stellwagen Bank in astronomical numbers. Whales depend on small organisms, such as krill or sand lances, in sufficient abundance to fuel their massive needs. Thus, for all their great size, they are dangerously vulnerable to any forces that reduce accessibility to traditionally abundant food or that deplete the food.

For all that the whales – cows, bulls and calves – fascinated me, so did the people. When whales surfaced almost within arm's reach, some people broke into spontaneous applause, although for whose benefit I wasn't sure. But they were not so much thinking as reacting in a rather primal way, the whales obviously touching something deep within them. Having ignored the seabirds I had found so fascinating, these people were now spellbound. Maybe, in time, future generations will have such positive feelings not only toward the most spectacular of the "charismatic megafauna," but also

SEAGULLS DON'T EXIST

Of all the lost causes I support I suspect none is more hopeless than my efforts to persuade people to drop the word *seagull* from their vocabularies. Each gull species has its own name, and none is called a seagull. In fact, most species of gulls are found on large bodies of water far from the sea. Although some do occur along sea coasts, they rarely go to sea. (The black-legged kittiwake is an exception, but there are few others.) Usually gulls are scavengers, patrolling shorelines, following tractors as they plow fields, visiting landfill sites or looking elsewhere for scraps or offal.

RED PHALAROPE

for a wider variety of this planet's wondrous species, including sooty shearwaters and double-crested cormorants.

As I turned my attention back to the birds, I noticed more northern gannets present, their white and black bodies flashing above the distant horizon. Binoculars revealed that some of the birds were showing patches of darker, immature plumage across the backs. These would have been two- or three-year-old birds, a little shy of the full adult plumage.

Once we saw a pod of Atlantic white-sided dolphins. These sleek cetaceans often associate with the huge humpbacks, although the nature of the relationship is not clear. The dolphins curved up out of the waves, not quite clearing the water, and then returned to the depths, with no indication that they had noticed either us or the whales. Given what we are learning about dolphin intelligence, I could not help but wonder what they thought of us as we pondered them. And what thoughts existed in the great brains of the whales all around?

My musings were interrupted by a flock of red phalaropes. These tiny birds were in the non-breeding gray plumage that gives them the name "gray phalarope" in Britain. They are also known as "whale birds" from their habit of accompanying cetaceans; they sometimes walk on the exposed backs of surfaced whales, apparently gleaning parasites from the whales' skin.

The most oceanic of all shorebirds, the three species of phalarope float on the water like corks. They dab their heads in delicate, bobbling movements to take food items from just under or on the water's surface as they swim about in abrupt little circles. These curious swimming movements are believed to stir up small organisms and edible debris from the bottoms of shallow ponds, although the same movements occur when the birds are floating in deep water. Red phalaropes are sometimes encountered in huge numbers. I only saw a few, and they were flying, not swimming, but I could easily have overlooked some birds on the water.

Later I wrote of my whale-watching experience, "My own, subjective impression of the whales was one of ponderous grace and gentleness, each animal a manifestation of the inherent dignity of wild creatures at peace in their native realms, with some of them briefly willing to share fragments of their lives with the small, noisy, colorfully garbed beings crowding the decks of the *Virginia C-II*."

We were back in Boston at about 5:30 p.m. that afternoon. The trip had taken nearly seven hours. A laughing gull was my last new species of bird for the day. Back at the World Society for the Protection of Animals conference that I was attending, someone said they had heard I had gone whale watching.

"That's right," I answered.

"Hmmm," the conference delegate replied. "And I thought you'd probably go birding."

I thought of the gannets, the shearwater and the cormorants, and the whales and the dolphins and the people on board the boat, and said nothing. Bird watching, whale watching or people watching, it had been fun.

PHALAROPES

Phalaropes are little shorebirds characterized by toes that have scalloped lobes down their lengths. The male, which has duller plumage than the female, incubates the eggs and tends the young without assistance from his mate. There are three species of phalarope. The red phalarope (*Phalaropus fulicaria*) is a Holarctic species that nests only in the far north. It has the thickest beak of the three and tends to winter at sea. The red-necked phalarope (*Ph. lobatus*) used to be called the northern phalarope in North America. It, too, is a Holarctic species that nests in the high latitudes and usually winters at sea. It is the smallest of the trio and combines the chunkiness of the red phalarope with the needle-thin bill of the Wilson's. The Wilson's phalarope (*Ph. tricolor*) breeds only in North America and winters only in South America. It nests on inland lakes and large prairie sloughs.

WOOD STORK

JEKYLL ISLAND, GEORGIA

Probably it can be traced to a couple of popular songs or *Gone with the Wind* or a plethora of southern fauna and lush flora to be found there. Whatever the reasons, my mother had always wanted to visit Georgia. Since I never mind going anywhere there is good birding, one autumn I took a holiday and drove my mother to Georgia, ending our journey at Jekyll Island.

We arrived at night, driving across the long, bleak causeway that crosses a huge salt marsh and bridges the Intra-coastal Waterway that separates the island from the mainland. Even in the darkness, as we sought and found the hotel, we could sense this was an exciting place for naturalists fleeing the early stages of a northern winter.

In the morning, just at sunrise, I took our two dogs, Buffy and Charm, to the beach on the far side of the great sand dunes, behind the hotel where we were staying. Both dogs had been trained from puppyhood not to disturb any wildlife. As it was late November and well past the usual tourist season, the shore was virtually deserted.

The beach extended some eight or nine miles (13 km) along the edge of the Atlantic. To the south I could see the water tower that is one of the low-lying island's major land-marks. The tide was out, revealing elongated tidal ponds, or runnels, that glinted in the low morning light and rippled when teased by stray sea breezes. A pale-colored ghost crab scuttled sideways, leaving behind a wonderfully delicate tracery of footprints in the sand.

As I continued along the beach, I encountered a variety of shells – clam, whelk and slipper – as well as the beautiful little coquina shells. Further along were the remains of plumed worms; bits of blue, calico and other species of crab shell; the round, white sand dollar remains that are called "tests"; skate egg cases; a dead puffer fish; long strands of marine algae; the curious, curved carapaces of horseshoe crabs; and much else to arouse my innate beachcombing instincts.

Overhead flew ring-billed gulls, their white underparts glowing peach-pink in the sun. The sun quickly warmed the air. The breezes became warm and fresh, and the sea was remarkably calm.

From time to time, one or more loons, both common and red-throated, would fly by. They are easily distinguished from other waterfowl in flight by the position of the wings – halfway between the tip of the pointed beak and the tips of the toes. The large, webbed feet extend out past the loon's short tail. Both species were in winter plumage, but the larger size, heavier bill and more uniform gray of the backs easily distinguished the commons from the smaller, more delicate red-throateds.

Out over the ocean, just above the wavetops, were three red-breasted mergansers, their forms superficially loon-like, but more trim and dashing. A flock of greater scaup passed by, plus several double-crested cormorants. These were all familiar species I enjoyed seeing in unfamiliar surroundings.

I continued walking south, more interested in birds than in breakfast, while the dogs playfully explored new sensations all around. Dunlin, sanderlings, ruddy turnstones, black-bellied plover and willets were the first shorebird species encountered.

In the distance I could see large flocks of birds on the sandbars paralleling the beach. As we approached, there were, as expected, numbers of laughing gulls, some still sporting the black heads of breeding plumage. The gulls stood out among swarming masses of small sandpipers. From an even closer vantage, the small shorebirds revealed themselves to be

VISITING JEKYLL ISLAND

Jekyll Island is everything coastal barrier islands should be, except, perhaps, uninhabited. But then, were it uninhabited, it would be less accessible to birders. Under Georgia law, two-thirds of the island, which is a state park, cannot be developed. Once privately owned by a group of millionaires, the island is about nine miles (14.5 km) long and one and one-quarter miles (2 km) wide, with eleven miles (17.7 km) of beach. It is separated from the rest of Georgia by an extensive area of salt marsh, intersected by Jekyll Creek and a meandering network of tidal creeks.

A paved road encircles the island, but birders often enjoy walking on the beach or following the extensive network of bicycle pathways. Tourist accommodation includes a campground, cottages and hotels.

western, semipalmated and least sandpipers, each very similar to the other in size, shape, pattern and color, and collectively known by birders as "peeps."

Royal terns, with shaggy crests, and the slightly larger and more compact Caspian terns perched on the sand in the company of laughing, ring-billed and herring gulls and a species high on my list of hoped-for species – black skimmers. There were only three skimmers that first morning, but early morning walks on the beach became a regular ritual and later I encountered hundreds of them. I enjoyed watching them skim tidal ponds, their elongated lower mandibles neatly slicing the surface for tiny fish or other aquatic organisms, as their long wings carried them just above the water.

As I trekked back to the hotel for breakfast, a bottle-nosed dolphin swam along beside me, about thirty feet (9 m) offshore. Later we saw many other dolphins, particularly from the vantage point of the towering fishing pier on the island's north end, overlooking St. Simons Sound.

On my second morning I added Sandwich and Forster's terns, semipalmated plover and killdeer to my list of beach birds, plus an endangered species, the piping plover. All my life I seem to have stumbled on piping plovers with disproportionate regularity and I was glad to maintain the tradition in Georgia. Just as the back of the similar, but very common, semipalmated plover is the color of wet sand, the piping plover's back is the paler color of dry sand.

About a week after our arrival we found one more shorebird species: the American oystercatcher. I spent a happy half hour sitting on the beach, sketching three oystercatchers as they posed at the water's edge. They held their long, red beaks on a slightly downward angle, almost as if they were too heavy to hold up. These beaks glowed as the light of the sun shone through them. The birds had a heavy, solid look that fit well with their stolid movements, in contrast to the tiny peeps and delicate sanderlings who ran on twinkling legs at the water's edge.

One morning as I walked up among the dunes, looking at yellow-rumped warblers in bushes behind the beach, I flushed a single snow bunting. Snow buntings and skimmers on the same beach? Jekyll Island is well south of the snow bunting's normal wintering range, and local birders declared my find to be worth noting. Also worth noting was another species I had not expected to see, a great crested flycatcher, north of its normal wintering range.

Back of the island's beach, at the south end where there is less human disturbance, there is a dune-based ecosystem that begins on the seaward side with incipient and primary dunes and builds up to an area of densely foliaged, wind-stunted shrubs and trees. Inland from that is maritime climax forest, dominated by the huge live oaks for which the island is so well known. That forest extends to the island's western, or inland, edge, which terminates abruptly at the saltwater tidal marshes.

The hotel grounds were shaded by big-leaf magnolias, live oaks and cabbage palms. A pileated woodpecker sometimes visited a palm in the back courtyard, and occasionally a pair of handsomely patterned red-bellied woodpeckers would put in an appearance. The boat-tailed grackles were quite tame and their strange assortment of squeaks, gurgles and whistles were frequently heard. They would strut about with a bold, proprietary attitude, their long, keel-shaped tails held at a jaunty angle.

While I always advise people not to feed wildlife, I'm guilty of not always following my own good advice. We learned that the grackles would take popcorn from our fingers, as would the gray squirrels. The squirrels would even climb a pantleg to reach a handout. They were a smaller and darker subspecies of the same gray squirrel species that occurs in my garden, back home.

In the middle of the island there is an area of huge houses that were once "cottages" of such famous rich folk as the Rockefellers, the Macys, the Goodyears and the Cranes. Richard Crane made his millions from the bathroom fixture

PEEPS AND STINTS

There is a group of small sandpipers, generally lacking in particularly distinctive markings, that are collectively known to birders as "peeps." In North America, the five species most often called peeps are the semipalmated, western, least, white-rumped and Baird's sandpipers. In the last two, the wing tips extend beyond the tail tip, but the rump of the white-rumped is white, while that of the Baird's is dark. The Baird's has a more scale-like pattern on the back and a buffier tone to the head and breast. The remaining three species are smaller, the least being the smallest of all. The western sandpiper is very similar to the semipalmated, but has a slightly longer beak that may seem to droop just a tiny bit at the tip. However, other small sandpipers (several species are called "stints") normally found in Europe or Asia occasionally show up in North America. A telescope is almost essential to shorebirding, and time spent learning the native peeps will help the birder find the rarer species.

MISNAMED WARBLERS

As a group, our North American wood warblers are notorious for having geographically meaningless names. For example, the Tennessee warbler only occurs in Tennessee, as well as in every other eastern state, during migration. It breeds almost exclusively in Canada and winters from tropical Mexico south into northern South America. Similarly, the Nashville warbler neither nests nor winters anywhere near Nashville. Although the first Cape May warbler known to science was shot in Cape May, New Jersey, it was about eighty years before the bird was found there again. The species is now known to breed almost exclusively in Canada and winters in the tropics. The Connecticut warbler is another species that nests in the forests of Canada and winters in the tropics. Its spring migration is mostly to the west of the Appalachians.

business, and his palatial cottage boasts seventeen bathrooms. Some of these mansions were open to the public and we toured their interiors in the company of well-informed volunteer guides.

We were wandering around the lawns of the great homes on a day when large numbers of wintering songbirds were present. We found eastern bluebirds, pine warblers, a prairie warbler, eastern phoebes, white-eyed vireos, Carolina wrens, northern mockingbirds, a yellow-throated warbler, Carolina chickadees, downy woodpeckers, white-throated sparrows, rufous-sided towhees, American robins, cardinals, blue jays, tufted titmouses, yellow-rumped warblers and various other species. The pine warblers, a species not always easy to see back home, were remarkably tame and remained low, at eye level, to provide some of the best views of the species my mother and I had ever enjoyed. Unstreaked brown above and yellow below, the pines are not the most brightly colored of warblers, but there is a subtle elegance to their appearance.

Wax myrtle is one of the most common shrubs on Jekyll Island, and the yellow-rumped warblers seemed to particularly favor it. They flitted about the bushes, flashing the yellow patches for which they were originally named by Audubon. Appropriately enough, the species had been called the myrtle warbler when I was a youngster, but since I lived outside the myrtle's range, I never saw the bird in association with its namesake.

Other common vegetation, particularly among the sand dunes, included Virginia creeper, red bay, catbrier, buckthorn, yaupon holly, Spanish bayonet, red cedar and saw palmetto. Groundsel, also called cotton brush, was distinctive by virtue of its fluffy, white seeding heads. It grows throughout the southeast. Handsome sea oats, protected by law because of their role in anchoring sand dunes, were common, as was sandspur, unfortunately. Its ubiquitous, bristling little seeds punctured my fingers each day as I tried to remove them from between the pads of the dogs' feet.

Water oaks, red maples, pignut hickories, live oaks, black gums, big-leaf magnolias, sycamores, hollies and saw palmetto dominated the mature forest, where birds were generally scarce. These woods hosted numerous white-tailed deer, which could be seen along road edges every night. Their footprints were in the beach sand each morning.

In one ecologically complex location where ancient dunes converged with what is called an inlet bluff beach, adjacent to the salt marsh, I found clumps of prickly pear cactus. They grew on the waist-to-shoulder-high "bluff" above a narrow strand of gritty beach, which sloped down to the muddy edge of the marsh, just a few feet away.

Everywhere in this area, at the southwest corner of the island, I could hear the songs of white-eyed vireos. Their five-to-seven-note phrases are a distinctive song of the south. They usually end with a sharp "chick" note and are quite unlike the familiar, rambling, slightly slurred songs of other, more widely distributed North American vireos, such as the red-eyed and the warbling.

The Virginia live oak was one of the most common trees – and the most impressive. Its huge branches spread out like massive arms, swooping down sometimes to the ground. The foliage invariably was a near equal blend of leaves and openings, creating a gloriously intricate and complex filigree of light and dark patterning. They were festooned with lichens, ferns and other epiphytes, particularly Spanish moss, which hung in gray or light green banners that swayed gently in the breeze. Resurrection ferns grew along the lengths of the branches, sending out blunt little fronds from the main stem.

The golf course in the island's middle features a large, man-made pond. Although trespass on the fairways was discouraged, birders were welcome to visit the pond. Anhingas perched in the trees at the water's edge. On the water swam a flock of beautiful male hooded mergansers, fanning their magnificent crests as part of their impressive breeding displays. Pied-billed grebes, brown in color and more business-like in

SOME BIRDS NAMED FOR OBSCURE FEATURES

Because woodpeckers usually perch up against tree trunks, the coloring of their lower underparts can be obscured. For this reason, the red belly of the red-bellied woodpecker is one of its least visible features. However, birds are often named by scientists examining preserved specimens. A stuffed skin of this species clearly shows the red belly. While the characteristic is of limited value in field identification, it is a quick and simple way to tell the bird from similar species when they are laid out on a museum tray.

The ring-necked duck has a beautifully distinctive ringed beak, but the colors of unfeathered anatomy are usually faded in preserved specimens. The plumage of the head and neck is black, but reflects colored highlights; a narrow ring around the neck reflects bronze tones. However, while the ring is easily seen in the hand, it requires excellent lighting conditions to be visible in the field.

behavior than the gaudy mergansers, were occupied with hunting for fish. They would sit low in the water, in typical grebe fashion, sometimes with their backs awash. Then suddenly they would perform an abrupt little dive, leaving only a few ripples on the surface where they had been.

Along the causeway we enjoyed excellent views of great egrets, American wood storks, great blue herons, white ibises, snowy egrets, little blue herons and tricolored herons. The birds festooned the trees that grew in scattered clumps about the marsh. Tree swallows swarmed overhead in great numbers. They winter farther north than any other North American swallow, and coastal Georgia is well below the normal northern limit of their wintering range.

The marshes extending to the horizon to either side of the causeway comprised the cordgrass and mud habitat of the clapper rail. I could hear rails calling, but after casual attempts to produce a sighting failed, I decided to make a concerted effort. This consisted of standing on the road's edge for a half hour in a light drizzle, staring intently at locations where the sounds of clappers originated. Eventually a clapper rail was kind enough to daintily step into plain view, looking quite clean and dry in spite of the rain and the mud exposed by the falling tide. The bird was the size of a small chicken. In every particular of shape and pattern, it resembled the Virginia rail and the king rail. But it was much larger than the Virginia and grayer than either. The king rail, unlike the clapper, can be found in freshwater marshes. But kings do sometimes share salt marsh habitat with clappers, and the two species are known to hybridize.

Before returning home, we made day trips to the mainland for some good coastal birding to the north, and once for a memorable visit to Okefenokee Swamp. Was Georgia what my mother had expected? Yes, and more, much more. She's returned there since that first visit and wants to do so again. She still has Georgia on her mind.

CLAPPER RAIL

NORTHERN MOCKINGBIRD

III
THE SOUTH

GRAY KINGBIRD

THE FLORIDA KEYS

The Animal Protection Institute (API) was holding its annual meeting in Orlando, Florida – home of Mickey Mouse, one of the very few animals I can't stand. The day the conference ended, API's Bruce Webb and I caught a flight to Miami. There we rented a car and, starting late in the afternoon, headed south through the Florida Keys until overtaken by darkness.

It was early October. The warm, humid night air that came through the open window of the restaurant where we had dinner was a reassuring confirmation of tropical influence. It promised new and wonderful things to be seen, beginning with the anole lizard that peered over the window sill at my elbow. Possibly it was the endemic form native to the Keys, *Anolis sagrei stejnegeri*, but it could also have been an introduced species from the West Indies or some hybrid form.

The next day at dawn we pulled into the parking lot of the National Key Deer Refuge, on Big Pine Key. Towering cloud masses glowed in the half light out over the Gulf of Mexico. Bruce, interested in looking for fall songbird migrants, particularly warblers, walked back up the road while I followed a flooded track into clumps of red mangroves to look for southern species. Recent rains had filled low areas over my boot tops, so I could only go a little way to look at three short-billed dowitchers and a tricolored heron.

I thought about the pleasure of seeing familiar species, such as the dowitchers, in unfamiliar settings when a tiny deer slowly trotted across my path. It was a white-tailed deer belonging to the endangered race that is endemic to the Florida Keys. Only about three hundred of these animals, known as the Key deer, survive. Many thousands were originally killed by hunters, who used dogs and bush fires to drive the deer into range of their guns or clubs. Hunting has long since been banned, but the remaining animals are subjected to the stresses of encroachment, with roadkills all too common.

One constantly hears sport hunting justified as a "management tool" for deer. Without such "control," deer populations increase until food resources available to each animal decrease. The animals then tend to become smaller. The smaller deer, with more modest food requirements, are better able to survive increased competition for finite food than the larger animals. Smallness is an inherited feature. The belief, familiar among wildlife managers, that smaller animals are inherently "wrong" is entirely subjective, reflecting some humans', not nature's, values. The Key deer were allowed to evolve in their food-impoverished environment in the absence of contemporary wildlife management practices.

When the rangers showed up for work, they kindly allowed me to photograph the tiny skull of a Key deer, my ruler beside it, and patiently answered questions about local fauna and flora. Bruce and I then strolled up and down the road. I tried to photograph a magnificently posed great blue heron against a backdrop of mangroves and spectacular cloud formations while Bruce continued to look for warblers.

When we finally drove away, we turned right, just outside the parking lot gate, to follow along beside a mangrove-studded inlet. Bruce slowed to a stop and indicated that I should take a second look at what I, still enthusing about the deer, had assumed was a little blue heron. I was chagrined. How could I have ever, even for an instant, failed to note the shaggy neck plumage and subtle color differences that distinguish the reddish egret from the little blue heron? I took out my telephoto lens and started taking pictures of the egret, which was perched on a weathered snag.

ON THE WIRES

The telephone and electric cable wires following the single highway through the Keys serve as perches for a variety of birds in an environment where perching sites are somewhat limited. Among the most conspicuous birds are the double-crested cormorants, which seem too large and clumsy to balance on such slender perches, as does the occasional egret or heron. Although most raptors prefer to sit upon the supporting posts, American kestrels are frequently seen perched on the cables. Belted kingfishers and eastern kingbirds also use these perches, but each kingbird should be looked at carefully as this is the one place in the United States where the gray kingbird and the even rarer loggerhead kingbird can be expected. Flocks of swallows sometimes line the wires.

Meanwhile, Bruce had spotted a peregrine falcon. Peregrines are endangered; reddish egrets are not. But through the years I have seen many peregrine falcons and will do so again; the reddish egret was my first, and so I did not even glance at the falcon. Bruce had a second peregrine in view. Then a third. I kept right on trying different exposures, snapping each movement the egret made in the morning light.

"You never even turned your head," Bruce said, with amazement. Although few birders would pass up three peregrines, I had no regrets. As so often happens in such situations, we soon found reddish egrets to be very common, but I never again was presented with quite so perfect a photo opportunity.

As we drove toward nearby Blue Hole, two Key deer trotted across the road in front of us. They vanished into slash pines and a jumble of palmetto palms.

Blue Hole is the name of a limestone sinkhole filled with wonderfully clear water. Signs needlessly warned us not to interfere with the alligators. We photographed a small, obliging alligator, which posed in glass-calm water, plus some fish I could not identify and the largest red-eared slider I had ever seen. Impressive, too, was a huge Florida soft-shelled turtle hauled out on the far bank. This animal seemed as wonderfully strange for its great size as the deer were for their smallness.

As we drove from Blue Hole along the famous Highway 1, dominant birds included double-crested cormorants, brown pelicans, magnificent frigatebirds, ospreys, belted kingfishers, American kestrels and sharp-shinned hawks, plus reddish egrets and numerous other herons.

One intriguing heron we searched for and found was a "Wurdemann's" heron, which is found almost exclusively in the Florida Keys. In appearance, the bird was like a normal great blue heron, but with a white head. At one time, "Wurdemann's" heron was thought to be a separate species, obviously related to the similar but very widely distributed great blue heron. Interestingly, the great blue has, in this area,

REDDISH EGRETS

The feeding displays of the reddish egret are spectacular. It can be seen flicking its wings, fluffing its plumage and erratically running about shallow tide pools as though not quite sane. Sometimes it will become airborne, jabbing down at prey on or near the water's surface. It may stir the water with its foot or spread one or both wings as if to shade the water, the better to see its prey.

The reddish egret is found in southern California, south along the coast of Mexico and around the edges of the Caribbean, as far south as northern South America. This is one of the most restricted ranges of our herons. The species seems to be most closely related to the reef herons of the Old World tropics.

FAMILY NAMES

North American bird families that birders often refer to by their scientific family names include the Procellarids (shearwaters, fulmars and petrels), Larids (gulls and terns), Alcids (razorbills, murres, dovekies, guillemots, murrelets, auklets and puffins), Tyrannids (kingbirds, flycatchers, phoebes, wood-pewees, kiskadees and tyrannulets) and Corvids (jays, crows, ravens, nutcrackers and magpies).

an all-white color phase. The "great white" heron was also once thought to be a separate species. There has been speculation that "Wurdemann's" is a hybrid between the great white and the great blue. However, current theory maintains that all three are color phases, or morphs, of one species, the great blue heron. In support of this theory scientists point out that other heron species show considerable color variation; for example, the reddish egret has a white color phase, and the immature little blue heron is white, while the adult is slate-gray with wine tones on the head and neck.

Highway 1, like the country, ends at Key West, some ninety miles (145 km) from the north shore of Cuba. Here we visited Audubon House, a lovingly restored, old southern home where Audubon once resided. While there he executed his magnificent painting of white-crowned pigeons, a West Indian species that occurs no farther north than extreme southern Florida. A volunteer custodian kindly discussed the history of the house with us. She explained that Audubon had chosen to portray the white-crowns among the foliage of the flowering geiger tree. A geiger tree, past blooming, grew by the front gate.

That was more than I could resist and I began taking measurements, doing sketches and taking photographs of the tree's foliage. The species belongs to the borage family (*Boraginaceae*), which includes the heliotrope and the forget-me-not. Its evergreen leaves are ovate, about five to six inches (13 to 15 cm) long and three to four inches (8 to 10 cm) wide. Small, trumpet-shaped, orange-red flowers grow in clusters at the ends of branches. Audubon portrayed a pair of white-crowned pigeons – blue-black birds with white forecrowns – with one bird feeding the other amid an arrangement of geiger tree leaves and blossoms. The artist caught the green of the foliage in the green iridescence of the pigeons' neck plumage. The red of the flowers is repeated in the red of the birds' beaks.

Many years earlier, Toronto birder J. E. "Red" Mason had given me a couple of dead white-crowned pigeons that

REDDISH EGRET

had been found as roadkills in southern Florida. I had preserved them in my collection. Now I knew that I would some day portray them in the same species of tree as was chosen by Audubon. There was only one thing left to do before I would feel comfortable about planning such a painting. I had yet to observe a living white-crowned pigeon.

"We can fix that," said Bruce. "They're supposed to be common in the Key West Botanical Gardens." That information, and much more, was contained in James Lane's book, *A Birder's Guide to Florida*.

Nature is cruel, though, even to a northern birder hot on the trail of a life bird. How else to explain the fact that we did, indeed, find a white-crowned pigeon? But it was dead. In fact, it wasn't even there except as a clump of feathers on the ground in the Botanical Gardens. We searched and found yet another clump of white-crowned pigeon feathers. Some predator was eating what I had come to see!

Apart from a rather tame black-throated blue warbler, few birds were in the garden. The site is most noteworthy for the fact that its trees are well labeled as to species. It would not do to be botanically naive here (particularly as I was in shorts and T-shirt); the featured vegetation includes the Florida poisonwood, *Metopium toxiferum*, a tree whose bark is stained with gooey-looking patches of black sap that is poisonous to the touch.

In the thickest part of this small, exotic woodland we found a single white ibis posed like a bird artist's model amid glossy mangrove foliage above a shallow pond. The same pond hosted a few Muscovy ducks, perched in a row along a horizontal limb. This species is native to Mexico and Central and South America, where it lives in habitat similar in appearance to the Botanical Gardens, although far more extensive. These were domesticated birds, showing odd patches of white plumage that distinguish them from the wild form, but they gave the impression of doing their best to revert to the wild.

Immediately adjacent the edge of the Botanical Gardens

TAMENESS IN BIRDS

Often birds with cryptic coloring "sit tight" when approached, the behavior appropriate for a bird that is likely to blend into its surroundings and go unnoticed. More brightly colored species, on the other hand, tend to be more quick to flee. Some species, such as nuthatches and chickadees, seem predisposed to tameness and can, with some effort, be taught to take food from the hand. Other birds, such as the black rail and the yellow rail, spend most of their time in thick habitat, keeping a screen of vegetation between themselves and birders who would very much like to see them.

MAGNIFICENT FRIGATEBIRD

NIGHTHAWKS

What North Americans call nighthawks are often known as nightjars in other parts of the world. The family to which they belong includes such species as the paraque, common poorwill, chuck-will's-widow and whip-poor-will – all named for their distinctive calls. When a family of birds has members with such diverse names, birders seek one name to apply to them all. Collectively, the members of the nighthawk and whip-poor-will family are sometimes called goatsuckers. That odd name derives from a quaint and quite incorrect belief that members of the family stole the milk of goats. Birders usually refer to these birds as Caprimulgids, which is derived from the family's scientific name, *Caprimulgidae*, meaning "big mouthed."

was a golf course, which explained why we were finding so many golf balls in this roughest of roughs. Pied-billed grebes hunted prey in a nearby water hazard; however, the number of balls landing all about encouraged us to stay in the woodlot, under cover of the trees.

Finally, Bruce spotted a living white-crowned pigeon, mostly hidden from view amid the huge leaves at the top of a tall tree. Later, in the Everglades, I would enjoy clear views of this species, but for now I was a little disappointed.

Disappointment ended abruptly on our way out of the Botanical Gardens. I noticed a tawny clump of leaves on a high limb that seemed worthy of a second look. They weren't leaves at all but my first chuck-will's-widow. I pointed to the bird just as it flew away, giving Bruce a glimpse. Like its close relative, the much smaller whip-poor-will, the chuck-will's-widow is colored and patterned in such a way that it tends to blend into its surroundings. Its reddish-brown coloring mimics bark and dead leaves. The bird often sits lengthwise on branches, its low profile looking like a knot of wood.

Although we were far from the mainland, the ocean water was filthy with oily residue and masses of plastic waste as it sloshed against the dirty beaches of Key West. This unappealing mess was the not-so-natural habitat of royal, Caspian and Sandwich terns, plus various shorebirds, including willets, ruddy turnstones, laughing gulls, short-billed dowitchers, semipalmated plovers and black-bellied plovers.

At Audubon House we had borrowed a key to a mangrove-fringed water reservoir near the airport, across the road from the beach. The key is kept there for birders' use. The pond was touted as a bird sanctuary, but while the viewing pier provided a pleasant place to rest, there were few birds about. An exception was a tricolored heron who posed for camera and sketchbook.

One other treat provided by Key West was in the form of a small gathering of white ibises on the lawn of a motel right beside the road. In so unnatural a setting the pictures I took of them can serve solely as reference material, but the opportunity to study the species at such close range was most welcome.

On our travels from Key to Key, we birded in thick, humid, mosquito-filled mangrove swamps one time and in cultivated gardens another. Sometimes we would work hard for little, enjoying the most productive birding where conditions were easiest.

I wanted to see southern species and had not been disappointed; Bruce's search for migrant warblers in the day and a half that we were in the Keys produced yellow-throated warblers, palm warblers, black-throated blue warblers, black-throated green warblers, northern parula warblers, prairie warblers, black and white warblers, ovenbirds, common yellowthroats and American redstarts.

There was so much else we would have liked to see. But it was time to turn around and head north, on to the Everglades.

RARE BIRDS OF THE KEYS

A West Indian vireo, the thick-billed, is known to make the odd appearance in southern Florida. Antillean nighthawks are other rare visitors to southern Florida from the West Indies. On warm summer evenings, they have been heard flying over the mangroves at the water reservoir, near the airport at Key West. The stray Bahama swallows that are so eagerly sought by visiting birders are more likely to be seen in pine trees, particularly at Big Pine Key.

ANHINGA

THE EVERGLADES

As naturalist Bruce Webb and I entered Everglades National Park, near Homestead, Florida, I had an odd sense of belonging. The feeling might have reflected the many books and articles I had read about the place or the various films about it I had seen. Now, finally, I was here.

Having explored the park before, Bruce drove, leaving me free to admire the scenery. For much of the drive along the one main road in the southern end of the park, we were on a causeway crossing a river about fifty miles (80 km) wide but only inches deep. This vast, slow-moving flood of fresh water is the dominant ecological feature of the Everglades. The water was so filled with saw grass and other emergent plants that, from the low angle of the car window, it often appeared as flat, dry prairie, with hammocks of trees scattered about. This was big sky country, with towering, ever-changing cloudscapes reflected intermittently in flat sheets of blue water.

The first stop was to examine a brown bird I had spotted in a distant entanglement of mangroves and palmetto. It was a limpkin, an aberrant marsh bird and sole member of its predominantly neotropical family. The Everglades are near the northern end of its range.

The limpkin is roughly ibis-like in shape and size and has taxonomic affinities to cranes and rails, but recent analysis of the bird's DNA indicates that its closest relatives are the very different-looking finfoots, or sun-grebes. Limpkins are generally nocturnal. Their calls consist of loud, strange sounds that might be expected of souls in hellish torment. More than one night visitor to the swamps of Florida has been unnerved by their "song."

Like the endangered snail kite, limpkins are particularly fond of eating *Pomacea* snails. The eggs of these snails cling to the bases of plant stalks where they emerge from the water. However, limpkins are less gastronomically limited than snail kites and will also eat frogs, crayfish and other aquatic fauna.

We made frequent stops on our way to Flamingo, at the park's southern end, where we would spend the night. Along the road, belted kingfishers perched on wires or out on exposed mangrove branches, or hovered above the water before plunging down after small fish. Black and turkey vultures were seldom absent from the sky. Eastern meadowlarks, northern mockingbirds, boat-tailed grackles, American kestrels and loggerhead shrikes were also frequently encountered.

The next morning, we headed for Snake Bight Trail. This four-mile-long (6.5 km-long) raised path extends through dense mangrove swamps and terminates at Florida Bay. A bewildering array of new visual sensations vied for attention as we walked along. The contrasts between light and shadow in the jungle-like vegetation confused the eye and made photography difficult. Bromeliads, or air plants, were abundant and an odd, elongated cactus sometimes looped across the trail, often at head height, ready to impale with its spines anyone who didn't look sharply.

Several crow-sized birds flew into the swamp, their forms quickly cloaked by vegetation, before we realized they were green-backed herons. Barred owls called from hidden places, sometimes reacting to Bruce's artful imitations, and we frequently heard alligators, although the great reptiles also kept hidden from view. We did enjoy excellent views of red-shouldered hawks, one of the most common raptors in Florida, as well as red-bellied woodpeckers and painted

THE CLASSIFICATION OF BIRDS

Beginning in the seventeenth century, bird classification was primarily based on physical (morphological) characteristics, such as bill and foot structure. Increasingly, a multitude of characteristics, including subtle aspects of anatomy, behavior, breeding biology and vocalization, have been used to determine bird species' relationships to each other. In the last decade or so, the pioneering work in DNA-DNA hybridization by John Sibley and Jon Ahlquist has allowed for direct comparison between genetic material of various kinds of birds. Many of the conclusions derived from their studies break strongly with traditional classification and have not been widely accepted as yet. For example, the new findings have broken up the Pelecaniformes order – seabirds that share the characteristic of having all four toes joined by webbing – into different groups that evolved the characteristic independently. The new classification thus places the pelicans and New World vultures and condors much closer to each other than to gannets and hawks, respectively.

buntings. The buntings, which were quite tame, were a particular treat for me, while Bruce was pleased to see several kinds of migrant eastern warblers. Most of the latter were species common in my part of the continent, but rare in Bruce's home state of California.

The trail lived up to its reputation for mosquitoes. The tiny insects swarmed through the damp, warm air. As we continued our hike, clouds built ominously into darkening masses and the air grew still with the threat of a rapidly developing storm. We finally reached the trail's end, where a boardwalk extended out over a tidal mudflat with the island-dotted expanse of Florida Bay and the Gulf of Mexico in the distance.

The dying light was luminous. Some roseate spoonbills with carmine red shoulders, bright pink wings and golden tails waded in the shallows or flew past us like images from a dream set in a birder's version of paradise. Tricolored and great blue herons, snowy and great egrets, white ibises, willets, black-bellied plovers and other shorebirds all milled about the mudflats, wading, feeding, preening, flying and sometimes approaching close to us.

Most exciting was a band of pink on the horizon – a flock of greater flamingos. This species, which is associated with Florida through neon-edged images and stylized caricatures or as captive, living ornaments at various tourist attractions, was extirpated from the state many years ago. The Bahamas, Caribbean, parts of South America and the Galápagos Islands are the historical home of the New World race of the greater flamingo. Whether this local flock on Florida Bay, which may be self-sustaining, derives naturally from wild birds from the West Indies or from escaped captive birds, is a matter of debate. The fact that at one time in the past enough of these birds reached the Galápagos Islands to establish a self-sustaining population there indicates that the species does have the potential to expand its range if allowed to do so. At any rate, they were a singularly appropriate part of our surroundings.

BIRDS AT LARGE

Among birders, Florida is famous, or infamous, for the birds that don't really belong there. Blessed of warm year-round climate, physically located near the neotropical sources of exotic pets for the legal and illegal animal trade, and filled with tourist attractions featuring exotic wildlife, the state is a rich source of escapees. Birders should look for scarlet ibis; various species of flamingo; black swan, bar-headed goose, muscovy, mandarin and other waterfowl species; black francolin; red-legged patridge; ringed turtle dove; rose-ringed parakeet, budgerigar, canary-winged parakeet, monk parakeet, red-crowned parrot, yellow-headed Amazon and other parrot species; spot-breasted oriole; red-whiskered bulbul; hill mynah; house finch; Java finch; and other species. When a hurricane hit the Miami Zoo and other animal parks in 1992, the number of exotic species at loose in Florida increased dramatically as birds fled cages destroyed by the wind. Time alone will tell how many will live and propagate.

When the storm broke with a blast of thunder that would have done justice to a nearby nuclear detonation, I suggested we try to wait it out. As there was no significant cover available anywhere, the boardwalk was as good a place as any to endure the storm. We were going to get soaked no matter what we did and given the amount of lightning exploding overhead, perhaps being on the boardwalk was safer than being under the trees on shore. We crouched lower than the railing, in the hope that this would make us less vulnerable to the lightning.

"These tropical rains," I said, "often end quickly."

We waited, and waited, and waited. My belongings were in a rubberized bag, but it was old and, I soon discovered, no longer waterproof. In an effort to protect it from the rain I sat on it, which, as I later learned, caused a bottle of sweetly scented and very oily insect repellent inside to leak onto my sodden airplane ticket. The ticket was creased, torn, oily and smelly when I presented it, two days later, to various airline employees who, gingerly holding the mess between thumb and forefinger, tried to read it and process the information. Field guide and sketchbooks were similarly affected. Camera, binoculars and film survived.

Two hours later, the lightning had abated, and we decided to walk the four miles (6.5 km) back to the car through the rain. I was a little worried about poisonous snakes on the trail, but the only reptile we saw was a large alligator, which crossed over in front of us. The rain stopped as we approached the car.

Otherwise the weather was splendid during our stay in the Everglades. Eco Pond, which, in the dry season, is a popular place for herons to congregate (to the joy of photographers) is near Flamingo. Although this was early October and not yet the dry season, the birding at the pond was good. A tricolored heron partly hidden in marshy vegetation at the edge of the water allowed me to approach closer with my camera than I had ever been to one before. Moorhens also cooperated, and

CATTLE EGRETS

One race of the cattle egret originated in Africa. Within historic times it has spread north into Europe and east as far as the Caucasus. Somehow the same race reached northern South America, where it was first recorded in 1880. It may have done so on its own or as a stowaway on board a transatlantic boat. From there it spread south in cattle ranges as far as Argentina, and north through Central America, Mexico and the West Indies. It reached the southern United States in the early 1950s, and continued north as far as Canada and west to the Pacific coast. Although cattle egrets traditionally follow herds of wild herbivores, such as antelope and elephants, it is thought that the wide spread of deforestation and subsequent development of the cattle industry are prime factors supporting its rapid dispersal throughout so much of the world.

"GATOR HOLES"

At the height of the winter dry season, water in the Everglades tends to be concentrated in potholes. These attract water-dependent wildlife, including fish, amphibians, turtles and, of course, birds. Beautifully plumed egrets and herons may flock to such sites in huge numbers, to the delight of photographers. What creates the potholes in the first place is the American alligator. It cleans out the "gator holes" of muck and debris, making them suitable for the animals that take refuge there during the dry season.

GREATER FLAMINGO

an adult bald eagle, the endangered southern race, flew by low overhead. A black vulture and a turkey vulture sat close to each other on a wooden railing beside the walk leading to a platform that provides an elevated view of the pond. It was as if the birds were posing for an illustration showing the differences between the species.

On a grass stem growing beside the path I found a grass frog, which hopped from view before I could call it to Bruce's attention or make a positive identification. The tiniest frog I can recall seeing, it may have been *Limnaoedus ocularis*. At about three-quarters of an inch (2 cm) in length, it is the smallest species in the country.

While other visitors watched the egrets and other showy species at Eco Pond, Bruce and I poked about the roadside vegetation at the entrance to the pond. We found brown thrashers, painted buntings, northern parula warblers, gray catbirds, white-eyed vireos and red-eyed vireos. I took great pleasure in the best view of a prairie warbler I'd ever had.

Yellow-breasted chats are rare back home, although not so rare that anything other than perverse luck had kept me from seeing one for most of my life. I had finally caught up with the species a few years earlier, but I still cherish each sighting. At Eco Pond I had a spectacular close-up look at a beautiful chat who posed in bright sunlight against a background of vibrant green, subtropical foliage. How transient, and therefore precious, such a moment can be.

In a closed, overgrown area of campground near the Flamingo Park Lodge, down the road from Eco Pond, we encountered more vultures that allowed us to approach closely. They sat on picnic tables and benches with their wings spread in the sunlight or strolled about in unconscious parody of picnicking tourists. Flocks of quite tame cattle egrets also strutted about in overgrown grass.

On that first day, and the next morning, as we slowly made our way from the park, we explored short nature trails.

Some took us on raised boardwalks through dense hammocks that were botanical and ecological delights. The Gumbo Limbo Trail, for instance, is named after the thick-limbed gumbo-limbo trees whose thin, peeling red bark is a highly distinctive counterpoint to the surrounding green vegetation. That hammock also hosted Florida royal palms. In the interiors of all of the hammocks we visited, intricate masses of aerial ferns, mosses, lichens, orchids and bromeliads constantly delighted the eye in the green-filtered sunlight.

On the Mahogany Hammock Trail, Bruce took a touristy photo of me standing next to the largest living mahogany tree in the United States, according to the sign next to it. Although on this brief visit, we failed to find the tree snails that live there, the exquisite zebra butterflies were a wonderful sight. In their description of the Everglades in *Wild America*, Roger Tory Peterson and the late James Fisher had this to say about the zebra butterfly: "It had the most curious delicate flight – it does not beat so much as quiver its wings, and with a shivering delicacy picks its way very slickly through undertangles of the most jungly complication." Just as the hauntingly beautiful blue morpho butterflies have come to symbolize the American tropics to me, so have the zebra butterflies come to symbolize the very essence of the beauty that is so abundantly distributed throughout the Everglades.

On the second night of our visit, we drove back along the main road, toward the Main Visitor Center, looking for whip-poor-wills and other nocturnal wildlife. We did, indeed, find a whip-poor-will perched in vegetation beside the road, its eyes glowing ruby-red. We also saw quite a few raccoons. They were foraging for frogs and snakes, which, as they crossed the road, were exposed to both cars and predators.

We soon realized that there were so many frogs on some sections of the road that we could not avoid them. Bruce slowed to a snail's pace and stopped several times so I could get out and move the amphibians. But many frogs took aimless leaps in our direction and sometimes we could hear them

WHITE IBIS

thumping into the side or bottom of the car.

Southern leopard frogs abounded. One of the larger frogs I caught was a pig frog, so named because its call sounds like the grunting of a hog. It looked to me like a slender version of the bullfrog. I released the handsome amphibian in the bushes safely back from the road and hoped it would survive.

The next morning we traveled along the same section of road, stopping twice, once to identify a southern ribbon snake that was dead on the road, and once to end the misery of a small diamond-back rattlesnake that had been partly crushed by a car's wheel. Some of the raccoons that had come to the edge of the lonely road to eat frogs or snakes hurt or killed by cars during the night had themselves been killed by cars. They would soon be food for vultures, as well as myriads of insects and other small scavengers for which the road's edge supplied a continuous source of nourishment.

White-crowned pigeons were at first difficult to see along the highway. They tended to fly rapidly across the road, from treetop to treetop, and sometimes seemed to take the form of large leaves when they came to rest. For such large birds – they are a little smaller and more slender than most common street pigeons – they could be surprisingly hard to detect. Eventually, however, we secured good views of these handsome birds.

The Anhinga Trail, one of the world's most famous nature trails, was featured in an Audubon Screen Tour film I attended when I was a child. I had been reading about it and looking at pictures taken from it ever since. Now it was my turn to walk along its famous boardwalk.

The trail itself is only a half mile (0.8 km) long, partly path, partly boardwalk. It curls around and through a reservoir of pure water in which Florida gar and various other native and non-native fish are clearly visible. The vegetation includes large numbers of small and large bromeliads growing on twisted branches in shaggy profusion.

VISITING THE EVERGLADES – A FEW DO'S AND DON'TS

Firearms and hunting are prohibited. Airboats, swamp buggies and all-terrain vehicles (ATVs) are potentially damaging to the fragile Everglades environment and are not permitted in the park. Pets must be caged or leashed and are not allowed on the trails. Off-trail hiking can be dangerous; if you do it, be sure someone knows where you're going and when you intend to return. Poison ivy, Florida poisonwood and manchineel can cause painful skin irritations; be sure you know what they look like. Mosquitoes can be a particular annoyance; do not go birding without wearing a good insect repellent. Do not smoke on the trails and restrict campfires to assigned areas. Under no circumstance should you remove plants or any wildlife, including invertebrates.

The trail does live up to its name. Anhingas abound. I find this species endlessly appealing, and, needless to say, I was in a state of high excitement at seeing so many so close. Some swam by underwater, practically at our feet. Their trim forms and the vigorous paddling of their large feet were easily studied through the glass-clear water. Others speared fish or swam with just their snaky necks and heads above water, a habit that earns them the colloquial name, snakebird.

The anhingas tended to sit about in small groupings, or they would pose in solitary splendor, sometimes with wings partly spread to dry. Great blue herons were common and tame, and like the anhingas, seemed to have developed the habit of striking picturesque poses. A volunteer naturalist pointed to a form curled beside the path, a handsome Florida banded kingsnake. Alligators were common.

We watched a flock of wood storks fly by overhead. Then one anhinga posed for me by sitting on the flat, wooden railing by the path. It allowed me to approach ever closer, snapping its picture. Bruce, who had been helping me do photographic studies of vegetation by holding a ruler up against some of my subjects, jokingly offered to hold the ruler up next to the cooperative bird.

Near the Anhinga Trail we visited the Pineland Trail. Also a half mile (0.8 km) long, it winds through slash pine forests. Like most of the shorter nature trails we were on, it is "self-guiding," with well-placed signs that provide information about the site. It is also accessible to the handicapped. There were odd sinkholes in the limestone bedrock, reminding me of similar habitat encountered in the West Indies.

A western kingbird flew to the top of a dead cypress snag as we were taking our last drive through the park. That was the last new bird species we saw during our visit. The Everglades was more than I had hoped it would be. As we drove out of the park, I felt a melancholy sense of leaving a good friend.

ANHINGAS

An anhinga's plumage is not very water resistant. That feature allows the bird to attain low buoyancy, and thus swim underwater after prey with ease. There are tradeoffs. The bird is restricted to areas where the water is warm enough for it to submerge without losing too much body heat to survive, and it must follow its dives with long periods of perching in the sun, wings spread, drying out. The plumage of cormorants is much more water resistant, but even they can often be seen perched with their wings spread. As well as drying their feathers, there are probably benefits to be derived from the touch of sunlight on bare skin. Many species of birds will spread out their wings or open their mouths and eyes to the sun in order to absorb the rays directly for short periods of time.

PROTHONOTARY WARBLER

THE GULF COAST

Things were not going at all well. It was the dregs of winter and I was tired of it. There were problems in my personal life, as well, and although I normally take few vacations, this time I thought it best to get away for awhile. My mother had been suggesting I take her and the dogs on a birding holiday in the south. Remembering earlier such adventures, I thought it was a good idea and a good time to get away. Whoever said you can't run away from your problems could not have been a birder. Surrounding myself with nature has never failed to put my problems into perspective.

Although I had been to Louisiana before, it was only for a long weekend in New Orleans. There had been little opportunity for birding; a city park had produced yellow-throated warblers and my first look at a seaside sparrow, a small, streaked bird appropriately located at the water's edge. I wanted to see some of the rural areas of the state, and my mother, who had never been to Louisiana, simply wanted to experience that part of the south.

However, it was not to be. We had Buffy and Charm with us and when we discovered that Louisiana had a law against dogs in motel rooms, we decided to change our plans. We did sneak the dogs into a motel for the one night we spent in the state, after a quick tour of the French Quarter of New Orleans. The next morning, following the flip of a coin to choose which direction we'd go, we headed east, to Mississippi.

Just across the state line into coastal Mississippi, we drove through Waveland, where we found Lydia's Audubon Shoppe by the side of the highway. The proprietor, Lydia Schultz, had gone birding for the day, but the clerk left in charge of the store displayed classic southern hospitality by lending us a book on birding in the three counties of the Mississippi that border on the Gulf of Mexico. With that book to guide us to nearby habitats, we spent many happy hours birding. Appropriately enough, our adventures included a brief glimpse of a Mississippi kite. We found northern mockingbirds, red-bellied woodpeckers, tufted titmouses and other southern species, but apart from the kite, these were all species already observed on our way south.

The Gulf Coast boasts long beaches and a series of barrier islands attractive to large numbers of avian migrants. It was March and we were just a little too early in the year to catch the greatest numbers of northbound songbirds, but the warm weather was still a welcome change from the cold back home, and the birds would be a bonus. As well as the beaches, sandy trails led us on explorations through inland loblolly pine forests. We drove through exotic bayou country with hidden swamps and lush tangles of foliage.

In Gulfport, Mississippi, our motel was across the road from a protected stretch of beach that hosted a nesting colony of least terns. Signs declared the site a refuge, not to be disturbed during the nesting season, with cords strung around rectangular sections of beach to discourage trespassing. Many of the small terns had started nesting and were easily observed and sketched. These dainty birds had the characteristic field marks of yellow bill with black tip, white forehead and yellow feet. However, they were not, as I had expected, shaped like miniature versions of common terns. There were subtle differences in proportion, which I tried to capture in quick sketches.

Traditional forms of beach use are incompatible with tern nesting, but here so much beach was available for human

SANDERLINGS

To find the delightful little sanderling on its nesting ground, one must travel to a few scattered locations in the far north, most of them above the arctic circle. There the bird can be seen in its rufous breeding plumage. However, most of us see it in its pale gray and white non-breeding plumage while it is migrating or on its wintering grounds. It seldom seems to matter where in the world a birder birds, if there is extensive shoreline, sanderlings will be encountered at one time or another. Shorelines on coasts and inland in North and South America; islands of the Pacific, Atlantic and Indian oceans; Europe, Asia, Africa and Australia all know the delicate footprints of this small traveler.

pleasure that it seemed unlikely anyone would begrudge the terns their portion of the sand. Sanderlings, some wearing their brightly ruddy breeding plumage, darted about on the wet sand as they followed receding wavelets. Considerable numbers of laughing gulls perched on the beach or on piers, accompanied by smaller numbers of ring-billed and herring gulls. Royal, common and Caspian terns patrolled offshore, or rested on slender sandbars, while black-bellied plovers flew by or stood in stolid isolation. Sandy gray willets would suddenly flash their bold black and white wing patterns as they took to the air, calling with a rapid series of alarm notes. Ruddy turnstones and other shorebird species were also present on the beach in small numbers.

On Dauphin Island, off the coast of Alabama, due south of Mobile, we found extensive areas of white sand, towering dunes and wide beaches, plus pine and palmetto woodlots. The island is about thirteen miles (21 km) long, but throughout most of that length it is less than a mile (1.6 km) wide. The barrier islands slowly move in a westerly direction as wind and currents push sand up from that direction and erode the islands from the east. Succeeding generations of plant life adapted to sand and salt provide anchorage for the wind-driven sand to build dunes. As in Georgia, sea oats, with their extensive root systems, are recognized here for their essential preliminary role in building dunes and are protected by law.

Dauphin Island provided the opportunity to finally see numbers of prothonotary warblers at close range. The males of this species have brilliant golden heads and breasts, greenish backs and gray wings. Set against their golden heads are black eyes and black beaks. We saw our first ones beside a small snack bar, just after we drove off the bridge and onto the island. Although these glowingly beautiful birds reach the northern limit of their range within a few hundred miles of where I live, they are not a species with which I have great familiarity. It is not only the opportunity to see new species that brings joy to traveling birders, but also the opportunity of seeing a species more closely than ever before.

That was the case, too, with the hooded warbler. We had certainly seen this species before at close range. Indeed, in the early 1960s my mother had captured one in our garden when she was banding birds. But hooded warblers are generally rare back home. Here they were common, and in an afternoon I watched as many individuals as I had during my entire life prior to that day.

Brown-headed nuthatches, like the closely related pygmy nuthatches of the west, are tiny birds that like to poke about on the upper limbs of huge pine trees. My previous experience with the species was limited to unsatisfactory glimpses of them in the pine forests of Georgia. Here, in an area of pine woods and palmetto, I enjoyed close views of these tiny birds as they busily went about their business in typical nuthatch fashion, like tiny, overwound mechanical toys.

After photographing a most cooperative speckled king snake, we drove to the low, flat west end of the island. Above a small, brackish pond flew a single gull-billed tern. The shape of the pond below determined the tern's oval flight path as it endlessly circled, ignoring the wide stretches of ocean nearby to focus on the shallow pond. Occasionally, the tern would dive into the water and emerge with what appeared to be a small crustacean.

The birding highlight of Dauphin Island was found at a seaside estate that was empty of inhabitants, other than a caretaker who graciously allowed us to wander about the grounds. In an area of cattail marsh we found a magnificent mottled duck. Although it is even more similar to the American black duck, the species is very closely related to the widely distributed mallard duck and resembles the female of that species. However, the beak is bright yellow, like that of a drake mallard. The tail of the mottled duck is darker than a female mallard's and the head a little paler and less streaked than that of a black duck. What is most outstanding is the speculum, the patch of iridescent color on the secondary feathers of the

MALLARD, BLACK AND MOTTLED DUCKS

The mallard is one of the most widely distributed and best known of all birds. It is native to most parts of the northern hemisphere. In North America, the two species most closely related to it are the American black duck and the mottled duck. Sophisticated genetic analysis shows that the black and the mallard are almost the same species. They hybridize in areas where range and habitat overlap, leading some to believe that the more numerous mallard will one day genetically swamp the black duck out of existence. The mottled duck, on the other hand, has a very restricted range, which is disjunct. The Florida race (*Anas fulvigula fulvigula*) was once considered a distinct species, called the Florida duck. The race found along the coasts of Louisiana, Texas and Mexico, *Anas f. maculosa*, is a little darker and more heavily patterned, on average, than the Florida subspecies.

wing. The speculum is blue in the mallard, closer to purple in the black duck, but it is a startling turquoise green in the mottled duck when seen at certain angles to the light. I had the pleasure of seeing the bird at close range in flight, the green of its speculum very conspicuous.

We spotted many songbirds on the estate, including white-eyed vireos, painted buntings and summer tanagers. The tanagers were so common that at times the rose-red males looked like large blossoms among the green foliage. It was here that we encountered the only Kentucky warbler seen on the entire journey, distinguished by the black "sideburn" markings on the side of its head.

Along the coast we primarily remained on well-traveled highways, but dirt roads and dead ends have always fascinated me, and when we reached bayou country, past Biloxi, we began to follow ever dwindling back roads deep into swampland. We saw our first of many marsh rabbits as it swam across a channel of water. The species is essentially a cottontail that has both the ability (as any rabbit does) and the inclination (as most rabbits do not) to swim.

At one point we stopped to look at a sign that warned trespassers against wild boars, cottonmouths, rattlesnakes, quicksand, poison ivy and alligators. All such dangers were hidden from view by a thick screen of foliage.

Finally, at the end of the road, we found a man working on a cottage placed high on stilts, looking over an open space of swampland. There were tools, some boards, doors and drywall scattered about beneath the building, plus a plugged-in refrigerator stocked with beer. The man turned out to be, appropriately enough, a writer. Certainly this place appeared to be right out of a Hollywood movie script's idea of where an iconoclastic writer might live. Unfortunately for him, his fiancée did not share his enthusiasm for the remote location and he was moving out. Would we like to see his alligator?

He took us over to the edge of a small patch of water

PAINTED BUNTING

and called into what seemed to be nothing more than dense underbrush. However, eventually a medium-sized alligator did emerge from the vegetation and started to swim toward us with just his eyes showing above the clear water.

"Normally," said the writer, "I'd throw him some dead chickens right about now, but since I don't have any, maybe we'd better back off."

During our travels through the Deep South, we also saw raccoons, white-tailed deer, opossums, gray squirrels and other mammals. We encountered large magnolias in full bloom, live oaks, Spanish moss, resurrection ferns, yellow pitcher plants, palmetto and other plant species so characteristic of the region. Meadowlarks, mourning doves, red-winged blackbirds, song sparrows, common crows, tree swallows, eastern phoebes, great blue herons, belted kingfishers and many other bird species that are common back home were also common here.

In this inland region we discovered that six species – northern mockingbirds, white-eyed vireos, rufous-sided towhees, tufted titmouses, brown thrashers and northern cardinals – made up by far the majority of songbirds seen. We enjoyed such southern specialties as red-bellied woodpeckers, fish crows and boat-tailed grackles. In Florida we watched a flotilla of white pelicans from the Pensacola Bay Bridge on our way to Santa Rosa Island, where Charm and Buffy romped among towering white dunes. Brown pelicans, the state bird of Louisiana and once considered endangered, were commonplace along the length of the Gulf Coast.

Black and turkey vultures, northern harriers, American kestrels, broad-winged hawks, sharp-shinned hawks and red-tailed hawks were among commonly encountered raptors. White-throated sparrows were common throughout the entire journey from Canada to the Gulf Coast and back again.

On our return north, we restricted travel to the secondary roads of Alabama, generally avoiding major highways until we reached Tennessee. In northern Alabama we spent a

BROWN AND WHITE PELICANS

Of the seven species of pelican found in the world, two occur in North America: the brown and the American white. The brown pelican is the state bird of Louisiana. It was locally reduced to endangered status during the 1970s, due to pesticide contamination from DDT that produced widespread reproductive failure. Fortunately, with partial banning of DDT, the species has staged a remarkable comeback. Brown pelicans are found along coastlines and rarely stray inland.

The American white pelican breeds in interior lakes and sloughs from Texas north into northern Canada, but spends the winter on the coasts of the southern United States, Mexico and parts of Central America. At such times, it can be seen in the same general habitat as the brown; however, it favors deeper water and is more aloof. Brown pelicans can become delightfully used to people and may beg for fish from fishermen.

beautiful afternoon at Rickwood State Park. On the way south we had visited some of Kentucky's famous caves, and here, in Rickwood State Park, there was another cave to visit, complete with bats of unknown species, presumably little brown myotis.

Spring had touched mountain landscapes with the visual magic of the delicate bloom of redbud and the showy white of flowering dogwood. They glowed amid the green mist of swelling buds suspended in dark networks of twigs and branches. Black swallowtail butterflies, the most elegant of native butterflies, were also the most common in this region.

Carolina chickadees, blue-gray gnatcatchers, ruby-crowned kinglets, yellow-rumped warblers, eastern bluebirds, pileated woodpeckers, red-bellied woodpeckers, white-eyed vireos, tufted titmouses and northern cardinals were common species in forests characterized by tulip trees, black gums, sycamores, silver maples, shagbark hickories and other typically Carolinian tree species.

As sorry as I was to see the vacation end, I was grateful for having taken it. We continued heading home, losing, one by one, those parts of the natural environment that define the south and gaining those that belong to the higher latitudes. We reached Ontario about the same time as the yellow-rumped warblers. Spring had arrived.

BROWN PELICAN

PRAIRIE FALCON

IV
THE WEST

BRITISH COLUMBIA

MOUNTAIN CHICKADEE

When I was a small child, I lived for nearly four years in southern California. But for more than a dozen years thereafter I never left the province of Ontario. From my eastern perspective I loved the West with a passion originating from golden memories of those ever more distant years in California. I studied the western bird paintings of Allan Brooks and other artists and dreamt of mountains, deserts, prairies and Pacific shorelines. Then, in late December, 1964, we finally headed west again, to spend Christmas with friends in the Okanagan Valley, British Columbia.

The long train ride across the snowbound prairies was itself an adventure. It was bitterly cold and the doors between the cars often froze solid. At one point we ran out of ice cubes, to the chagrin of those adults who saw the trip as an ordeal to be endured only with the assistance of chilled cocktails. How could we be without ice when the stuff was several feet thick on the outside of the train? Christmas plum pudding became a twice-a-day mainstay of our diet as other food failed to materialize due to missed schedules and deliveries at stops along the way. Once we became snowbound for nearly half a day, and another time the side of the train was struck by a truck at a level crossing. Through it all, my mother and I spent most of the daylight hours looking out windows at the passing scenery. West of the wooded monotony of Ontario, the land became strangely, hauntingly beautiful. Although I am now a lover of the rich, earthy variety of tropical forests, the simplicity of the winter prairies wove a different kind of spell for me on that journey.

We sometimes saw snow buntings, and sharp-tailed grouse were fairly common, the latter a life bird. The black-billed magpie was also a life bird. This crisply black and white patterned bird seemed to suit the prairies in winter. I shall always associate it with that severe landscape, even though I have since seen it in a variety of habitats in Europe and Asia as well as in North America. We spotted ruffed grouse, perched in willows beside the train tracks, and the odd red-tailed hawk. Rough-legged hawks, the white undersides of their wings glowing with light reflected up off snowy fields, hovered in their search for rodent prey.

Birding from a train is frustrating. One keeps wanting to stop beside good habitat. The open spaces of the prairies provided us with longer opportunities to see birds than would most other forms of terrain. We would start at the front of a coach, looking out the windows, one on each side, and then yell out if something was spotted. By running back to the end of the coach, we could keep the bird in view the maximum length of time – usually only four or five seconds when the train was traveling at top speeds. Flocks of sharp-tailed grouse would fly outward from the front of the engine, and we could sometimes watch long enough to see them settle some distance away. Magpies sometimes flew parallel to the train tracks. If they were going in the same direction as the train, we could keep them in view a little longer. Snow buntings were usually seen swirling out over the fields.

For this odd form of high-speed birding we chose coaches nearly empty of fellow travelers. Those who were present viewed our antics with bemused tolerance, wondering what the excitement was all about when a particularly good look at a magpie or a snowy owl elicited excited comments and finger pointing.

Eventually we reached Kamloops, where we left the train in the middle of the night in the middle of a blizzard.

BLACK-BILLED MAGPIES

The black-billed magpie is a Holarctic species, meaning it is found throughout much of the northern hemisphere. However, there is a curious gap in its range. For some reason, the species has yet to occupy eastern North America. In Europe and Asia, the bird is found in urban areas, and in North America it lives in mountains, forests and prairies. There seems to be no reason why it could not find sufficient food and shelter in the diverse habitats east of the great plains. From time to time strays do show up in the East, and I suspect that one day the floodgate will open and the species will become common in eastern North America.

Howard and Peggy Strong and their daughter, Louise, were our hosts. They had arranged for a rental car at the station. On the long drive south to Penticton, where we would be staying, I could see little of the passing countryside, beyond my first glimpses of sage and yellow pine. I stayed awake in excited anticipation as Howard drove and was rewarded with the sight of a great horned owl perched on the sign that announced our arrival at Penticton. A very good omen, indeed.

The Strongs dropped us off at a motel that backed onto an apple orchard. It was that orchard, at first light the next morning, where I began to meet the western birds I had dreamed of seeing all my life.

Here were "Oregon" juncos, then generally considered to be a species separate from the "slate-colored" junco of the east. "Oregons" sometimes showed up in the east, but except for the most brightly colored adult males, they could be diffi-cult to distinguish from the brownish immature and female eastern birds. Now both forms are considered races of the one species, called the dark-eyed junco.

Song sparrows were common. Their darker coloring marked them as subspecies distinctive from those of the east. They hopped about in the bottoms of ornamental shrubs in typical song sparrow fashion. House finches, now common in Toronto, were unheard of in Ontario in my youth. The ones I saw before breakfast did not quite qualify as life birds, being one of the very few species I remembered from when I was a small child in California.

After these sightings, I excitedly turned my binoculars to a bulky shape in a hedge. It was a varied thrush, one of the most beautiful of all western birds and one I had hardly dared to hope I might one day see. The species is the sole member of its genus, *Ixoreus*, and a little more similar in form, color and pattern to some of the Asian thrushes than to any North American species. It is beautifully marked in a balanced pattern of dark gray and burnt orange. These colors seemed to glow in the low sunlight reflected off the surrounding snow.

AMERICAN DIPPER

As I was admiring the varied thrush, another bird entered the same binocular field: a flicker. This was the "red-shafted" race that was then considered to be a species distinct from the eastern "yellow-shafted" form I had seen all my life. Where the yellow-shafted has yellow undersides to the wings and tail, this bird was salmon-red. The face was gray, with a brown cap and red "moustache" markings. Where the two forms overlap, hybrids now occur with enough regularity to cause scientists to classify them as distinctive races of one species, called the northern flicker.

The atypically deep snow in the valley was a mixed blessing. While it hampered travel and observation of ground cover, it had, local birders told us, increased the numbers of birds driven down from the surrounding mountains. Most winters there was milder weather, less snow and fewer birds in the valley. We found so many more birds than one does during winter in the east that we did not mind the snow.

The richly textured and muted cloudscapes and the valley's tawny cliffs and gently sculpted bluffs reminded me of paintings by Allan Brooks, who lived and painted in the Okanagan most of his long life. Softly gray clumps of sage and the evenly spaced yellow pines, with their broadly scaled orange-brown bark and long needles, came to symbolize the West for me then and forever after. I wasn't surprised to learn, years later, that the yellow, or Ponderosa, pine was one of Major Brooks's favorite trees.

In the higher country, where we drove in spite of warnings about the snow, my mother and I were treated to the sight of a magnificent lynx prowling through the shadows of the forest. At the edge of a dark mountain stream that tumbled through softly curved mounds of snow, a sinuous mink failed in his attempts to catch one of several American dippers. Chunky and gray with short tails, these fascinating, vaguely thrush-like songbirds swam about in the current or flew on buzzing wings along the banks. They bobbed and tilted on precarious, mid-stream perches of ice, snow or rock, their

VASEUX LAKE

Just south of Penticton is the northern tip of an extension of arid, intermontane basin habitat that brings several wildlife species across the border into Canada. The shores of Vaseux Lake have become a favorite location for birders in British Columbia. Bird species of special interest include the white-throated swift, canyon wren, yellow-breasted chat, white-headed woodpecker, chukar, California quail and large numbers of waterfowl, particularly during migration. Although difficult to find, sage grouse also occur there in small numbers. The California race of the bighorn sheep and the Pacific rattlesnake are among other southern wildlife species that occur in this interesting region.

white eyelids flashing each time they blinked.

Later that day, while we walked across the parking lot of a small mall in downtown Penticton, a prairie falcon flew overhead, a dead California quail clutched in its talons. We spent some time to the south of the city, where we saw a number of California quail, running about the apple orchards with the curious, upright curved feathers of their crests looking more like a cartoonist's invention than reality. Large flocks of Bohemian waxwings decorated the bare branches of orchard trees like so many Christmas tree ornaments. They would huddle quietly or turn their attention to any dried fruit that clung to surrounding twigs. Also encountered were northern shrikes, a distinctly marked western race of the fox sparrow, the hairy woodpecker and various other species.

A few days after our arrival, we turned our attention north, to Summerland, where we took part in a local Christmas bird count under the direction of well-known birder Steve Cannings. Early on the morning of the bird census, even before we were out of Penticton to travel north, we watched a territorial dispute between a handsome pileated woodpecker and two "red-shafted" flickers. For reasons that remain a mystery, the birds chased each other around tree trunks, between tree trunks and over rooftops. It was a thrilling display of colorful woodpeckers.

A bigger thrill came a moment later when our first Lewis' woodpecker appeared. The species is unique in its blend of oily green, dark red, pale gray and softly pink markings. It turned out to be the only one of its species on the local Christmas count that day.

To our list of life birds we also added Cassin's finch, Clark's nutcracker, Townsend's solitaire and Steller's jay, all species whose names honor the pioneer naturalists and explorers of the Pacific region.

In the afternoon we stopped along a road overlooking the gray waters of Okanagan Lake. Flocks of waterfowl were spread out on the waters below but of even greater interest

BOHEMIAN WAXWING

were the massed flocks of American coots. It was my first experience with coots in such huge numbers – hundreds in a single flock. A bald eagle made several low-level passes at them, forcing the birds to scatter and dive with much splattering and splashing.

Throughout that memorable day, I constantly called out, "Red-shafted flicker," for the sake of counters. Finally Steve patiently said to me, "Barry, just saying 'flicker' is enough. They're *all* red-shafted." So they were, but that was, for me, a wonderful thing.

On our return, we saw our first pygmy nuthatches and mountain chickadees in massive yellow, or Ponderosa, pines, just as Allan Brooks would have seen and painted them, many decades earlier. We nearly caused a rear-end collision when we braked to admire the sight of an adult bald eagle sitting in a roadside tree. Surrounded by a small flock of black-billed magpies, it was an avian study in black and white against soft gray clouds. The driver behind us did not seem to share our enthusiasm.

The published results of the count would become part of the store of raw data used in understanding changes in the population dynamics of birds; computer-assisted comparisons are made from year to year. But for two eastern birders there was more fun than science in being part of the 1964 Lower Okanagan Valley Christmas Bird Count.

Many years later I was again in British Columbia, this time on business. While in Vancouver I contacted Jude and Al Grass, who picked me up at my hotel one morning and introduced me to Vancouver birding, or rather, birding just outside of Vancouver. I had already poked about streets and parks of the city and met some life birds, including the northwestern crow, which is a very slightly smaller version of the widely distributed American crow; the glaucous-winged gull, a Pacific coast relative of the herring gull; and the crested myna, originally from Asia and introduced into Vancouver in the 1890s. A little

EAGLES

Eagles have long held a reputation for killing the young of livestock and big game animals. Tens of thousands of golden and bald eagles have been shot, trapped and poisoned by people who think such actions will protect young livestock. An eagle can kill a weak or unprotected lamb, for example, but will rarely do so. However, both eagle species are scavengers and when seen feeding on a carcass are wrongly assumed by many people to be the cause of the animal's death. Although bald eagles are members of a group of eagles that are predominantly piscivorous, they are not adept at catching fish. Sometimes they will swoop upon an osprey carrying a fish, trying to use their greater size and strength to take the fish from the other bird. More often they will feast on dead or dying fish washed up on shore.

larger than its familiar relative, the European starling, the myna has remained in the city.

It was mid-winter, but already the weather was exceptionally mild. It was also foggy when we arrived at the dock for the ferry to Vancouver Island. We started with a life bird for me, a pelagic cormorant, perched on a stout piling nearby. Next to it was a double-crested cormorant. Close to shore swam a noisy little flock of brightly colored harlequin ducks.

As we had driven out on the foggy causeway, we had seen all three species of scoter, red-breasted and common mergansers, scaup, wigeon, mallards and both species of goldeneye. Posed on the rocks at the water's edge were some mew gulls, whose dark eyes, slender bills, long wings and medium-small size made them seem quite elegant.

BLACK-HEADED GROSBEAK

Close to shore swam a western grebe, its lower mandible shattered and hanging from a flap of skin. I've seen that kind of damage before, caused by shotgun pellets, and my hosts confirmed that waterfowl hunting was commonplace in the area. The sight of the grebe saddened me all the more because there was no way to prevent the bird's inevitable end from starvation. Driven by instinct, the grebe had no ability to understand that all its endeavors to catch fish would be useless.

Boggy flatlands near Delta were our next stop. This place is touted as hosting more wintering raptors than anywhere else in Canada. The soggy, driftwood-strewn fields host huge numbers of Townsend's voles, which, in turn, attract birds of prey. One of the first ones we saw was a long-eared owl perched on a stub out in the open, something I had never seen one do before as they normally hide in deep foliage. Later we spotted some short-eared owls in the open, as is more typical of that species.

To the east the sun began to burn off the fog to reveal the coastal mountains. Red-winged blackbirds were calling. The weather was growing increasingly warm and wonderfully spring-like.

Birds of prey were abundant. Rough-legged hawks

were the most common buteo. A fine representative of the western *calurus* race of the red-tailed hawk perched on a driftwood root, in full view. Northern harriers lived up to their name as they quartered the fields, searching for prey. American kestrels, a merlin and bald eagles were also tabulated on this part of our outing. The large vole population also attracted many great blue herons, which patrolled the fields with stately grace.

By this time in my career as a birder, I had somehow managed to visit barn owl habitat in Ontario, the United States, Central and South America, the Galápagos, Europe and Africa without ever seeing a wild barn owl. Finally, in Delta, I was taken to a large, empty barn where we found a pair of the pale tawny and white-colored owls. It was a species I had frequently seen in captivity, but how appropriate that I should see my first wild barn owls flying about the rafters of a barn.

Although the lower mainland forest was mostly cleared, a few small patches of it remained, hosting distinctive western races of song, fox and white-crowned sparrows. We found a red-breasted nuthatch, black-capped chickadees and the first of the spotted race of the rufous-sided towhee I had ever seen; I had heard one years earlier in California.

We concluded the outing at Boundary Bay, where tidal flats hosted northwestern crows and glaucous-winged gulls. Large numbers of robins and song sparrows were manifestations of spring. And as always, traveling presents variations on the familiar. Here I found a small cluster of beautifully plumaged green-winged teal in mist-filtered sunlight out on the dark tidal flats. They were a delightful vision of a well-known species back home.

My next visit to Vancouver took place in the summer. This time I rented a car and drove inland, up the Fraser River Valley, seeking new and different habitat. What most impressed me was the lack of birds. I was too far west to encounter many of the songbird species I associate with British

BUTEOS

In English-speaking countries outside of North America, the term *buzzard* is usually used for species of hawk in the genus *Buteo*. Unfortunately, in North America, the word *buzzard* is often incorrectly applied to turkey or black vultures. Buteos, which tend to be medium to medium-large in size, have rounded wings and tails. The tails are usually short to medium-long, depending on the species. Buteos frequently soar, like vultures, or perch on exposed sites to look for prey. Unlike vultures, they catch live prey and only rarely eat carrion. North American Buteos include the red-shouldered, red-tailed, broad-winged, gray, Swainson's, rough-legged, ferruginous, white-tailed, zone-tailed and short-tailed hawks.

Columbia, and as I headed east I was tempted to throw my schedules and commitments to the wind and continue all the way back to the Okanagan Valley I remembered so fondly from that one Christmas visit so many years earlier.

Instead, I drove about as far as I felt I could go and still leave time for a little hiking before returning to Vancouver. Sasquatch Provincial Park provided me with the opportunity to explore mountain forest beside a sparkling lake. A highlight for me was the opportunity to observe families of Steller's jays. Adults fed fluttering fledglings amid the broad branches of fir trees hanging over a lakeside campground. The species, which ranges through the mountains of the West from Alaska deep into Mexico, symbolizes the entire western region for me. The Steller's is a close relative of the blue jay, and between them they are found in most of North America, below the tree line.

Mountain and black-capped chickadees, red-breasted nuthatches, breeding pine siskins, black-headed grosbeaks and other bird species, along with mule deer, were to be found in the woods, while violet-green swallows swooped low over open water.

I saw other species, mostly ones that also occur in the east. But it was not so much the birds and other wildlife, the scenery or the vegetation that I remember, as it was the pleasure derived from the ambience of the West they all created. I carried that memory of a single afternoon in southern British Columbia back east with me, eager for yet another visit to the West.

GROOVE-BILLED ANI

DEEP BELOW THE HEART OF TEXAS

Roger Tory Peterson identified the 100th meridian as a convenient division between east and west for birders, and Dallas is east of that line, but others have chosen the Mississippi River as a good dividing line, and Dallas is west of that. Although there is no absolute beginning to the American West as defined by terrain and wildlife, to my eastern eyes the natural features encountered in and near the Dallas area are definitely western.

On a Sunday afternoon in October, after attending a weekend conference in Dallas, I flew south to Harlingen, where I rented a car and drove the short distance to Brownsville, at the southernmost tip of the U.S. mainland. With only a few hours of daylight left, I booked into a motel, quickly changed my clothes and headed for the dump. In U.S. birding circles, the Brownsville dump is famous.

I drove across the flat, dry landscape, toward a dark column of smoke, which I assumed came from a dump fire. I was wrong. The fire, on vacant land, had been set to train firefighters. I had missed the landfill site. Compensation came in the form of some golden-fronted woodpeckers. The birds perched on telephone poles and allowed close observation. The species is heavily barred black and white above, with a white rump patch that is conspicuous in flight. The top of the head is red in the male, brown in the female. There is a golden color to the nape and to the small clump of feathers that cover the nostrils. The latter feature gives the bird its name. Apart from a small section of Oklahoma, golden-fronted woodpeckers are rarely encountered outside of Texas or Mexico.

Finally I found the dump. It was an enormous area of hills and valleys manufactured from accumulated waste and dotted with clumps of prickly pear cactus. As this is one place where the Mexican crow – unknown in the United States prior to the 1960s – occurs in numbers, the dump is frequently visited by birders. In fact, when the guard at the gate found out what I wanted, he cheerfully let me drive onto the dumpsite, but told me that the crows had left a few days earlier.

I was disappointed, but there was another species of crow here that I was just as anxious to see, the Chihuahuan raven. This species is only slightly larger than the familiar American crow; however, it has the characteristic wedge-shaped tail, shaggy throat plumage and heavy bill of most species of raven. When the wind ruffled the feathers at the side of the bird's neck, I could see the white bases of the feathers that inspired its former name of white-necked raven.

Great-tailed grackles strutted about at close range. This was a species familiar to me from Central America, a "mega-grackle" in comparison to the common grackle back home or the small and quite delicate grackle species I had seen in the West Indies. There was little else around and darkness was setting in. Reluctant to give up searching for the Mexican crow, I waited until it was dark before heading for the motel.

Before dawn the next day, I left Brownsville and drove to the Falcon State Recreation Area. I left my car in a dusty parking lot and paused to enjoy the sensation of being in the midst of a desert thorn-scrub habitat, surrounded by wonderfully unfamiliar birdsong. The large Falcon Dam reservoir was a sheet of luminous water in the morning light, its eastern end abruptly terminated by the curving sweep of the dam.

The first bird I spotted flashed about in the tops of the highest bushes, the early sunlight shining through the

VISITING BROWNSVILLE

Along the Texan Gulf coast, Padre Island is a famed birding location, noted for shorebirds and herons. Boca Chica is a good headquarters for birders visiting the coast. Nearby is the National Audubon Society's Sabal Palm Grove Sanctuary, the largest refuge for the native sabal palm and home to many native songbirds, as well as an excellent spot to look for migrants.

In addition to the Brownsville dump, birders staying in Brownsville might want to check out the Municipal Golf Course for local and migrant songbirds. Highway 281, also called the Military Highway, is the birder's best route west, for it passes several good birding sites. Although agriculture has obliterated much of the original habitat, there are native sabal and fan palms growing along the route. James Lane reports that evening travelers might see barn owls or yellow bats, which employ the palms as roosts.

For a complete list of the area's birding locations, obtain a copy of *A Birder's Guide to the Rio Grande Valley of Texas*, by James A. Lane and Harold R. Holt.

translucent brown of its wing and tail feathers and highlighting the pale yellow tint of its lower underparts. A little checking in my field guide identified the bird as a brown-crested flycatcher. While not a life bird, it was certainly a good bird with which to begin the day, his loud calls welcoming me to the north shore of the lower Rio Grande.

A useful trick when birding, particularly in new regions, is to listen for an unfamiliar birdcall or song and then try to locate its source. As I left the flycatcher, I sought the origin of faint chirping in dense, thorny thickets. The bird was closer than I thought, perched in its bristling covert, staring back at me with something of the appearance of a northern cardinal. But the short, blunt orange beak of this bird was all I needed to tell me that at last I had come upon a bird I had wanted to see since childhood, a pyrrhuloxia. The bird was a female, tan below and gray above, with tints of rose in its plumage.

I heard the calls of a scaled quail, another bird high on my list of what I most wanted to see, but I failed to find it. I did enjoy seeing blue-gray gnatcatchers and northern mockingbirds. A bird the same size as the mockingbirds but with a different song was calling from the top of a tree. My binoculars brought the bird into focus: a curve-billed thrasher. That was my second life bird of the day. As is typical of desert birds, the curve-bill is colored in muted tones – gray, with a hint of tan on the lower underparts. The form in Texas is the nominate race, distinguished by vague spotting on the breast.

As I watched the thrasher, a small group of white-tailed deer sauntered through the thick mesquite. Desert cottontails hopped about on the ground.

Although this protected area is only a few square miles in size, it provided easy access to a broad cross-section of desert birds in something resembling the original native Texas landscape and flora. There were a few campers about and some sport anglers attracted to the reservoir; however, for the most part I had the park to myself.

WHAT TO TAKE INTO THE FIELD

The birder must strike a balance between taking enough to assist in enjoyment and too much. In new areas I usually carry some sort of bag in which I have a field guide, notebook, sketchbook, camera, a separate telephoto lens, extra film and, in warm weather, insect repellent and sunscreen. There may also be lunch, a water canteen and, in winter, an extra pair of socks. Sometimes a map and compass can be useful, plus waterproof matches and extra provisions; however, most birding does not require deep penetration of wilderness areas.

128

October is not the best time of year for birding; rather, late spring or early summer is. It hardly mattered, though. I was on an adrenalin high, fueled by new birds and habitat.

Harris' hawks perched on many treetops, fence posts and telephone poles in or near the park. These beautiful birds are sought by falconers. There is an illegal trade in wild-caught birds, as well as legal trade in captive-bred birds. Partly because of this, the species has declined seriously in some parts of its U.S. range. Fortunately, it is widely distributed from the southwestern States down through most parts of Central and South America. Certainly the species is not endangered. But aware of declines that have occurred elsewhere, I was pleased to find that here it was common.

Other common raptors included turkey vultures, American kestrels and crested caracaras. Technically a member of the falcon family, the caracara is too weak-footed to overpower any but the frailest prey and is generally a scavenger. With its rather slender form, bold black and white patterning and red face patch, the crested caracara is one of the most handsome of our native raptors. It is also called the Mexican Eagle and is featured on the flag of Mexico.

The lake provided an ideal habitat for ospreys. Damming the river had flooded out some trees, leaving standing snags that the large birds like to perch upon. The water had also attracted double-crested cormorants, great blue herons, great and snowy egrets, laughing gulls and Forster's terns. Cliff, barn and northern rough-winged swallows swooped low over the lake's calm surface in search of tiny insects.

I walked along the edge of a small picnic ground. Here a family of cactus wrens, including both adults and newly fledged young, scolded and chattered with intense, if unfocused, enthusiasm. Inca doves, with delicate scaled patterns on their plumage, strutted about or flew up ahead of me. Common ground doves, the smallest of our native doves, were numerous and like the Inca doves, they showed ruddy

BIRD RECORDINGS AND RECORDING BIRDS

Beginning birders are often surprised to learn that most bird identification is actually done by ear. This can be far from easy, particularly as some bird species, such as the magnolia warbler, have many variations of their song. There are numerous recordings available (usually through naturalists' groups and stores catering to birders) to help birders learn songs and calls. Those featuring a specific region usually work best because they allow the birder to concentrate on the species most likely to be encountered. During the breeding season, many birders will play the songs of those species that tend to keep hidden in likely looking habitat or near where the bird has been heard, in the hope of enticing the bird into view. This practice is harmless if done in moderation. However, there have been instances when a rare species has been kept so busy responding to recordings that it has been unable to attend to nesting duties, to the detriment of the young.

CRESTED CARACARA

patches in the primary feathers of their wings when they flew. A third dove, the mourning dove, was also present.

As I followed random, path-like open areas between clumps of thorny scrub, I flushed a sandy-colored bird with long wings. The bird's flight was erratic, but when it banked sharply, it presented its complete dorsal aspect as if posing quickly for an illustration in a field guide before vanishing amid the gray vegetation. The bold white wing markings and white feathers in its long, rounded tail identified the bird as a common pauraque. I had often heard this close relative of the whip-poor-will and the chuck-will's-widow as it called in the tropical nights of Costa Rica, but I had never before actually seen it.

When planning my day, I had assumed that the visit to Falcon Dam would be fairly brief. It was just supposed to be a starting point. But each time I thought it was time to leave, another interesting bird or other animal appeared.

Three groove-billed anis came into view. These black cuckoos with their long tails and angular, disjointed movements are among my favorite birds. Next came a male pyrrhuloxia. It was a wonderfully soft gray color with dark rose markings down its breast, just as artist Allan Brooks had shown it in the library copy of the old National Geographic Society's *The Book of Birds* I had borrowed so often as a child. There is an understated elegance to the bird's appearance I had long admired in pictures and preserved specimens.

Black-throated sparrows personify, for me, the American Southwest. I did not expect them here, on what must be the easternmost edge of their range. With their solid black throat patches, conspicuous face patterns and rounded tails, they don't remind me of most other North American species of sparrow as much as they do the smaller, flighty tropical species of finches and seedeaters. In *The Book of Birds*, the black-throated sparrow is called the desert sparrow, and Brooks's plate captures the essence of the bird – its small, delicate form contrasted with its bold pattern and manner.

Brooks shows the bird atop a sprig of chapparal, head back, mouth open in song. Its sprightly song, consisting of a couple of sharp chips followed by a rapid trill, is one of the most characteristic sounds of the arid Southwest.

Once more I found golden-fronted woodpeckers, these birds in more aesthetically pleasing surroundings than I had seen them the previous evening. However, while some perched in trees, in common with the closely related red-headed woodpecker of the east and the acorn woodpecker of the west, most did seem to have a fondness for telephone poles and tall posts.

A wide, sloping field of small bushes hosted a large number of scissor-tailed flycatchers. These elegant, soft gray birds with their touches of salmon-red coloring and long, sweeping tail streamers allowed close scrutiny. As I admired them, I regretted not having brought my camera. But with my camera or sketchbook at hand, I might not have left Falcon Dam until nightfall.

It was a hot, beautiful day and I was thoroughly enjoying myself. A giant swallowtail butterfly drifted by on broad black and yellow wings. A roadrunner darted through an empty campground, pausing to pose atop a wooden stake, crest raised, tail down, rounded wings hanging loosely.

Finally, I made it down to the dam itself. Looking across the spillway, I could see black and turkey vultures as they perched in another country: Mexico. If I were one of those birders who keep lists by jurisdictions, they would have been my first Mexican birds, or would they count as such when my feet were planted on U.S. soil?

I found some small, dull sparrows in an otherwise uninteresting field beside the dam. One was quite tame and posed at close range, allowing me to identify it clearly as a Cassin's sparrow.

A path that ran along the bank of the Rio Grande was just too promising to pass up, but as I started along it I saw no birds. Suddenly I heard a shout, off to my left, followed by the rapid banging of automatic weapons' fire. A faded sign indicated that somewhere nearby was a firing range for the agents of the U.S. customs' service. I waited to see if I could hear the hissing sound of bullets cutting through nearby vegetation. Nothing. I decided it was safe to continue. A Swainson's hawk flew ahead of me, into a grove of tall trees. I followed, hoping for a better look at the raptor.

It was with a feeling of intense joy that I turned toward a movement in the branches above my head and beheld one of the loveliest birds I've ever seen: a green jay. Again a series of images and memories flooded my mind as I recalled Brooks's handsome painting of a green jay published in *The Book of Birds*. I also remembered how, as a child, I watched captive green jays in an aviary. After the birds died, one of the bodies had been given to me, and I painstakingly preserved it as a study skin. But captive birds, a preserved specimen and pictures in books are never enough to truly represent a species. Here the bird was alive and in front of me, in native habitat where it belonged.

There were several, in fact, hopping about amid the intricate foliage of acacia trees. They are beautiful birds. The black bib pattern found in most neotropical jay species contrasts with their light blue heads. Their bodies are yellowish-green, ranging from a pale shade on the soft feathers of their ventral surfaces to a darker tone on their backs and wings. The inner tail feathers are green, the outer bright yellow.

The various members of the Corvidae family – jays, crows, ravens, magpies, nutcrackers, jackdaws, rooks and treepies – invariably fascinate me. All Corvids express a vibrant character that implies intelligence, curiosity and even humor. Were I a scientist, I could not voice this opinion without proof. But as a lay admirer of birds, I can say that I have the impression that Corvids, like parrots, have a distinct intellectual edge over most other birds.

Down the bank beside me flowed the sluggish green water of the Rio Grande. Least grebes, great egrets and double-

BLACK-THROATED SPARROW

crested cormorants hunted the river for fish. I checked each cormorant in search of olivaceous cormorants, but saw none.

I briefly glimpsed a zone-tailed hawk, characteristically holdings its wings at a slight angle as if trying to imitate the flight of a turkey vulture. Once a wood stork flew across the river to the Mexican side. Golden-fronted woodpeckers were doing the same, the river simply an element of their environment rather than an international boundary. Yet for many tropical and subtropical species of wildlife that occur this far north, the Rio Grande is a permeable biological boundary. They reach the river valley, but go no further.

Finally, with great reluctance, I drove out of the park and turned onto the highway. A Mississippi kite flew over my car, the last species to be seen at Falcon Dam. There were numerous other places to visit, but it was late in the afternoon and I knew there was only time for one more major stop – the Santa Ana National Wildlife Refuge.

It was 4:00 p.m. when I reached the gate of the refuge. The sign said that the park closed at that time, but, having come from so far, I hoped no one would mind if I visited. I drove slowly down the road, which was lined with exotic subtropical dry forest vegetation. Acacias seemed to dominate, and many of the overhead limbs were festooned with gray banners of Spanish moss. It was fascinating habitat, and I wished I had more time to explore it. One of my favorite fantasies is that a benefactor will hire me to do paintings of the birds of the American Southwest. Were my dream to come true, I would begin my field studies in this area.

My daydreams were interrupted by a rustling sound and I applied the brake. I turned my head to look out the open window and found myself staring directly at a chachalaca, too close for binoculars and posed magnificently on a branch. The bird, with stately dignity, hopped down and walked off into the woods. In fact, the species proved to be common in the park, and I soon saw others as I drove at a snail's pace along the sun-and-shade-dappled road.

BORDER CROSSINGS

There is a tale, the truthfulness of which I cannot verify, about a birder who perched upon a stool by the bank of a river and watched a small bird on the far side, hour after hour. As the bird had been identified, he was asked why it was still under such intense observation. The answer was that the bird was flying out over the river in pursuit of insects. The river was a political boundary. Its species had not been recorded in the jurisdiction where the birder sat. The man did not expect the bird to cross the river; he only wanted it to reach the midway point, at which time it could then be added to his list of birds of the jurisdiction in which he was comfortably seated.

The plain chachalaca is the northernmost member of the family Cracidae, and the only Cracid found in the United States. I had seen other Cracids but never this species, which occurs in the States only in this small corner of Texas. As Cracids are widely regarded as gamebirds, the other species I had seen had been few and far between and understandably nervous. These birds, presumably fully protected, were abundant and easy to observe. The word "plain" does them a disservice. In my opinion they are quite beautiful, with their subtle shades of brown and tan and delicate touches of iridescence to the wings and back.

I stopped for an armadillo as it ran across the road, looking like an intense, wind-up toy. Large fox squirrels with ocher-colored bellies scrambled along thick, curving tree limbs. These squirrels were the southern, most richly colored race of a species I had first observed in Illinois. At that time I probably annoyed the zookeeper who was proudly showing a group of us his zoo when I became as interested in the wild fox squirrels begging for handouts on the lawns between the cages as I was in the animals behind bars.

The light was low. There was no one else around, and no sound except the sounds of birds. The park was only about two miles (3.2 km) at its greatest width. I knew that I really had to explore a little on foot, so I parked and began to follow a nature trail through the legume- and acacia-dominated forest.

Some chachalacas fluttered awkwardly in my direction, almost hitting me. Green jays flew to the tops of low, nearby trees and looked down at me. Great-tailed grackles led me on. I stopped to look at a house wren, a familiar bird in most unfamiliar surroundings.

Doves were extremely elusive, but I finally got my binoculars focused on some and identified them as white-tipped doves, another species that reaches its northern limit in this corner of Texas. I was looking at these birds when a ranger walked up to me and offered to drive me back to my

PLAIN CHACHALACA

car so that I could leave. But, bound as he was to the rules of the park, which said that only cars had to be out by 4:00 p.m., there was nothing he could do to stop me from returning on foot for the last hour or so of twilight. I assured the ranger that I would be careful and that I would leave the park as soon as it was dark. After he reluctantly agreed, I had the entire park to myself.

In a small pond a female black-bellied whistling duck was surrounded by her brood of ducklings. I counted twenty of the tiny ducklings bobbing cork-like on the flat, green water. The same pond hosted pied-billed grebes, tricolored herons, great and snowy egrets, blue-winged teal, mallards, common moorhens and northern shovelers.

Suddenly I heard a sound from the past. It was the call of a green kingfisher, which I hadn't heard in the fifteen years since I had encountered the species in Costa Rica. I spotted the bird as it perched on a small snag above a dark pond. Kingfishers are noted for the variety of their bill shapes, and the green's beak is exceptional for its relative length and slender proportions.

I thought as I watched the bird that green plumage is clearly a tropical characteristic. Of all the birds in eastern temperate North America only the ruby-throated humming-bird has a significant amount of iridescent green plumage. Here, in southernmost Texas, were two species named for their color: the green jay and this handsome little kingfisher. Moving south into the tropics, green becomes a common color in birds.

A ringed kingfisher, the largest American member of the kingfisher family and found in the States only in this corner of Texas, looked down from a tall snag, its feathers glowing in the light of the setting sun. Its colors are nearly the same as those of the widely distributed belted kingfisher, but the proportions are different, with nearly all of the underparts chestnut. In the belted that color is largely restricted to a narrow breast band in the female.

FIELD GUIDES AND CHECKLISTS

A good field guide is important, and there is now a wide selection to choose from. Personally, I prefer those illustrated by art, not photographs, as the illustrations are more consistent. Field guides to other fauna and flora often enhance the birding experience.

Most birders carry local checklists to record each day's finds. I prefer a notebook, but checklists are handy to let one know what occurs in a given area.

Finally a belted kingfisher arrived, completing a southern Texas grand slam: all three kingfishers that are found in the States together at the same place at the same time.

As I walked along the trail, stray gleams of light still reached the leaf-covered ground. I paused to identify one of the many small lizards that were scampering about. This one was a keeled earless lizard. From the woods all around came the chattering and squealing sounds of green jays and great-tailed grackles. I saw some blue-gray gnatcatchers, another house wren and some more groove-billed anis.

Then I found a heavyset bird that was sitting quietly on a branch, not too far above me. My binoculars resolved the image into that of a long-billed thrasher. The bird superficially resembles the brown thrasher, but is larger. It has an orange, not yellow, iris, more gray about the head and neck and, as its name implies, a longer, more curved beak. All of these field marks were clearly evident in the bird before me. Although its range extends north of the lower Rio Grande River, the species is another bird normally not encountered in the States outside of southern Texas.

The final bird species I saw was another not normally found in the States outside of southern Texas, but one that, unlike the long-billed thrasher, is so widely distributed in Central and South America that I think of it as an old friend: the great kiskadee. This glorious flycatcher has a bright yellow breast, a distinctive black and white head pattern and a brown back and tail with strong rufous tints to the flight feathers.

Bold, noisy, colorful and conspicuous, the great kiskadee is a bird I admire and a good one to mark the end of one of my most pleasant days of birding.

BINOCULARS AND TELESCOPES

Modern technology has created some small, lightweight binoculars of excellent quality. Even so, I find that a thin binocular strap will, in time, give me a headache by pressing on the back of my neck, so I prefer a broad strap to better distribute the weight. I also like one that is long enough to allow me to sling the binoculars over one shoulder, but short enough to prevent the binoculars from bumping against nearby objects.

Telescopes are necessary for much shorebird, gull and waterfowl viewing. I prefer tripod mounts, but some birders use hand-held 'scopes mounted on gunstocks. The advantage of tripods for me, in winter, is that when I shiver, they don't.

SOUTHERN CALIFORNIA

My first adulthood journey to southern California was in late September to attend an Animal Protection Institute (API) conference in Anaheim, California. At the time I was working on many projects back home and could spend only one full extra day in the state. With that single day at my disposal, I briefly considered visiting Knott's Berry Farm, Mount Wilson or other places I remembered from childhood. But there was one place I particularly wanted to see again – the Mojave Desert.

I drove for several hours, frustrated by the expanse of urban sprawl that had engulfed what had been discreet communities, orange groves and open countryside in my childhood. The flat, dreary urbanscape was intersected by a network of highways constituting the infamous Los Angeles Freeway system. It took hours of highway driving before I saw my first open field, and with it the first signs of native vegetation and the odd animal. At the town of Twentynine Palms, just as it was getting dark, I found a wonderful motel on the edge of a desert habitat characterized by Joshua trees and other yuccas. Flocks of white-crowned sparrows busily flitted about in the bushes and there were intriguing avian call notes from the surrounding desert. But room rates were way outside my budget and I eventually wound up in an unappealing but affordable place on the other side of town.

It really didn't matter because I was back in my car well before dawn. In darkness I drove into the Joshua Tree National Monument Park, parked and walked at a more or less

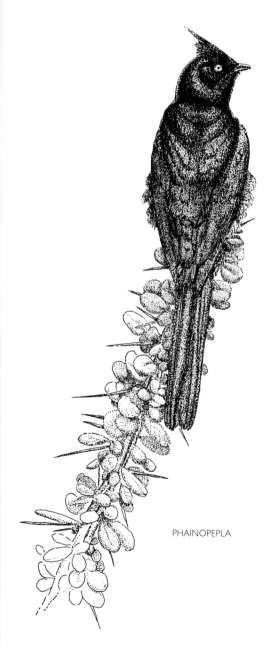

PHAINOPEPLA

right angle into the desert. I had no flashlight, preferring to let my eyes become adjusted to the night. In any case, with a clear, starry sky above and light-colored sand and rock below, it was quite bright. I had selected a place where the land gradually sloped upward from the road, so that there was no chance of my becoming lost. I also took careful note of the taller rocks and angular crags that stood in silhouette against the sky, suitable as landmarks to guide me.

The black horizon slowly lightened as dawn approached and the stars faded. There was absolute silence, but for the noise of my shoes crunching on the gritty soil. I found a comfortably contoured rock and sat down just as the top of a barren mountain to the west caught the very first rays of morning sun and glowed a bright orange. At almost that moment I began to hear birds calling. This was autumn and I was hearing call notes, not songs, and I wasn't sure of the species. As the sky rapidly lightened, I saw some small sparrows darting about in thickets. Eventually one of the birds paused in the open. It was a white-crowned sparrow.

I felt a bit foolish for not recognizing the call notes of a familiar species – the same species I had noted the previous evening at the first motel I had visited – but in such circumstances I'm always so primed for the unexpected that I sometimes fail to immediately identify the familiar. These birds were of the Gambel's race, which is found in the west, although sharp-eyed birders will see the odd one in the east, during migration.

The identity of another bird call also eluded me, and I was sure that this one was not familiar. The bird, which was small, managed to keep massive boulders between us. Finally, as if deciding that the game was up and it was time to reveal itself, the bird perched on a huge, nearby boulder in full view and was easily identified as a rock wren.

By now the surrounding terrain had completely changed color, with rich gold and ocher shades predominating. The rocks continued to change their color throughout the day.

VISITING JOSHUA TREE NATIONAL MONUMENT

In the hottest weather, visitors to Joshua Tree National Monument should have with them a gallon of water per person per day. Even if no hiking is planned, car trouble can be disastrous if one does not make a few preparations. Maps, guide books and camping information can be obtained at the visitor's centers on the Utah Trail, the main road into the park (at the east end of the town of Twentynine Palms) or at the Cottonwood Visitor Center (just north of Interstate 10, a few miles west of Chiriaco Summit). There are roads for four-wheel drive use only, and, of course, walking trails and campgrounds. At some campsites rangers conduct nature hikes, history tours and other activities. There are no service stations or restaurants in the park, so stock up on fuel and food. As long as you are on a main road, you are nowhere too far from park boundaries and communities that provide all the amenities.

I made my way back to the car, trying to take everything in but knowing that I would, at best, just have time to sample this fondly remembered environment from my childhood.

I drove on a few miles and stopped again. I had seen a bird flitting about in some dense bushes on the right-hand shoulder of the road. It is a wonderful feeling for a birder to know that a bird has been located that will almost certainly soon be in full view and will almost certainly be a new species. I even had a feeling I knew exactly what new species. I was right. The slender, glossy black, crested bird was one I had wanted to see all my life: a phainopepla.

I had long been an admirer of the tropical members of this bird's small family, usually known as the silky flycatchers. Now, finally, I had a wild phainopepla in its native habitat in front of me. This one was feeding on thick clusters of minute, red parasitic berries.

Although I am a birder, it is often botany that defines a region for me. I must have seen, or at least passed, phainopeplas and rock wrens when I was five and six years of age, but I don't recall them. However, I never forgot the magnificent Joshua trees of the Mojave Desert. They aren't really trees, but yuccas, which stand as tall as the smaller tree species and have stout central trunks that branch out in heavy, angular limbs. The limbs terminate in clumps of long, thick, pointed leaves.

In 1844, John C. Frémont described the plant as ". . . the most repulsive tree in the vegetable kingdom." In 1919, J. Smeaton Chase said of the species: "It is a weird, menacing object . . . One can scarcely find a term of ugliness that is not apt for this plant. A misshapen pirate with the belt, boots, hands, and teeth stuck full of daggers is as near as I can come to a human analogy. The wood is a harsh, rasping fiber; knife-blades, long, hard, and keen, fill the place of leaves; the flower is greenish white and ill-smelling; and the fruit a cluster of nubbly pods, bitter and useless. A landscape filled with Joshua trees has a nightmare effect even in broad daylight; at the witching hour it can be almost infernal."

THE JOSHUA TREE AND THE YUCCA MOTH

In order to pollinate, the Joshua tree requires the services of the yucca moth (*Pronuba synthetica*). In order to survive, the yucca moth requires the Joshua tree. The giant yucca's pollen is sticky and cannot be carried by the wind. The moth can gather this pollen easily and carries it to another flower. The moth thus fertilizes the flower and then lays its eggs in the ovary. The caterpillars hatch by the time the seeds are developed, and eat the seeds, leaving enough to guarantee the continuation of the species. The Joshua tree is guaranteed fertilization and the moth is guaranteed food for its offspring.

One of those "nubbly pods" was a cherished souvenir of the desert for many years. That day I did what I had dreamed of doing since I had been removed from this wonderful environment in my childhood; I walked up to a living Joshua tree in the Mojave Desert. I placed the palm of my hand flat against the trunk of the plant, glad that I was alone. (I've been known to be a little intolerant of the "touchy-feely" school of nature appreciation characterized by those who play flutes to dolphins or meditate on mountain-tops.) Yet here I was in unintended parody of the famous scene from the movie *2001: A Space Odyssey*, where the space-suited scientist approaches the alien monolith on the surface of the moon and puts the flat of his gloved hand upon its enigmatic surface. There was nothing enigmatic about this surface, which had the dry, rough texture of the desert. No message passed from monolithic plant to awe-struck human's skin, but the intimacy symbolized by this contact was the strongest affirmation I could think of that I was finally, if only briefly, back in the Mojave Desert.

I continued deeper into the desert, fully enjoying a landscape that was silent, orderly and peaceful. I paused to admire a cactus wren. This is North America's largest wren and its boldly speckled patterning and equally bold manner make it a favorite of mine on the special occasions when our paths cross.

As the wren perched on the top of a Mojave yucca, a swift movement nearby caught my attention and I turned to see a beautifully patterned black and white bird fly by. Its crest was scarlet. The bird alit and allowed me to admire it, my very first ladder-backed woodpecker. It perched vertically on the rough trunk of a medium-sized yucca, alertly looking around and bobbing his head before taking a few pecks at the plant. House finches and black-throated sparrows were also present. The sparrows were singing with crystal-edged songs that seemed as clear as the desert air.

Overhead, common ravens flew by, uttering their

familiar, croaking calls. The discontinuous North American range of this species has always interested me. It is close to being the only bird, particularly songbird (for taxonomically, its voice notwithstanding, that's what it is), that can be found in winter north of the arctic circle. Much of my own experience with the bird has been in boreal forest habitat within a two-hour drive of home. However, while it is absent from most of temperate eastern North America, a discreet population lives in the upper altitudes of the eastern mountains. In the West, the raven occurs in the drier, desert regions and in the mountains, from the high Arctic deep into Mexico.

The raven seems to prefer wilderness areas, and although it's a prominent inhabitant of human settlements in the north and in mountainous terrain, it is not a species I normally associate with major urban areas. Here, a few hours from Los Angeles, the raven seemed a part of the rugged and natural landscape of the high desert.

Most of the area's plants were armed with spines or thorns or sharply pointed twigs. However, dry washes formed paths through many of the thorny thickets, and even though I was wearing shorts I could walk considerable distances without worrying about the hostile nature of the vegetation. The senna, creosote, jojoba, smoketrees and various species of cactus, on the other hand, tended to space themselves in an arrangement that was fundamentally harmonious, each individual given enough room to grow. There was competition here no less than in the rankest rain forest, but it was competition of a slow-growing, stately quality.

As I hiked through one dry wash, a blacktail jackrabbit appeared, stood tall on its hind legs, then casually loped ahead of me for a minute or two before finally vanishing into vegetation off to the side of the wash. A northern mockingbird uttered some hesitant call notes from the crown of what appeared to be a species of willow.

Further on, a softly colored Say's phoebe perched on a rock. This highly migratory species of flycatcher breeds from

DESERT WOOD RATS

The desert wood rat is a small brown rat with a finely furred tail. Like many desert rodents, it is able to metabolize water directly from seeds. The wood rat makes a large nest out of piles of debris, including the spine-covered joints of the cholla cactus. It earned its popular name, packrat, by gathering up small objects left by humans at campsites or in cabins and packing them into the structure of the nest. While footprints, droppings and nests are easily found, the rat is usually nocturnal.

Alaska south as far as Mexico, and winters in the southern part of that extensive range. It occurs in many habitats, but with its sandy-brown and ocher-tawny coloring, the bird seems to me to belong in desert habitat.

Black phoebes, another western species — although one whose range extends deep into the tropics — were also present. They are typical phoebes in shape, size and habits, but are black, not brown. The U.S. race has a white belly. In the tropics, where I first encountered the species, their bellies are nearly all black. Black phoebes, like eastern phoebes, are usually found in the vicinity of water, but these migrant birds had to make do with the dry wash.

As I walked along, I passed holes that undoubtedly housed various species of desert fauna I longed to see, including snakes, lizards, spiders, scorpions, wood rats and kangaroo rats. I managed to identify one ground squirrel and a couple of lizard species, but apart from birds there were few animals to be seen.

Although the temperature was climbing up into the nineties, where it would peak, in the summer it could reach as high as 150°F (65°C) at ground level. The main strategy many species have for coping with these oven temperatures is to remain underground. I dug down a little into the soil with my hands and found that just below its hot, dry surface the earth was finer and cooler, feeling almost damp.

Loggerhead shrikes sat on the tops of rocks, on the tips of branches and on other exposed places, searching for large insects, small rodents or other prey. The kestrels I saw were also hunters, with tastes similar to the shrikes'. Death sustains life, and suffering is an inevitable component of sentience. Nevertheless, in this unpeopled place cruelty was absent. In contrast, throughout the day the skies above were penetrated by the dark, low forms of fighter aircraft, practicing war. Armed helicopters from a nearby military installation traveled in rigid formation in contrast to the curves and angles of the natural elements of the desert below. Jets screamed and the earth shook to distant bomb blasts. As I continued my explorations of this wondrous place, I tried to ignore the death machines of a species so efficient at killing its own kind.

I alternated between driving and walking through the morning and into the afternoon. What most impressed me was the degree of ecological change encountered from place to place as I moved through the transitional zone between the higher, more northern Mojave Desert and the lower, more southern Sonoran Desert. The appearance of the land kept changing and so did the composition of the vegetation. Sometimes there were massive jumbles of shattered rock and huge boulders. Elsewhere the land was flat or gently contoured. Everywhere erosion, fueled by extremes of weather, was the dominating force shaping the terrain.

A sudden turn in the road brought into view a truly bleak panorama, the flat expanse of the Pinto Basin and the low desert. Many thousands of years before Europeans invaded the continent, this valley was green with grass and trees and inhabited by a wide array of large fauna, including humans. Now it is a burning panorama of scorched scrub and rock thinly populated by desert-adapted wildlife and devoid of human habitation.

I stopped next to a dense stand of cholla cactus. The cholla is one of the most notorious of cactus species for painfully assaulting the human skin. It is so thickly covered with spines that it has a furry look. But cholla consists of loosely attached segments that break off with the slightest provocation, leading to claims that cholla clumps jump onto passersby. The spines dig deeply into clothing or skin, or so I've always heard. I had no problems as I admired, sketched and photographed these interesting plants.

Farther down the road leading to the Pinto Basin, I stopped abruptly when I saw my first ocotilla. This weird plant grows as a series of long, more or less upright wands that radiate out from a common base. The wands were covered with small green leaves and evenly spaced spines. Some

BIRDS AND CACTI

Birds freely hop about on cacti because their scaled feet, horn-textured beaks and feathered bodies offer no surface a cactus spine can penetrate. Several species take advantage of cactus spines by placing their nests within them. The nests are often bulky and easily visible, but they are well protected from many predators.

Few birds are as well named as the cactus wren, whose range corresponds with the distribution of various cactus species. In common with desert wood rats, which make large dens at the base of cactus clumps, cactus wrens will sometimes huddle, several together, in the interior of their nests for the sake of warmth.

terminated in clumps of tiny scarlet flowers. What seemed so out of place was the luminous brightness of the leaves, which had erupted in response to a recent, unseasonal and very local rain shower whose water had long since evaporated or drained into the porous soil. The presence of the cactus nearby was indication that this particular corner of the desert received more rain than other parts of the region I had visited. Cactus are often, though not always, desert plants, but they do require settings where there are reasonably high levels of rainfall on a seasonal basis.

I visited the Cottonwood Campground and explored a little of the Lost Palms Trail, but I didn't have time to pay a proper visit. Desert birds are generally quiet in the heat of the day, although I did briefly glimpse a sage sparrow beside the road.

All good things end, and by late afternoon I left the southern boundary of the park. The last bird I saw in the park was a magnificent red-tailed hawk, perched on a signpost near the road at the park's exit, as if standing sentry duty.

I would have stayed until after dark, but there was one more place to visit. Among North American birders few places are better known than the Salton Sea, one of California's largest lakes. It is a somewhat mysterious, land-locked body of water that formed in 1905-6 in this desert country, some two hundred feet (61 m) below sea level. It formed in unanticipated and uncontrolled response to irrigation measures in the Southwest. As an ecological experiment, it has proved to be fascinating, starting, from an ornithological perspective, with the unexpected appearance of a colony of gull-billed terns, in the 1920s.

The brackish water attracts seabirds and birders and thus not surprisingly has a long list of improbable rarities to its credit. It's frequently mentioned in reports of avifaunal rarities and, although I had no specific information on what unexpected bird might currently be there, I thought I really ought to see the place.

JOSHUA TREE

The drive there included a stretch of road through magnificent canyons I would like to visit again some day. When I arrived at the Salton Sea, it looked like a very large lake, but the birds reminded me of an ocean beach. In the fading daylight I admired both white and brown pelicans; great and snowy egrets; black-crowned night herons; pied-billed grebes; Caspian and common terns; California gulls; American coots; common moorhens; a black-bellied plover; and killdeer.

After a long day in the dry desert, I enjoyed seeing these water birds, but an unexpected treat showed up in the form of a mountain bluebird, which fluttered about at my feet. The bird's clear, blue plumage was a visual delight. As I left the Salton Sea, a roadrunner flashed by in front of the car, the last species of bird seen during one of my most memorable days afield.

HEERMANN'S GULL

THE COAST OF NORTHERN CALIFORNIA

Although I had returned to California several times in conjunction with my duties for the Animal Protection Institute, this was my mother's first visit in thirty years. Once more there was an API annual conference, this one in San Francisco. While my first visits to new places, particularly in North America, are usually hurried, this time I decided to make a week-long holiday of it.

We began with a visit to the annual meeting of the Western Field Ornithologists, at San Rafael. The lectures given at the meetings were interesting and I did fairly well on the traditional identification quiz, particularly when it came to identifying the eastern warblers that western birders seem to cherish. Pacific shorebirds left me floundering a little and I'd rather not talk about my ability to identify the species pictured in softly focused slides of Pacific seabirds.

A trip to Point Reyes was announced for the following morning. However, as so often seems to happen in coastal California, a great rarity appeared. It was a Siberian species called a dusky warbler. Now, although I frequently claim that I am no longer a lister and that I prefer to see birds in their native habitat, I wasn't about to pass up a chance to see this tiny, dull-brown native of Siberia, if for no other reason than it was the only way I could go birding in the company of some of the West's top birders.

Well before dawn the next morning there was a mad rush across the tarmac of the motel parking lot. The dusky warbler had been found in a sewage treatment area in the opposite direction from Point Reyes. It was only the second time one had been found in California.

We wound up in an odoriferous region of mudflats and settling ponds intersected by a convenient grid of road-wide dikes. There were about two hundred birders present, and the excitement was like an electric current flickering within the crowd as people peered intently into the patches of scrub where the warbler had appeared the day before. It seemed improbable that this five-and-a-half-inch-long (14 cm) bird would bother hanging around amid all this fuss and bother, but songbirds are sometimes difficult to perturb.

Orange-crowned warblers are very similar to the unrelated dusky warbler in size, shape and color and are common in the region. Sightings of orange-crowns occasionally triggered some birders to charge in the direction indicated. In time, however, everyone did see the rare visitor. The little bird calmly and with polite dignity put in an appearance, hunting for insects in a shrub at the edge of a shallow basin between two dikes. It remained in plain view, tolerated the inevitable attentions of photographers who just had to get closer than anyone else, and displayed its determinedly nondescript field marks for all to dutifully note as it flitted about the foliage.

After enjoying good views of the dusky warbler, my mother and I wandered off to explore this unscenic but bird-filled landscape. We were among the few easterners present and for us species others thought of as commonplace were quite special.

The broad mudflats hosted large numbers of shorebirds, including our first long-billed curlews. They seem almost top-heavy, so long are their downcurved beaks. Marbled godwits, buff-colored birds with slightly upturned bills, probed in muck and shallow ponds for invertebrate food in the company of greater yellowlegs, western sandpipers and various other species of shorebird. Black and Say's phoebes obligingly posed in full view, usually on rocks or the tips of

ASIAN ACCIDENTALS

The dusky warbler is one of several Asian species that appear in North America often enough to justify birders' taking the time to learn what they look like, just in case one is encountered. The West Coast and Alaska, particularly the Aleutian and Pribilof islands, are the best places to look for Asian accidentals. Asian species known to occur in North America include the common crane; garganey and other waterfowl; Mongolian plover, black-tailed godwit and other shorebirds; slaty-backed gull and white-winged tern; Steller's sea eagle and other raptors; common and Oriental cuckoos; fork-tailed swift; Eurasian skylark; Middendorf's warbler, dusky thrush and other members of the family, *Muscicapidae*; black-backed and gray wagtails; plus the brambling, little bunting and various other finches.

vegetation, from where they would occasionally dart out in pursuit of flying insects.

A peregrine falcon flew by low overhead, its bold form sending a shockwave of excited response through the shore-bird flocks. More exciting for my mother was her very first view of a black-shouldered kite, a species I have always considered to be one of the most elegant of raptors. Although generally hawk-like in form, the bird is colored like a gull in shades of light gray above, with a white head, underparts and tail. The inner wing coverts are black, forming the patches that give the species its name. (The former name of the American form was the white-tailed kite.) The eyes are large, with bright orange-red irises, set off by touches of black plumage. Once rare in California, the species has made a remarkable comeback and is now widely distributed, particularly in brushy grasslands and low foothills, throughout much of the state. Various races and closely related forms are distributed throughout much of the world.

A lark bunting, partly in non-breeding winter plumage and partly in its black breeding plumage, perched on a wire fence. The white wing markings that characterize both plumages were clearly evident. The species is the state bird of Colorado, but this migrant was just outside its normal migration route and wintering range. A trim little Sprague's pipit strutted by us on the grassy edge of one of the dikes. The bird was close, and we had ample time to examine it carefully and make sure of its identity. Our field guide map put it well outside its normal range, too.

In the afternoon we drove up into Coyote Hills Regional Park at the south end of San Francisco Bay. Although I would return to this park eight years later and explore the salt marshes of its lower reaches, on this sun-drenched afternoon we restricted ourselves to the hills. This area is surrounded by city, but once in the hills, one is in dry scrub and oak-studded grasslands, which vaguely recall the natural world in this beautiful corner of the planet before it

LBJs

Birders can sometimes be heard referring to "LBJs." An LBJ is a little brown job – any species of bird that is characterized by small size, generally drab brownish plumage and very little in terms of distinguishing features. Few are actually brown; most are either greenish or grayish in color. The Asian dusky warbler is a classic LBJ.

was so heavily burdened by human endeavor.

On this glorious September afternoon, the heat of the sun was delicately tempered by stray wisps of cooler air from the nearby Pacific Ocean. Townsend's and black-throated gray warblers flitted about in the oak trees. Brown towhees, one of California's most common species, hopped about on the ground at our feet. The species is now called the California towhee, to distinguish it as a separate species from the paler, rufous-crowned inland form, which is called the canyon towhee. Scrub jays, golden-crowned sparrows, Brewer's black-birds and other common western species kept me busy with camera and sketchpad. California ground squirrels competed with the birds for the crumbs of our picnic lunch and boldly begged for handouts.

The next morning, having seen the dusky warbler, our birding companions were more relaxed as we joined them on board the fifty-five-foot (16.7 m) *Merry Jane*, which the Western Field Ornithologists had chartered for a twenty-three-mile (37 km) trip out of Bodega Bay to the waters over Cordel Bank.

Both common and red-throated loons swam in the more sheltered waters of the bay. We sailed past the headlands with their populations of sea lions, harbor seals, pelicans and cormorants and headed out to sea. Although there was a significant swell and jokes about sea sickness, everyone seemed comfortable and in high spirits. Hot sun and cool sea breezes combined to make this a pleasant excursion. Soon we were accompanied by pods of Pacific white-sided dolphins.

In contrast to the previous morning, this was birding at its social best, with the more experienced helping the less experienced and everyone having fun. I was extremely grateful that we had some expert seabirders on board. They were able to locate Buller's, pink-footed and black-vented shearwaters, all life birds for my mother and me, as well as pormarine jaegers and Arctic terns. Flying among the shifting forms of the dark waves were small flocks of dainty

PIPITS

Pipits have the same general colors and markings as the grassland sparrows. They tend to be colored in shades of brown, buff, tan and sometimes rufous, and they are usually streaked, with light edges to their wing feathers. Unlike sparrows, they have very slender bills and they walk, rather than hop, often pumping their tails as they do so.

The red-throated pipit, the rarest native pipit, nests in extreme western Alaska, as well as in Asia. It can be seen on the Pacific coast during migration and in the winter. It has light-pinkish-colored feet and usually shows some reddish coloring about the head and throat, which is quite pronounced in breeding plumage. The back is streaked. The most widely distributed pipit in North America is the water pipit, a Holarctic species. It has dark brown or blackish feet and a plain or lightly streaked back. There is always the possibility of Asian pipits showing up, particularly in Alaska, where both the petchora pipit and the olive tree pipit have occurred.

red-necked and red phalaropes, both species colored in the gray of their winter plumages.

The boat's crew was apparently used to birders and so they paused, without being asked to do so, among a flock of Sabine's gulls, a fitting species to see at such a time as it is featured on the logo of the Western Field Ornithologists. It's a species we had seen before and once again we found ourselves enjoying its elegant, graceful form. Later a group of Dall's porpoises paced our boat with exuberant displays of rapid swimming.

The trip was a great success. As we headed back to shore, we sailed beneath some attractive cliffs where we had close views of common murres and pigeon guillemots. The pigeon guillemot of the Pacific is nearly identical to the black guillemot of the Atlantic, but its white wing patch is bisected by a black bar. Although each species remains in its respective ocean, I was pleased when we approached the guillemots closely enough to see that distinguishing black bar.

Our plan for the rest of the holiday was to drive south along the coastal highway from San Francisco to Los Angeles and visit the places my family used to live. But we never made it anywhere near that far. What was supposed to be a very brief visit to Muir Woods National Monument park, just north of San Francisco, turned into several very pleasant hours among towering redwoods. In common with millions of others before us, we were captivated by the stillness and cathedral-like atmosphere of the forest.

As is so often the case with deep forest, there were few birds. Birds are usually most evident at the forest edge, where there is a greater variety of vegetation, hence more food, roosting sites and nesting locations. Beneath the tallest, oldest trees the most easily seen birds were some Steller's jays, along with chickadees, song sparrows and bushtits.

We finally left the park and paid a visit to Bolinas Bay. This region of backwater marshes provides good habitat for

VISITING THE BAY'S MARSHES

The saltwater marshes of the southern San Francisco Bay region are a birder's delight. Pied-billed, horned and eared grebes are found there, while western grebes prefer deeper, more open water and the kelp beds of the nearby ocean. Egrets, other herons and brown and American white pelicans are among the most distinctive of the area's common birds. On the other hand, the species easiest to miss is the black rail. This is one of the very few places anywhere on the continent where one can hope to find this tiny, elusive bird, which is known to winter in the marshes. The marshes are also home to a western race of the clapper rail, now protected as an endangered species. Both short- and long-billed dowitchers occur there, along with long-billed curlews, stilts, marbled godwits, willets and other shorebirds, including huge wintering flocks of avocets. The Bay region as a whole is famous among birders as the home of extremely localized races of the song sparrow.

shorebirds. We spent enjoyable hours in the company of a variety of terns and shorebirds, including the first elegant terns I had seen in many years. Stilts, avocets, western sandpipers and other species that are rare and absent in my home birding grounds were common here. Northern pintails, ruddy ducks and other waterfowl were also present in significant numbers, while great and snowy egrets hunted in the shallow waters.

By late afternoon we were on our way along the highway south of San Francisco. Although our route took us past a magnificent shorescape that was familiar from movies, picture books and even TV commercials, nothing had prepared us for the wondrous grandeur now before us. The contrast between the massive size of the cliffs and headlands and the intricate detail of the mats of coastal chaparral and the stones and pebbles imbedded in the rock matrix gives this place its timeless appeal. The rocks have been carved by the elements into a bewilderingly diverse variety of textured forms. The most abundant bird in the dense chaparral cloaking this wonderfully convoluted environment was the grayish-brown western race of the Bewick's wren.

SAY'S PHOEBE

The life of the seashore is so much more complex than its freshwater counterpart that I found it impossible to resist frequently stopping the car, getting out and having a look. I also enjoyed the novelty of simply being able to stroll out to the ocean's edge. Among the birds we encountered was a magnolia warbler, an eastern species quite out of place in this setting of yellow willows on the edge of the Pacific Ocean, which it shared with bushtits, plain titmouses and a Say's phoebe. The brown pelicans, willets, western gulls and other commonplace birds were becoming "the usual" to us, although I was still stopping to sketch and photograph these western birds.

The juxtaposition of familiar birds, such as the magnolia warbler, with unfamiliar settings continued to be a source of pleasure. At one beach we spent a half hour in the company of an American crow. This ubiquitous species was hardly new, but the bird was beautifully feathered and quite tame as it perched in picturesque fashion on the tip of a gracefully curved driftwood log. I photographed and sketched him in the low light of late afternoon.

WRENTIT

The next day we reached the Monterey Peninsula. For $4.00 we were allowed into the enclave of the rich who live near 17-Mile Drive. This is a marked highway through the peninsula. Millionaires' estates, carefully guarded, are interspersed with patches of native woods that feature the Monterey pine, the world's fastest growing pine. It is widely planted around the world as an ornamental tree and a commercial timber species. The Monterey cypress is endemic to this one location but is also widely planted elsewhere. Cliffside cypress trees take on strange, angular shapes decreed by the wind, and these forms have become something of an icon for the region.

Handsome scrub jays, with their russet backs and blue wings, were common. We often saw the gray-colored western form of the fox sparrow, hopping about on the ground beneath shrubs and bushes. We also found wrentits, a species of uncertain taxonomic affinity. Some consider it to be the only New World representative of a huge Old World family of birds collectively known as babblers. Others place the bird in the Old World flycatcher family. It's a small, long-tailed brown bird that loves to climb about in chaparral thickets. The curious wrentit can't resist a little people-watching, though, and usually makes itself visible to the patient birder.

Along the rock-bordered beach at the tip of the peninsula, near the area's famous Pebble Beach golf course, we discovered birds and mammals in such abundance that the scene before us resembled a museum diorama that had come to life. Western, Heermann's and California gulls flocked at our feet. California ground squirrels were bold and abundant, climbing about on the rocks amid the gulls and Brewer's blackbirds. The blackbirds love to frequent areas of the West where people tend to picnic. Because they are common, they're taken for granted by many western birders. I consider them to be quite beautiful, with their finely balanced forms and the delicate shades of iridescence in the plumage of the males, and the subtle tones of gray in the females.

With my telephoto lens I took pictures of Brewer's blackbirds, marbled godwits, black turnstones, willets and sanderlings. Often the birds were too close to focus upon. I wasn't after masterful portraits, just snapshots showing details of form and behavior that could be used as reference material for future artwork. To my delight, a nearby whimbrel posed long enough for a quick sketch. In fact, Pacific whimbrels, on the whole, seem to be more tolerant of people than the ones that briefly visit the shores of Lake Ontario.

We made little forward progress, taking all of one day to cover only thirty miles (48 km). Four days into the journey, after constant stops for birding, sightseeing and souvenir buying, we reached Big Sur National Park, where I would love to return one day for an extended stay. The region possesses natural beauty in luxuriant abundance.

We parked the car and set out on foot. I left the road and went off into the woods for a couple of miles, working my way down into a heavily forested valley. Here, beneath towering redwoods that were growing during the lifetime of Christ, there was a sense of how it must have been before the arrival of Europeans. I was constantly shifting my attention from such details as a dried fern frond or a bit of lichen on a rock to the overall forest environment. Mule deer shuffled through the woods on the far side of a clear stream, where I had stopped to cool myself in the dappled filigree of moss and leaf-filtered sun and shadow. A curious Steller's jay looked down at me from an overhead limb, head cocked, observing me as I observed it.

I retraced my steps back through the gathering gloom of the forest to find the car. My mother had birded along the road during my absence and had seen more bird species than I, including beautiful lazuli buntings and western tanagers.

EASTERN WARBLERS OUT WEST

Eastern wood warblers are a major attraction for California birders. Fall, winter or spring there's always a chance of seeing a vagrant prothonotary, Tennessee, northern parula, black-and-white, black-throated blue, blackburnian, chestnut-sided, Cape May, magnolia, bay-breasted, palm, Kentucky, Canada, hooded, worm-eating or other eastern warbler.

However, I had not regretted my time deep in the redwood forest. We made it back to the motel parking lot just in time for me to do some quick sketches of some lovely little chestnut-backed chickadees in a nearby shrub. The next morning, the fifth and final day of our driving holiday, we began our return journey to San Francisco.

While we were now on a tight schedule and forcing ourselves not to dawdle, we did make one final birding stop at Point Lobos State Reserve. It was worthwhile for the charming sight of white snowy egrets delicately perched on floating rafts of kelp at low tide. The elegant birds would step carefully, balancing themselves on uncertain footing that rose and fell with the gentle roll of the surf. Occasionally there would be a quick jab, and then, usually, a small fish or crustacean would appear briefly in a beak, before being swallowed.

The highlight of the reserve was, however, not birds, but two sea otters who were floating on their backs among the kelp beds of Whaler's Cove. We watched them for a pleasant half hour, reluctant to acknowledge that our week-long holiday was already ended. It was dark, foggy and time to be back in San Francisco, where the conference was about to begin.

CALIFORNIA GROUND SQUIRREL

SACRAMENTO AND THE SIERRAS

YELLOW-BILLED MAGPIE

Sacramento, California's state capital, is located on hot, flat valleylands where the Sacramento and the American rivers join. Although well inland, the city is only a little above sea level and on a direct waterway route to San Francisco Bay. I made a quick business trip there one August, leaving Toronto behind enshrouded in a humid heat wave. It was just as hot in Sacramento, but the lack of humidity plus the cooling breezes that flowed up the broad valley from the Pacific most evenings made this a very pleasant climate.

Everywhere I went I couldn't help but see one of the city's most distinctive birds, the yellow-billed magpie. It is closely related to the black-billed magpie, which is found throughout most of the northern hemisphere, except eastern North America. The yellow-billed is found only in central California, in an area where the black-billed does not occur.

Other common urban wildlife species included Brewer's blackbirds, house finches, scrub jays, northern mockingbirds and American robins. California ground squirrels and a pale, western race of the gray squirrel were also common.

Tim Manolis, then an employee of the Animal Protection Institute, as well as a top birder and a fellow bird artist, took me to see some of the valley avifauna. As we left the city, he cautioned that this was one of the worst times of the year for birding in the area. Maybe, but since that time I've birded in the valley several more times with Tim or with Bruce Webb, and I'd argue that there is no really "bad" time there for an eastern birder.

At dawn we stood overlooking a small, backwater marsh that was still within the tidal zone. A marsh wren sang its gurgling repertoire of jumbled notes and trills from nearby reeds. We heard a blue grosbeak singing but the bird remained hidden from view. Although they were in summer eclipse plumages, some cinnamon teal drakes showed chestnut tones as they puddled about in the shallow water. Mallards were also present, dabbling amid mats of duckweed, and a Swainson's hawk soared by overhead. At one point we were a little startled to see a ruddy shelduck. The species is native to the Old World but is widely kept by bird fanciers and zoos. No doubt this was an escaped bird.

We next went to a sewage settling pond where there were flocks of American avocets and black-necked stilts. The avocets were showing both the gray heads and necks of winter plumages and the lovely tawny-buff coloring of their breeding plumages, with some birds displaying almost completely buff or completely gray heads. A large, mixed flock of western and least sandpipers waded in shallow water, probing for invertebrates. Killdeer, migrant barn swallows and California gulls were also common in this area.

One species I saw with some frequency was the loggerhead shrike. In my childhood the bird was reasonably common in the hawthorn hedgerows of the fields north of Toronto, but in the intervening years its numbers have fallen to endangered status in Ontario. Loggerheads hold their own in the south and the southwest and it's always a pleasure to be where these handsome gray, black and white birds are common.

We ended the outing with a visit to riparian habitat where Tim identified blue, California live, valley and black oaks. Oaks and cottonwoods dominated this habitat to form a pleasant, park-like setting. Black-chinned hummingbirds, Nuttall's woodpeckers, plain titmouses and bushtits, all species that would eventually become familiar to me, added themselves to my life list that memorable morning.

Overhead we saw white-throated swifts, which Tim said were a little unexpected so early in the season, when they usually are still in higher, mountain country. Black-shouldered kites perched in treetops or hovered above open areas. Busy little coveys of California quail ran about on the ground. The park also hosted belted kingfishers, northern flickers, western kingbirds, acorn woodpeckers, ash-throated flycatchers, black phoebes and various other species.

The next day I was scheduled to fly home, but Tim, perhaps sensing that my pleasure in the new birds I had seen was a little blunted by the fact that I had encountered little in the way of interesting habitat, drove me up into the foothills of the Sierras. Nostalgia can be an overwhelming emotion and it flooded me as I viewed the kind of rocky outcroppings and pine forests I recalled from childhood visits to the mountains.

Details varied, no doubt, but my childhood memories were not clear enough for it to matter. What did matter was that these foothills and mountains looked like the California I remembered. We saw digger pines, golden-colored fields and foothills cloaked in chaparral. We watched a mule deer with her fawn, a species of wildlife I could clearly recall from my childhood.

We found such delightfully western bird species as the lazuli bunting, the western wood-pewee, the western tanager, the lesser goldfinch, the lark sparrow and California towhees. Wrentits called from brush-covered hillsides, although on that trip I was frustrated by an inability to spot one. Acorn woodpeckers were abundant. The scenery changed with each twist and turn of the road, and every direction held its own distinct view in this ruggedly contoured landscape, which was so very different from the valley floor.

A few hours later I was in the air, flying over the mountains and hoping some day to return.

Several years and several visits to California later, I finally managed to return for a longer visit to the Sierras. I had flown

MULE DEER

over them that first time in August. Looking down from the airplane window, I had seen the characteristic western oak and pine forests and stands of poplars. The undergrowth and canopy cover looked sparser than what one encounters in eastern forests. I remember admiring the contrast between the glaring white patches of snow and the hot land further down the slopes. How I longed to go there.

It was again August, but many years later, when I joined my good friends Kathy Strain and Teri Barnato, Kathy's daughter, Erin, and Teri's friend, Kay Inks, for a trip into the mountains inland from Sacramento. None of my companions was a birder, but all loved animals and were prepared to be tolerant of my eccentricities. That included allowing me to take the wheel for most of the journey so that I could stop for birds, although my tendency to do so rather abruptly, or to follow a bird's flight as I drove, did make them a little nervous.

We travelled up through the region where the first digger pines occur. These handsome trees tend to grow in small, well-spaced groves. Their needles are arranged in bundles of three and their foliage is always sparse and feathery. Scrub jays, showing bright blue wings and tails, often flew in and out of the pines. Acorn woodpeckers were also frequently encountered at this altitude.

Going higher we began to see ponderosa (or yellow) pine, Douglas fir, sequoia, mountain hemlock, sugar pines, western white pines and knobcone pines. These grew amid the golds, ambers, ochers and yellows that are the predominant colors of the rock and dead pine needle ground cover of the mountain forest. Eventually we reached the high passes where posted warnings of the need for chains on tires seemed out of place in this clear, warm weather. But in the highest reaches of the uppermost slopes there were still patches of snow, just as I had seen from my airplane window years earlier.

Lake Tahoe sparkled in the distance, and Teri spoke in glowing terms of its beauty. But we headed more or less

ACORN WOODPECKERS

Acorn woodpeckers hammer holes into tree trunks, then wedge acorns into the holes, where they are stored for winter use. In the cold months, the bird will break the outer layer of the wedged acorn with its beak to obtain the soft food inside. Some trees (or even wooden telephone poles) may become quite riddled with these holes, a sight characteristic of any area where the acorn woodpecker is common. The same holes may be used over and over again, year after year. This habit is even practiced by acorn woodpeckers in Central America, where there is no winter shortage of insects. While it procures insect larvae buried in the bark by drilling in a manner typical of woodpeckers, this active species is also skilled in the somewhat un-woodpecker-like behavior of catching insects on the wing.

south, toward a place called Twin Lakes, near Bridgeport, in Mono County, where the Barnato family owned property. We stopped once so I could go back along the road to admire a Clark's nutcracker. In dense willows beside a broad mountain stream, some song sparrows led me on a bit of a chase until one finally had the courtesy to pop into view and reveal its identity. A busy family grouping of Wilson's warblers were more cooperative, allowing me to admire their yellow and olive plumage. The fledglings were just about old enough to be on their own, but couldn't resist begging food from passing parents. Continuing on, we began to see our first black-billed magpies.

Bridgeport sounds as though it ought to be the name of a coastal city, but this tiny town stands in a flat valley primarily given over to cattle ranching. We passed through the town and drove up the valley into higher country where two small lakes lured tourists such as ourselves. The Barnato property overlooked Upper Twin Lake and the mountains on the other side.

The property itself, reached by an inconspicuous driveway angling up off the main road, had once included a cottage. An avalanche had destroyed the building a few winters earlier. As we parked the car and I was opening the door, a brownish bird with a tomato-red cap flew up beside me. It was a green-tailed towhee. He posed briefly and then flitted upslope to vanish in the silvery sagebrush.

The sage itself was important to me, defining an area I had very much wanted to see. In fact, so beautiful was this place and so interesting its rich assortment of geological and botanical forms, that I fell into something resembling a daze as I wandered off into the brush and tumbled boulders above the picnic site.

By making "pishing" noises I was able to call a rock wren from cover. Sparrows sometimes flew across the top of the sage, but vanished before I could make an identification. Lizards seemed equally elusive, at first, but I've found that the

SQUEAKING AND PISHING

In addition to recordings that trigger responses, birders use other aids to bring birds into view. Some make their own "generic" squeaking noises, either vocally or by rubbing their hands together in a fashion I've never mastered. Blowing on a grass stem can also make the requisite noise. Others are skilled at doing vocal imitations of birds. "Pishing" is the fine art of making a hissing "*pisssshhh*" sound that seems to sound enough like a distress call to attract birds from vegetation.

GREEN-TAILED TOWHEE

trick to lizard watching is to simply exercise patience. Sure enough, some eventually appeared in the open and paused long enough for me to identify them as sagebrush lizards. More than twenty years earlier I had been commissioned to paint pictures of four species of the lizard genus, *Sceloporus*. I had worked from pickled specimens, captive animals and photographs. Now, finally, I was seeing the genus in the field, this species being *Sceloporus graciosus*.

Our picnic site became the center of attraction for a few golden-mantled ground squirrels. These large chipmunks are possibly the prettiest of America's squirrel species and a species I had always longed to see. The only other ones I had ever encountered were laboratory animals in deep hibernation in a university's cold room.

After lunch we traveled the short distance up to the head of the lake. We crossed a stream and followed a switchback trail up the slope of the mountainside a short distance to a magnificent waterfall. On the way there I was always well behind the others, pausing to touch or photograph this or that plant. I saw chipmunks I couldn't identify, there apparently being several species in the region. Chickarees, which are the western equivalent of the eastern red squirrel, chattered from the branches overhead.

At one point I spent several minutes peering through my binoculars at an immature sapsucker. In this plumage the three species found in California are similar. That's not a problem in the east where only one species, the yellow-bellied, occurs. I was, in fact, looking at my first red-breasted sapsucker. Although it was in immature plumage, there was enough red to make its identification quite certain. At one time the red-breasted was considered to be a race of the yellow-bellied but it is now given status as a full species. The third sapsucker species, the Williamson's, also occurs in the Sierras.

Western wood-pewees, mountain chickadees, red-breasted and white-breasted nuthatches, brown creepers and

Steller's jays were some of the species we saw in the forest. In relative terms the pewees were far more abundant than their eastern counterparts. In the willows and bog-like tussocks that bordered a stream flowing into the lake's upper end, we found song sparrows, house wrens and yellow warblers. A mother common merganser swam up the creek with two of her brood on her back, the third in the water beside her. The ducklings were a little larger than starlings, and two were all that would fit on the mother bird's back. Brewer's blackbirds splashed in the shallows of the lake. There were mallards farther out and a pair of belted kingfishers flew out over the water, rattling noisily.

There is a lovely campground at the head of the lake, with inviting cottages for rent. We paused to watch a tame mule deer as it came to a trailer to be fed. The woman doing the feeding saw the look of pleasure on young Erin's face and gave her some food for the deer. Tree swallows twittered on overhead wires, their backs glittering like shattered emeralds in the pine-filtered sunlight.

We spent the night in Bridgeport. The others assured me that they were early risers, but their version of early rising was different from that of a birder's. And so I was alone when I began walking up the road toward the edge of town. As the sky turned light in the east, I could see flat, green pastures stretched out on either side of me.

This open country had its own appeal and its own accompaniment of birds. California gulls flew by overhead. Blackbirds flocked about me. Most were Brewer's blackbirds, but there were also large numbers of yellow-headed blackbirds. Among the most beautiful of our native songbirds, they range across the West, normally appearing no further east than the border region between Michigan and Ontario. Because it was August, the birds were in molt, with many juvenile males showing varying degrees of yellow on their heads. Some of the adult males, however, were still fully feathered in their bold black and yellow coloring, with white wing patches.

YELLOW WARBLERS

The yellow warbler nests throughout most of the continent, below the tree line, although it is absent as a breeding species in much of Texas and the extreme southeastern United States. Nevertheless, it is common in those areas, spring and fall, as a migrant. The bird often nests in willows. It makes a bulky nest, sometimes with enough white plant down woven into the structure to make it among the easiest of all warbler nests to find. If a cowbird lays its egg among the eggs of the yellow warbler, the warbler builds another layer over top of the cowbird egg. If it happens again, another layer is added. Some yellow warbler nests have been found that were many layers deep.

RED-BREASTED SAPSUCKER

Western meadowlarks, whose range tends to coincide with that of the yellow-headed blackbird, were also common and in song. The species is very similar in appearance to the eastern meadowlark, but the song is a distinctive series of clear, bubbling notes, hurried at the end and entirely unlike the sweet, double-noted song of the eastern meadowlark, the first note rising upward, the second slurring downward. As is the case of three other common California birds – the wrentit, the northern mockingbird and the California quail – the song of the western meadowlark tends to find its way onto the soundtracks of movies and television shows featuring out-of-doors scenes.

After a bit of souvenir shopping and some more hiking with my companions later that day, it was time to start back to Sacramento. As we drove down onto the flats approaching Bridgeport, I finally saw a bird fly across the road that I had been hoping to see. I pulled over, jumped out and enjoyed close looks at several sage thrashers as they perched in typical fashion on the tips of sagebrush clumps. Placed in its own genus, *Oreoscoptes*, with our other North American thrashers in the genus *Toxostoma*, the sage is an atypical bearer of the name "thrasher." It has the shortest relative tail length of any thrasher and the shortest, straightest beak. Heavily streaked below, like the brown and long-billed thrashers, it differs from them in being brownish gray above.

Although that was one of the most pleasing birds for me to see, the ornithological rarity of our three-day excursion was, oddly enough, a yellow-billed magpie, seen below Twin Lakes, within sight of Bridgeport. The species is not supposed to occur at all on the eastern slope of the Sierras, but here was one, in association with black-billed magpies.

On the way back to Sacramento, I drove – which meant that I got to pick the place to stop for a late meal. I chose well, I think. Although we had to pay a fee just to use a roadside picnic site, it was worth it for the pleasure of the company of the California gulls, Steller's jays, California ground squirrels and black-billed magpies who came to share our lunch.

The next weekend I was a guest of Tim and Annette
Manolis, in Sacramento. Tim and I went in search of some
of the life birds I might reasonably hope to see in the area.
We drove up past Folsom Lake, which is formed by a dam
across the American River. Its sandy beaches are a popular
playground.

We continued up into the hills behind the lake, onto a
high area known as the Folsom Peninsula. The attraction here
was chamise chaparral, which grows on the upper reaches of
the peninsula, where there is a spectacular view of the lake.
We could see all the way across the golden grasslands, their
undulating expanse dotted with dark clumps of oaks, to
the gray smudge in the distance that was all that was visible
of Sacramento.

Chaparral always intrigues me, with its dense, intricate
networks of branches and twigs and small, generally leathery
and often strongly aromatic leaves. Among the chaparral there
were a few stands of digger pines, whose wispy needles provided almost no shade on this hot, dry upland. Typically,
the individual plants that constituted the chaparral were
spaced fairly evenly so that with a little care one could walk
a fair distance into the habitat before inevitably finding the
way blocked.

Manzanita (*Arctostaphylos*) was one of the most common
species of chaparral – and one of the most distinctive. It has
twisting, dark red branches with thin, smooth bark that peels
off in an odd scaly pattern. It seemed, in places, to push out
the chamise, a heather-like plant of the genus *Adenostoma*.
A third common species was toyon (*Photinia*), which is in the
rose family. Its dark red berries remain on the plant through
the winter, giving the species its alternative name of
Christmas berry.

We were too late for the nesting season and the birds
were generally quiet, apart from the ubiquitous wrentits,
heard many more times than they were seen. However,

occasionally one of the little birds would obligingly make a brief appearance before ducking back out of sight in the thick foliage. Tim assured me that this was a good place for winter birding, with large flocks of hermit thrushes and other migrants sometimes attracted to the berries growing on some of the vegetation.

Bewick's wrens were common, though, and scrub jays flew among the pines that grew amid the chamise chaparral. We found some rufous-sided towhees, members of the spotted race, which used to be considered a distinct species. Not only does the "spotted" towhee look quite different from the eastern form, with its white wing bars and white spots on its back, but it is also a little bolder in its habits.

Driving back through lower levels of these foothills, we entered grassland and oak tree habitat. The hills to the side of the road were dominated by the bright red foliage of poison oak. We found California towhees, cliff swallows and a family of acorn woodpeckers, the young just out of the nest.

We stopped to admire some lesser goldfinches. These small, yellow-breasted birds often associate with the star thistle, an accidentally introduced species that is originally native to the Mediterranean. The prickly plant grows abundantly, pushing out native species and ruining livestock fodder. But the lesser goldfinches are attracted to the low-growing weed, the yellow of their own plumage matching the blooms of the thistle. When a small flock of goldfinches flew up from the weeds, it looked as though half the blossoms of a star thistle patch had suddenly taken to the air. It was the seeds, not the camouflage value of the plant, that attracted the birds, but I couldn't help but think the plants were of serendipitous value to the tiny birds.

There was no time to sketch vegetation, but I did photograph the star thistle and some of the native flora, particularly the California buckeye, a tree that is endemic to California. The tree has spectacular spring blooms, which form in panicles some five to ten inches (13 to 25 cm) long,

GOLDFINCHES

Goldfinches are not gold. The name was originally applied to a pretty Eurasian species of finch that has yellow bands on its wings, but is otherwise colored in brown, black and white, with a red face. The name has been given to other, closely related Old World species. In North America there are three native species of goldfinch – the American, the lesser and the Lawrence's. In southern California and central and southern Arizona, where their ranges overlap in winter, the three species may be seen in the same locality.

made up of white to rose-pink blossoms. The trees were in fruit and in the process of dropping their leaves, which, in these arid foothills, fall rather suddenly in mid-summer.

In the late afternoon we were back on the floor of the central valley. Tim took me to a small cattail marsh across the road from a subdivision. The marsh had hosted a nesting colony of tricolored redwings up until about a fortnight before my arrival. There were plenty of red-winged blackbirds about, and we checked the closer ones. Apart from the adult male tricolored in breeding plumage, which has white middle wing coverts in contrast to the buff coloring of the corresponding feathers in the red-winged blackbird, separating the two species can be very difficult. Tricolored females, young and non-breeding males resemble the red-wing, but have slightly different bill shapes. In their markings overall, immature and females are slightly darker than red-wings. Unfortunately, no tricoloreds were to be seen. Wire fences bordering the marsh and fields provided perch space for red-wings, western kingbirds, brown-headed cowbirds and Brewer's blackbirds.

We visited a nearly dry riverbed. Its standing patches of brown water had attracted black-necked stilts, American avocets, dowitchers, yellowlegs, killdeer and other shorebirds. Western meadowlarks were extremely abundant in this area, constantly flying across in front of us, some in such heavy molt that it seemed as though they had to beat their ragged wings with extra vigor to remain in flight.

Tim turned down a road that bisected flooded rice fields. Muddy irrigation ditches hosted great and snowy egrets; black-crowned night, great blue and green-backed herons; mallards; moorhens; and pied-billed grebes. The habitat attracted white-faced ibises, whose down-curved beaks give them the appearance of large, dark curlews. The ibises are chestnut-maroon, with bronze highlights and iridescent green and purple tones to their plumage that are visible under appropriate lighting conditions.

A sandy area, just inside a roadside fence, had a small

BURROWING OWLS

Nineteenth-century naturalists found some large colonies of burrowing owls on the plains. The owls used burrows originally dug by prairie dogs. Burrowing owls and prairie dogs would also be found living in the same colonies. As both species sometimes sought refuge in the same hole in times of danger, some people incorrectly believed the two species shared the same sites to raise their young.

In the absence of prairie dogs, the burrowing owl can use holes originally dug by such species as ground squirrels, badgers, woodchucks, skunks, foxes, wolves, tortoises and armadillos. There is a race of the species found in Florida, which usually digs its own burrow. The Miami airport is a sanctuary for the burrowing owls that live there – they can sometimes be seen out the windows of airplanes during landings and take-offs. Indeed, that was how I first made the acquaintance of this charming owl.

ANNA'S HUMMINGBIRD

bank with a hole in its base. Sitting on a nearby fence post was a burrowing owl. With binoculars we could just make out the face of another owl peering out from the darkness of the nesting hole.

Although it was my first view of the western race of the burrowing owl in the wild, I realized with some chagrin that I had spent a good part of the day in Tim's company in California and not seen a single life bird. However, then I remembered how, when I was a youngster, James L. Baillie, a consummate lister of local birds, told me he envied me the freshness of each new sighting. I hadn't seen any life birds that day, but there would be other opportunities and so much still to anticipate.

WILLOW PTARMIGAN

V
Prairie and Polar Birding

THE INTERIOR PRAIRIES

DOUBLE-CRESTED CORMORANT

It's fitting that I saw my first wild cinnamon teal on the same cold, clear fall morning that I saw my first wild prairie dogs. Both species are associated with the prairies. But it wasn't my first look at the prairies. That came in very early childhood, during a long drive across America, much of it on the old Route 66, to a new home near Los Angeles, and, nearly four years later, the long drive back east. Apart from coyotes and turkey vultures, there are few wildlife species I recall from those very early childhood journeys – I have few memories of any kind beyond a sort of general recollection of broad, open spaces and the narrow, cloth-scented confines of the back seat of the car.

In my early twenties, my mother and I made our cross-country journey by train. Most of the route was not as flat as popular conception would have it, but contoured, at times passing steep-sided river valleys. It was endlessly beautiful, clean and pure, the sky a burning blue and the snow a sharp white in a world where slush, dirt and pollution seemed to be alien concepts. There were patches of scrubby bushes and stiff cattails and reeds to mark the sloughs frozen beneath the snow.

However much I find myself drawn to the vibrant life of the tropics, ever since that winter journey the prairies have represented to me the essence of travel into other environments: my first new ecosystem to visit. They are the western edge of my home environment in the way that the Atlantic Ocean is its eastern edge. One spring or early summer day

THERMALS AND VULTURES

When the sun warms the ground, the air above that patch of ground expands, becoming less dense than the surrounding cooler air. This heated air starts to rise. It does not necessarily rise straight up, but may be moved by the wind on a horizontal axis at the same time it is rising vertically.

This rising air mass is called a thermal. Vultures and other birds take advantage of rising thermals to stay airborne. If the thermal can be visualized as a huge bubble, the soaring birds circle the circumference of the bubble. They fall as the air rises, but if the air bubble rises at the same speed as they fall, the birds will remain at the same altitude until they reach the bottom of the bubble, at which time they will glide to the next thermal. Glider pilots have learned to look for circling vultures as indicators of rising air thermals.

I hope to drive west from where I live and slowly fill my memory with prairie images, but, to date, I feel I've only touched the edges of the great central plains, learning a little here and seeing a bit there.

In a sense, there's not much left to touch. Most of the prairie ecosystem has been thoroughly degraded by the removal of its keystone species, the bison, and by the usurpation of agriculture, with most of the damage coming from the beef industry. In the interest of an earlier generation of beef producers, the bison is gone, as is much of the culture of the people of the First Nations who depended upon it to provide them with food, clothing and shelter. Gone, too, are scenes of grasses spreading from one horizon to another, like an undulating wind-ruffled sea where herds of bison passed like great, dark cloud shadows.

No ecosystem on the continent has a greater proportion of vulnerable, threatened, endangered or extinct species of wildlife relative to its size and human population than does the prairie ecosystem. Greater prairie-chickens, mountain and piping plovers, Baird's sparrow, burrowing owls, ferruginous hawks and loggerhead shrikes are bird species from the northern prairies that have experienced declines – or even extirpation. The Eskimo curlew once migrated over the prairies in vast flocks, but now it is nearly extinct. The whooping crane is a prairie migrant that has become an icon for endangered species on this continent. The black-footed ferret, slender hunter of prairie dogs, may be our rarest mammal. The swift fox, black-tailed prairie dog and the plains pocket gopher are in decline, or gone. And the prairie race of the gray wolf is extinct.

There is no hard edge of demarcation where the prairies begin. We can, even as far east as my home, see tiny remnants and accidentally created patches of prairie habitat, as defined by carefully cherished stands of plant species, now too often listed as rare or endangered. The animals that can adapt to the loss of the bison and the intrusion of agriculture are still found on the western plains, along with multitudes of new species of grassland flora. The landform endures but it is ever less supportive of species that are native to the region.

Most of the bird species that are predominantly native to the prairies I've managed to see, either during brief visits or in places outside the actual prairie interior of the continent. However, the mountain plover (a prairie bird, its name notwithstanding) has eluded me the times I've been where it might be. The chestnut-collared longspur, which favors tallgrass prairie, and the McCown's longspur, which prefers shortgrass prairie, both occur where I have never been at a time when I might see them. The Baird's sparrow, a species that, like McCown's longspur, is in decline, is another prairie specialty I long to see.

The prairies are divided by ecologists into the shortgrass prairie, the tallgrass prairie and the aspen parkland transition zone, with its light cover of delicately beautiful aspen trees. Key to understanding prairies, veldts, savannahs, steppes, plains and other grasslands is knowledge of certain characteristics of prairie grasses. These are plants that have evolved to be cropped by grazing animals and fires.

In a sense each lawn in suburbia is a miniature prairie, with the lawn mower taking the place of teeth or flames, removing the tops of the lawn plants. The grass plants continue to grow, green and healthy, in spite of constantly being cut back – indeed, precisely because they are frequently cropped. Left uncut, the grass and other plants grow tall and turn dry and brown as they go to flower and seed.

In a more natural grassland situation, grazing animals cut the grass down, possibly as low as ground level, and move on, leaving the plants to grow back, nourished by excrement and carrion the herds leave behind. Occasionally lightning will ignite the older, drier grass and start a fire that will snake across the landscape until it burns itself out. Ash-covered ground is left behind, which soon turns a misty green with regrowth from the roots left untouched by the fire.

MOUNTAIN PLOVERS

The mountain plover is a shorebird that usually avoids the shore. Its name notwithstanding, it is not a bird of the mountains, either, but rather, one that breeds in short-grass prairies and prefers dry fields and desert as its wintering grounds. The male is known to incubate the first-laid clutch of eggs, while the female goes on to lay a second clutch, which she broods herself. Following nesting, beginning as early as mid-June, flocks start to form and range the southern midwest and southwest, where they may be found in dry agricultural communities and hot, semi-desert country. Like gulls, mountain plovers may follow the plow in search of grubs turned up with the soil.

Intentional fire setting is one of the oldest hunting techniques employed by humans and one that appears in early cultures throughout the world. Grass fires drive (or kill) game as the flames burn back older grass to make room for tender, new grass that is more supportive of both wild and domesticated grazing animals. Some bird species have learned to take advantage of grass fires as sources of food in the form of fleeing insects, snakes, mice and other small animals, or partly cooked carrion.

A major ecological component to the prairies, and one of special interest to birders, is the prairie slough. These shallow, water-filled depressions nourish luxurious growths of vegetation — emergent reeds, rushes and cattails and fringing screens of willows, alders and other shrubs and trees. The open water hosts a variety of waterfowl and other wetland avifauna. Riparian floodplain habitats also snake across the plains, marked by maples, cottonwoods and other trees and often badly degraded by human encroachment.

The number of prairie marshes has been greatly reduced as water tables are lowered or contaminated to service agricultural needs. As a result, many prairie duck species are in serious decline. While hunters blame wetland depletion for the decline of prairie waterfowl, in fact, there are wetlands in which the birds are absent. Some species, such as the gadwall, show a resilience in their nesting site preferences that suggests that they would fill much more wetland breeding habitat if so many of them were not annually removed from the population by hunters. There are few or no "surplus" prairie ducks to be "harvested" within this shrinking habitat.

Apart from a few species they may wish to see, birders seeking to add prairie species to their lists are unlikely to be negatively affected by either situation now or in the near future. To a birder, the sloughs of the prairie usually continue to be oases where interesting species are to be encountered.

Western, red-necked, horned, eared and pied-billed grebes all may be found nesting in prairie sloughs and lakes.

NORTHERN PINTAIL

The latter two species range farther south, as well, and favor smaller bodies of water. Grebes' nests are mounds of vegetation that tend to float while lightly anchored to emergent vegetation. This arrangement accommodates rising and falling water levels.

The spectacular American white pelican nests in large colonies in prairie lakes and those of adjoining boreal forests, often to the surprise of non-birders who associate pelicans with more tropical, seaside habitats. The central prairie states and provinces also host a significant proportion of the world's population of another species of oceanic affinity: the double-crested cormorant. Pelicans and cormorants both require adequate amounts of water to support their piscivorous appetites, but the pelicans are less dependent on the larger lakes and rivers for nest sites as they may fly a hundred miles or so from their breeding colonies to their feeding grounds. The cormorant does not travel as far between nest and feeding grounds.

American bitterns, great blue herons and, in the south-central prairie region, the white-faced ibis may all nest in larger prairie sloughs, marshes and lakes. Sandhill cranes also breed in some prairie wetlands.

The prairies, particularly to the north, are sometimes called "duck factories" by hunters. The ponds, marshes, sloughs, lakes and rivers host breeding Canada geese; mallards; gadwalls; green-winged, blue-winged and cinnamon teal; American wigeon; northern pintails; northern shovelers; ruddy ducks; canvasbacks; redheads; lesser scaup; buffleheads; common goldeneyes; common mergansers; and other species.

Virginia, sora and the elusive yellow rails can be found nesting in some prairie wetlands, where the superficially duck-like American coot reaches its largest breeding concentrations. The sight of nesting American avocets almost defines the central and southern prairie wetland. Piping and mountain plover, killdeer, marbled godwit, the western race of the willet, greater and lesser yellowlegs, solitary and spotted sandpipers, Wilson's phalarope and common snipe are found

AMERICAN AVOCETS

The American avocet is a singularly elegant bird. The beak is very slender and distinctly upcurved near the tip. This bill shape is the only easily observed external part of the bird that allows birders to identify the sex of the individual. In females the bill tends to be relatively short and more abruptly upcurved. Males have, on average, longer, less acutely upturned beaks.

SANDHILL CRANE

nesting in prairie wetland habitats or adjoining woodland bogs. The breeding range of the Franklin's gull is almost completely within the prairie marsh ecosystem, as is that of the long-billed curlew, which often prefers drier, upland habitat. So does the upland sandpiper, whose breeding range extends to field habitat far east of the prairies.

Migrant shorebird species, such as western and semi-palmated sandpipers, may swirl above prairie sloughs or probe their muddy edges during migrations between arctic nesting grounds and southern wintering quarters. Migrating short-billed dowitchers probe mudflats or briefly and jauntily swim in the shallows of the sloughs. Noisy flocks of greater white-fronted and snow geese also visit prairie sloughs on migration.

Bonaparte's gulls tend to nest in more wooded areas adjoining the northern limits of the prairies. Its name notwithstanding, apart from wintering along the west coast, the California gull's wide distribution incorporates much of the high plains country. The Forster's and the black tern both nest in prairie sloughs, while the common tern may breed on prairie lake sandbars, particularly in the north.

Each slough has its own characteristics, with its own blend and proportions of bird and other wildlife species, but among the more reliable inhabitants are the spectacularly colorful yellow-headed blackbirds and their more widely distributed relatives, the red-winged blackbirds. Both species have distinctive, if not musical, songs that are as much a part of the marsh as the sparkling glint of sunlight on rippling water.

The enthusiastic, bubbling song of the marsh wren is another audible feature of many prairie wetlands. The small bird may become so enthused in its performance as to virtually ignore the visiting birder paddling in a canoe or patiently wading in the shallows. Usually more elusive, the pretty little common yellowthroat adds its own distinctive song to the prairie slough medley.

The LeConte's sparrow, one of the most prettily patterned of our small, native sparrows, likes the wet edges of

GIZZARDS

Birds lack teeth. Thus, while they may render food into small pieces, they do not chew it. The stomach includes a large, muscular organ called the gizzard. Coarse-textured elements of the bird's diet lodge there to help grind up the partly digested food before it enters the intestines. A few species that specialize in easily digested, liquid or soft foods, such as nectar, have virtually no gizzard. Insectivorous birds have weak gizzards where the tough, chitinous material of insects' exoskeletons help digest their food. Birds that eat seeds will swallow gravel to assist in digestion. This habit causes millions of waterfowl to be poisoned each year when they mistakenly swallow spent lead shot picked up from the bottoms of ponds where there has been extensive waterfowl hunting. Hawks and owls swallow the indigestible parts of their prey, such as fur, feathers, scales and bones, to assist in digestion. Grebes, which are almost exclusively fish eaters, swallow fish whole, and also swallow their own feathers.

sloughs and adjoining bogs at the northern end of the prairie ecosystem, where its short, buzzing song is easily overlooked by anyone other than experienced birders.

The prairie uplands are part of an ecological continuum that ultimately includes the wetlands, but that provides distinctive environments harboring different species. If one bird characterizes the uplands for me, it is the western meadowlark. Its range extends east to Ontario, and each year I hear one or two near my home. Where I live, though, their numbers are overwhelmed by the eastern meadowlark.

The two meadowlark species are very similar in appearance, but their voices are markedly different. Hearing western meadowlarks in the west is different from in the east because their voices are much more frequent, filling the clear, prairie air with glorious songs that overlap each other and come from many directions.

A list of songbirds characteristic of most of the prairies and plains might include the eastern and the western kingbirds; Say's phoebe; several species of swallow; black-billed magpie; American crow; house and rock wrens; mountain bluebird; sage and brown thrashers; Sprague's pipit; grasshopper, sharp-tailed, vesper, Savannah, song, lark, Brewer's and clay-colored sparrows; dickcissel; and lark bunting.

If one moves into adjoining alder and willow thickets, aspen woodlands or spruce and sphagnum bogs to the north, or sage brush and chaparral to the south, the variety of bird species increases accordingly. Rivers, and now highways and rail lines, support corridors of non-prairie vegetation, facilitating movements of still more species. Some birds, like the distinctive western race of the yellow-billed cuckoo, are dependent upon riparian woodland habitat in the West. The decline in such habitat has had serious repercussions for some of these species.

Although the most terrestrial of our woodpeckers, with a taste for ants in ant hills on the ground, flickers also need trees, and the number of trees limits the range of the species

PELLETS, LARGE AND SMALL

All species that swallow roughage occasionally cast it back up, sometimes in the form of pellets. These range in size from the discreet little clusters of gravel that a songbird may regurgitate to the large, oblong pellets of fur and bones that birders look for as indications that owls are roosting nearby.

on the prairies. It's been suggested that the increase in trees associated with roads, rail lines, town and city parks and farmland windbreaks has greatly increased the prairies' ability to sustain flickers from both the western race and the eastern, with subsequent increases of hybrid birds.

Western films often have someone refer laconically to circling "buzzards." Cowboys aren't noted for ornithological acumen, and the birds they refer to are usually turkey vultures. These are widely distributed throughout the contiguous forty-eight states, including the prairies. There, however, in the vast bowl of an empty sky, they are particularly noticeable as they soar on long, outstretched wings held in a shallow "V," circling in broad spirals on rising thermals. Their bare heads sometimes impart an almost "headless" look. Their naked red heads and medium-long tails are responsible for their name, "turkey" vulture, although apart from such features, there is almost nothing about them that suggests a turkey.

Raptors more characteristic of the prairie states and provinces include the golden eagle; northern harrier; the light-toned "Krider's" race of the red-tailed hawk; the abundant Swainson's hawk; the ferruginous hawk; the American kestrel; the pale "Richardson's" race of the merlin; and the prairie falcon. In winter, as most birds of the prairies migrate south, the list changes to include such species as the rough-legged hawk and snowy owl.

Although several owl species can be found in suitable habitat within the prairie ecosystem, particularly in the aspen-dominated foothills and riparian woodlands, the burrowing owl, which sometimes nests in prairie dog burrows, is a prairie specialty. The much more widely distributed short-eared owl is also at home on the open grasslands. Both species may be active in daylight.

The ranges of both the greater and the lesser prairie-chickens have been so reduced that these grassland species can only be found in a few, usually protected, predominantly grassland prairie environments. The greater prairie-chicken is

SWAINSON'S HAWKS

The Swainson's hawk undergoes one of the longest migrations of any Buteo, all the way to the pampas country of Argentina – an ecosystem replicating the hawk's high plains nesting grounds. The migrating birds, fattened on grasshoppers, don't appear to eat until they reach South America, where their propensity for catching grasshoppers has earned them the colloquial name, locust hawk. A small population of mostly juvenile birds winters in Florida, and there are other records of birds wintering in southern Texas. Although the Swainson's can soar in the best of Buteo fashion – teetering slightly on up-tipped wings, a little like a vulture – it often hunts from stationary perches, often close to the ground. It even hunts on the ground, running after crickets and grasshoppers in a rather unhawk-like, and somewhat undignified, manner.

a tallgrass prairie species that also moves into forest openings, while the lesser prairie-chicken favors shortgrass prairie and is more specialized in its requirements. These birds, whose mating displays are so dramatically incorporated into some of the traditional dance rituals of the Plains Indians, were once extremely abundant.

The more northern and much more widely distributed sharp-tailed grouse survives in both agricultural land and in open settings in northern forests, far from what is usually considered to be traditional prairie habitat. It has been known to hybridize with the dissimilar greater prairie chicken in the east, and even the much more dissimilar blue grouse in the west. The sage grouse, which is nearly equal to the wild turkey in size, does live up to its name and is still fairly widely distributed in sage-covered foothills and high plains. Wild turkeys occur in some adjacent oak and other woodland habitat within some prairie states. Three introduced species of game-bird, the ring-necked pheasant, the chukar and the gray partridge, also live in prairie habitat.

The prairies are the heartland of the continent. They are not merely flat spaces that provide agricultural products, but a vibrant range of intermeshing ecosystems that support an immense diversity of plants and animals. We have treated them harshly, destroyed much of what they had to offer and imposed new floras and faunas of alien species. But the prairies still have virtually every species of bird that was there when herds of bison extended to the horizon, although some of those species are now critically endangered.

No one can predict what the future holds, but with more conservation initiatives to protect the prairies and support prairie species underway now than at any time in history, we can dare to hope that the birds and other wildlife of the region will take their rightful places beneath clear western skies for generations to come.

CALIFORNIA GULL

THE FAR NORTH

HORNED LARK

When you're a Canadian naturalist you're expected to be
so . . . well . . . Canadian. I love my country and all that, and
I've seen it from sea to shining sea, but I have not yet seen
the third shining sea – the northern one. Most of the keenest
birders I know who share my nationality have at least visited
Churchill, Manitoba, where the tree line dips south, paralleling the Hudson Bay coast. Southerners can take the train to
Churchill and visit true tundra, complete with polar bears,
ptarmigan, nesting shorebirds and hoards of mosquitoes that
show up as clouds on slides projected on screens for the
benefit of people like myself. Birding is one of Churchill's
prime tourist attractions.

On the other hand, when I once complained to an
American friend of my limited experience in the north, he was
incredulous. "But," he sputtered, "you *live* in the north!" He
went on to define the north in terms of moose pasture, northern pike and loons. Yes, I can relate to that, as the "north" of
my friend's definition has never been far from where I've lived
most of my life. It is a place I've visited often. It is the north of
childhood summer memories, of days that glitter in my mind
like the sun on the water of the small, clear lakes I could see as
I picked blueberries and hoped, while secretly wishing otherwise, that I would not run into a black bear.

That north services a spiritual need for clean and basic
things – a frozen lake at night when the frost splits trees with
bangs like rifle shots and the stars are glowing dust scattered

across the cosmos above the shifting curtains of northern lights. I have found peace walking out onto the ice on still, bitterly cold winter nights. At such moments I've had a feeling almost of being under water, at the bottom of the sea of air that fades out not too far overhead, into the empty realm of the stars. It is then that the sound, sight, smell, taste and feel of human endeavor are absent and I fully realize that I am standing on a planet hung in space where there are other planets, other solar systems and other galaxies.

Spruce bogs and sphagnum moss; Labrador tea and the sweet call of a white-throated sparrow; a canoe easing past the ancient rocks of the Precambrian shield on a frost-rimmed morning when the mist floats low over silver water. That part of the north I have encountered, often to the scent of mosquito lotion blended with sweat as I've hiked through the still, hot summer forest or plunged into dense bogs or eaten a lunch while sitting on lichen-encrusted rock outcroppings, a raven calling in the distance.

A vast band of boreal forest extends around the world and is called the taiga, although when you are actually there it is likely to be called either the "woods" or the "bush." I have traveled by car or train great distances along narrow routes through what seemed to be endless, black-spruce-dominated forest laced by lakes and rivers. At some point, though, the road or track simply ends, and no similar road or track is to be encountered again until you reach the other side of the world.

Water then becomes the main means of transportation, either as a route for a canoe or other vessel, or as a surface that an airplane can use for takeoffs and landings. Cross-country transportation, either on foot (with the assistance in winter of skis or snowshoes) or on snowmobiles or all-terrain vehicles, is another option.

For all that a stream or a forest trail lures one on to see what comes next, there is a sameness to the intricate complexities of the northern woods, with species variety tending to decrease as northward progress increases. This great expanse of

HOLARCTIC, NEARCTIC AND PALEARCTIC

The term *Holarctic* is used to describe animals and plants that are found around the northern hemisphere. The term *Nearctic* is used for those species found only in the northern half of the western hemisphere, while *Palearctic* refers to those species exclusive to the northern half of the eastern hemisphere. Thus, the grouse family is a Holarctic bird family, and the willow ptarmigan, the same species as the "red grouse" of Scotland, is a Holarctic species. The black grouse, found only in Eurasia, is a Palearctic species, while the spruce grouse, found only in North America, is a Nearctic species.

relatively similar mixtures of terrain, fauna and flora is in sharp contrast to many parts of the tropics, where an hour's drive, or less, or even a short hike over a ridge or into a valley can plunge one into a markedly different and specialized ecosystem.

The life-limiting force of winter, more than any other single ecological factor, defines the birds of the north in terms of what they are and what they do. One of the things most of them must do is migrate. Thus the birder who, like me, is usually stationed near the southern edge of wherever we might think the north begins has the opportunity to encounter regularly many of the birds of the far north.

In 1957 the University of Toronto Press published Lester Snyder's book, *Arctic Birds of Canada*, wonderfully illustrated by the scratchboard drawings of Terence M. Shortt. Snyder defined arctic birds as those nesting well above that somewhat vague boundary of ecological demarcation known as the tree line. Compared to the south, or the boreal forest, a disproportionate number of those birds are water birds, shorebirds and birds of prey. It isn't until page 246 of a book whose species descriptions run from page 21 to page 279 that we encounter the songbirds, a group that usually occupies a third to nearly half of the avifauna of most non-polar regions, apart from small, isolated oceanic islands dominated by seabirds.

The songbirds given full species account by Snyder are the horned lark and the Savannah sparrow, two species that nest within a short walk of my home; the northern raven, to be found within a two-hour's drive of my home, or closer; the water pipit, white-crowned sparrow and American tree sparrow, all of which occur on migration where I live, often in large numbers; the common redpoll, Lapland longspur and snow bunting, all of which appear in my area more or less regularly each winter; the hoary redpoll, which is rare enough to warrant a mention on the local birders' hotlines when it appears in my region; and the northern wheatear, which normally migrates to ancestral homes in Europe or Asia each winter and is considered an extreme rarity in the south. The

ARCTIC LOON

GRAY JAYS

This large, fluffy jay is well known for its boldness, which leads it to frequent camps in the north woods, particularly when the snow lies deep. It is likely to snatch any food it finds available and will even enter tents or take snacks from people's fingers. The gray jay nests as early as February or March. Its nest is cup-shaped, with thin walls and a soft lining. It usually lays three or four eggs, which have a pale, off-green or gray-green ground color and are covered with irregularly shaped spots, speckles and splotches of brown, olive and pale gray. Only the female incubates, a process that takes sixteen to eighteen days. The young leave the nest after about two weeks. In their immature plumages the young jays are dark, sooty-gray with a faint suggestion of a pale gray moustache stripe. Their beaks are light blue with black and pink markings.

wheatear is the only member of this select group I've not seen near my home.

Snyder's list of "arctic" songbirds is extremely restricted. To it might be added such "subarctic" songbird species as the Say's phoebe, alder flycatcher, tree swallow, bank swallow, cliff swallow, gray jay, boreal chickadee, ruby-crowned kinglet, varied thrush, American robin, northern shrike, Bohemian waxwing, orange-crowned warbler, yellow-rumped warbler, blackpoll warbler, yellow warbler, Wilson's warbler, northern waterthrush, dark-eyed junco, Harris' sparrow, fox sparrow, Smith's longspur, rusty blackbird, white-winged crossbill, pine grosbeak, rosy finch and other species that, while not normally to be found in the open, treeless tundra, are most certainly birds of the far north. Many of them may occur just north of the Arctic Circle, in the relatively biologically rich Mackenzie Delta on or near the shores of the Arctic Ocean. Almost all of these species can be encountered throughout significant parts of North America as either breeding species with wide ranges or as migrants.

The arctic warbler, bluethroat, red-throated pipit, white wagtail, yellow wagtail and the Siberian tit (whose normal nesting range extends east into the Yukon) are all Asian species whose breeding range includes parts of Alaska. The McKay's bunting is special to birders who keep regional lists. This close relative of the very widely distributed snow bunting nests only on a few islands in the Bering Sea and can sometimes be encountered along Alaska's west coast or in the Aleutians in winter. There are many other "Alaskan" specialties that are Eurasian species whose range includes Alaska.

The remaining birds of the tundra, mostly shorebirds and waterbirds, are species whose ranges either extend far to the south or species that migrate regularly into warmer climes. All of the tundra-nesting shorebirds identified by Snyder migrate through my area or other parts of North America, although the critically endangered Eskimo curlew is far too rare to be expected anywhere with certainty.

Indeed, the arctic shorebirds spend little of their lives in the Arctic (where they nest, lay eggs and raise young with startling rapidity) to take advantage of the abundance of invertebrate life on the tundra during the brief, arctic summer. In my area one sees northbound arctic shorebirds up until June, with southbound migrants beginning to appear in July.

With a few exceptions from Alaska, such as the emperor goose, spectacled eider and Steller's eider, virtually all the far northern waterfowl species can be encountered rather widely as breeding birds or migrants elsewhere in North America. Similarly such northern seafowl as the thick-billed murre, dovekie, northern fulmar, jaegers and several gulls and terns show up elsewhere. Fortunately for the birders in my region, the Great Lakes often seem to substitute for the ocean in the needs of such wintering birds. A significant percentage of the gulls that visit the Niagara Gorge each winter are from the Arctic.

There are some exceptions. Few arctic birds appearing in the more populated parts of the continent can draw more birders than the ivory gull, so seldom does it wander out of the far north. Usually one must visit the high Arctic to have any expectation of seeing this pure white species that regularly includes polar bear dung in its diet. When Ross' gulls nested in Churchill, the town's tourist population boomed with southern birders. Even a twenty-four-hour guard couldn't prevent the eggs in one nest from being stolen by collectors who might otherwise have to search the distant regions of the Old World arctic to find the nest of this species.

All of the birds of prey that nest in the far north – the golden eagle, bald eagle, northern harrier, sharp-shinned hawk, northern goshawk, red-tailed hawk, rough-legged hawk, osprey, American kestrel, merlin, peregrine falcon, gyrfalcon, short-eared owl, great horned owl, great gray owl, snowy owl, northern hawk-owl and boreal owl – are species I've seen near where I live. Some, such as the short-eared owl and the great horned owl, have many races and geographical

EIDERS

Eiders are in trouble. Once abundant, all four species seem to be in decline, although the king eider is still plentiful. The common eider may not live up to its name, but it is still not endangered. However, the remaining two species, the spectacled and the Steller's, have restricted ranges in the area of the Bering Sea. There have been such dramatic declines that both species of eider should have full status under appropriate legislation as endangered species. This decline has probably been happening for many years, but it has only been in the early 1990s that authorities have realized that losses are heavy enough to cause fear that the species may not survive.

KING EIDER

variations distributed through extraordinarily extensive ranges and varieties of habitats.

Just as hunters sometimes refer to the northern prairies as the great duck factory, so do birders sometimes refer to the north woods as the warbler factory. In the Americas, several groups of birds (usually defined taxonomically as families or subfamilies) reach their greatest numbers of species diversity in the tropics, but have representatives whose breeding range extends as far north as Alaska and the Yukon.

The tropical affinities of some of these species are symbolized by their brightly colored plumage. Among the wood warblers there are hues and patterns that seem apt for tropical forests where, in fact, many of the species spend significant parts of their life cycles. There are about 114 species of wood warbler, of which approximately two dozen can be found nesting in northern forests or adjacent habitat.

Tanagers are also noted for their bright colors. There are approximately 215 species of tanager, of which one, the western tanager, ranges north through the mountains and valleys of the West as far as southern Alaska and the southwestern corner of the Northwest Territories. The scarlet tanager also nests well up into the southern boreal forests of eastern United States and southeastern Canada.

The vireos are of a more somber color. They are another group of New World birds with approximately forty-three species in the family. Most are tropical, subtropical or temperate in their breeding range, but the solitary vireo, red-eyed vireo, warbling vireo and Philadelphia vireo can all be found nesting in the taiga. Even the yellow-throated vireo, an attractive, Carolinian species, reaches the very southern fringe of the taiga.

Among the approximately 256 species of tyrant fly-catchers, all found in the Americas, most are tropical, but about ten species occur as far north as Alaska, the Yukon or the Northwest Territories. All of these birds leave the north woods each fall and return each spring. One need not go too

LIMITED BREEDING RANGES IN THE NORTH

Some birds of the far north have limited breeding ranges. The Ross' goose breeds only in the central region of the Canadian arctic, mostly in the Perry River region of the Northwest Territories. The hardy emperor goose breeds in a fairly restricted coastal area of eastern Siberia and western Alaska. The Hudsonian godwit has a disjunct breeding range, with breeding populations in Alaska, the Mackenzie Delta, and the western shores of Hudson and James bays. The once abundant Eskimo curlew is nearly extinct. If any nest has been found this century, the information has not been made public. Presumably nesting occurs somewhere in the Northwest Territories or the northern Yukon. The red-legged kittiwake nests only on islands of the Bering Sea. The breeding ranges of the Aleutian tern and the red-faced cormorant are almost as restricted. The breeding range of the Harris' sparrow is limited to the area of stunted growth in the tree line, from the Northwest Territories to northern Manitoba.

far north to see most of them, although a few of these highly migratory songbird species nest almost exclusively in northern or mountain forests. Many nest in temperate North America.

None of this is to imply that there is little need for birders to travel north. On the contrary, some do as often as they can. The land is too vast, too dramatic and too interesting to be dismissed on the grounds that many of its birds can be encountered elsewhere. There is something incomplete in only knowing a species as a transient migrant or because it sometimes occurs nearby in the dead of winter.

Photographers, particularly, extol the virtues of nearly day-long periods of daylight when there is an abundance of birds to be seen in beautiful wilderness settings.

I yearn to return to the north woods and to see the birds of the high Arctic, familiar or otherwise, in the context of that fascinating ecosystem. For all the uncounted thousands of snow buntings I've seen, I've yet to see one in full breeding plumage gathering nesting materials on its tundra breeding grounds. I've seen oldsquaws in breeding plumage, but not as they cared for their young. I would like to see nesting shorebirds and ptarmigan, and I want to view arctic ground squirrels, belugas and lemmings in their natural habitats. Jaegers are birds I associate with distant views on pelagic trips. I'd like to see them up close, in breeding plumage. I would like to make the acquaintance of the yellow-billed loon and rock ptarmigan, and I'd like to sail past thick-billed murres in their huge breeding colonies on cliffs towering over arctic seas.

There's always much more to birding than mere lists. Someday I'll travel further north than I've been thus far, birding all the way.

OLIVE-SIDED FLYCATCHER

J O U R N A L

DATE / TIME

LOCALE

SPECIES

IMPRESSIONS

DATE / TIME

LOCALE

SPECIES

IMPRESSIONS

DATE / TIME

LOCALE

SPECIES

IMPRESSIONS

J O U R N A L

DATE / TIME

LOCALE

SPECIES

IMPRESSIONS

DATE / TIME

LOCALE

SPECIES

IMPRESSIONS

DATE / TIME

LOCALE

SPECIES

IMPRESSIONS

J O U R N A L

DATE / TIME

LOCALE

SPECIES

IMPRESSIONS

DATE / TIME

LOCALE

SPECIES

IMPRESSIONS

DATE / TIME

LOCALE

SPECIES

IMPRESSIONS

J O U R N A L

DATE / TIME

LOCALE

SPECIES

IMPRESSIONS

DATE / TIME

LOCALE

SPECIES

IMPRESSIONS

DATE / TIME

LOCALE

SPECIES

IMPRESSIONS

J O U R N A L

DATE / TIME

LOCALE

SPECIES

IMPRESSIONS

DATE / TIME

LOCALE

SPECIES

IMPRESSIONS

DATE / TIME

LOCALE

SPECIES

IMPRESSIONS

J O U R N A L

DATE / TIME

LOCALE

SPECIES

IMPRESSIONS

DATE / TIME

LOCALE

SPECIES

IMPRESSIONS

DATE / TIME

LOCALE

SPECIES

IMPRESSIONS

J O U R N A L

DATE / TIME

LOCALE

SPECIES

IMPRESSIONS

DATE / TIME

LOCALE

SPECIES

IMPRESSIONS

DATE / TIME

LOCALE

SPECIES

IMPRESSIONS

J O U R N A L

DATE / TIME

LOCALE

SPECIES

IMPRESSIONS

DATE / TIME

LOCALE

SPECIES

IMPRESSIONS

DATE / TIME

LOCALE

SPECIES

IMPRESSIONS

J O U R N A L

DATE / TIME

LOCALE

SPECIES

IMPRESSIONS

DATE / TIME

LOCALE

SPECIES

IMPRESSIONS

DATE / TIME

LOCALE

SPECIES

IMPRESSIONS

J O U R N A L

DATE / TIME

LOCALE

SPECIES

IMPRESSIONS

DATE / TIME

LOCALE

SPECIES

IMPRESSIONS

DATE / TIME

LOCALE

SPECIES

IMPRESSIONS

J O U R N A L

DATE / TIME

LOCALE

SPECIES

IMPRESSIONS

DATE / TIME

LOCALE

SPECIES

IMPRESSIONS

DATE / TIME

LOCALE

SPECIES

IMPRESSIONS

J O U R N A L

DATE / TIME

LOCALE

SPECIES

IMPRESSIONS

DATE / TIME

LOCALE

SPECIES

IMPRESSIONS

DATE / TIME

LOCALE

SPECIES

IMPRESSIONS

J O U R N A L

DATE / TIME

LOCALE

SPECIES

IMPRESSIONS

DATE / TIME

LOCALE

SPECIES

IMPRESSIONS

DATE / TIME

LOCALE

SPECIES

IMPRESSIONS

J O U R N A L

DATE / TIME

LOCALE

SPECIES

IMPRESSIONS

DATE / TIME

LOCALE

SPECIES

IMPRESSIONS

DATE / TIME

LOCALE

SPECIES

IMPRESSIONS

J O U R N A L

DATE / TIME

LOCALE

SPECIES

IMPRESSIONS

DATE / TIME

LOCALE

SPECIES

IMPRESSIONS

DATE / TIME

LOCALE

SPECIES

IMPRESSIONS

J O U R N A L

DATE / TIME

LOCALE

SPECIES

IMPRESSIONS

DATE / TIME

LOCALE

SPECIES

IMPRESSIONS

DATE / TIME

LOCALE

SPECIES

IMPRESSIONS

J O U R N A L

DATE / TIME

LOCALE

SPECIES

IMPRESSIONS

DATE / TIME

LOCALE

SPECIES

IMPRESSIONS

DATE / TIME

LOCALE

SPECIES

IMPRESSIONS

J O U R N A L

DATE / TIME

LOCALE

SPECIES

IMPRESSIONS

DATE / TIME

LOCALE

SPECIES

IMPRESSIONS

DATE / TIME

LOCALE

SPECIES

IMPRESSIONS

J O U R N A L

DATE / TIME

LOCALE

SPECIES

IMPRESSIONS

DATE / TIME

LOCALE

SPECIES

IMPRESSIONS

DATE / TIME

LOCALE

SPECIES

IMPRESSIONS

J O U R N A L

DATE / TIME

LOCALE

SPECIES

IMPRESSIONS

DATE / TIME

LOCALE

SPECIES

IMPRESSIONS

DATE / TIME

LOCALE

SPECIES

IMPRESSIONS

J O U R N A L

DATE / TIME

LOCALE

SPECIES

IMPRESSIONS

DATE / TIME

LOCALE

SPECIES

IMPRESSIONS

DATE / TIME

LOCALE

SPECIES

IMPRESSIONS

J O U R N A L

DATE / TIME

LOCALE

SPECIES

IMPRESSIONS

DATE / TIME

LOCALE

SPECIES

IMPRESSIONS

DATE / TIME

LOCALE

SPECIES

IMPRESSIONS

J O U R N A L

DATE / TIME

LOCALE

SPECIES

IMPRESSIONS

DATE / TIME

LOCALE

SPECIES

IMPRESSIONS

DATE / TIME

LOCALE

SPECIES

IMPRESSIONS

J O U R N A L

DATE / TIME

LOCALE

SPECIES

IMPRESSIONS

DATE / TIME

LOCALE

SPECIES

IMPRESSIONS

DATE / TIME

LOCALE

SPECIES

IMPRESSIONS

J O U R N A L

DATE / TIME

LOCALE

SPECIES

IMPRESSIONS

DATE / TIME

LOCALE

SPECIES

IMPRESSIONS

DATE / TIME

LOCALE

SPECIES

IMPRESSIONS

J O U R N A L

DATE / TIME

LOCALE

SPECIES

IMPRESSIONS

DATE / TIME

LOCALE

SPECIES

IMPRESSIONS

DATE / TIME

LOCALE

SPECIES

IMPRESSIONS

INDEX

Page numbers of illustrations are indicated in italics.

Accidentals, Asian, 146
Acorn woodpecker, 130, 156, 157, 163
Ahlquist, Jon, 100
Ajax, Ont., 2, 37, 45
Alabama, 109-11, 112-13
Alcids, 62, 64, 95
Alder flycatcher, 181
Aleutians, 146, 181
Aleutian tern, 183
Alligator, 94, 100, 102, 103, 106, 111, 112
American avocet, 155, 164, 172
American bittern, 172
American black duck, 33, 34, 55, 110, 111
American coot, 121, 144, 172
American crow, 112, 121, 126, 150, 175
American dipper, *118*, 119
American kestrel, 3, 42, 56, 76, 93, 94, 100, 112, 123, 128, 176, 182
American oystercatcher, 85
American redstart, 98
American robin, 44, 57, 87, 154, 181
American swallow-tailed kite, 14
American tree sparrow, 180
American white pelican, 44, 112, 149, 172
American woodcock, 24, 29, 35, 40, 43
Anhinga, 1, 88, *99*, 106
Anhinga Trail, Fla., 105
Ani, groove-billed, *125*, 129, 135
Animal Protection Institute, 92, 136, 145, 154
Anna's hummingbird, *165*
Anole lizard, 92
Antillean nighthawk, 98
Arctic Birds of Canada, 180
Arctic loon, *180*
Arctic tern, 148
Arctic warbler, 181
Ash-throated flycatcher, 156
Atlantic puffin, 67, 69
Audubon House, 95, 97
Audubon, John James, 87, 95, 96
Auklet, 95
Avocet, American, 149, 150, 155, 164, 172

Backus Mill Conservation Area, 19
Bahama swallow, 98
Baillie, James L., 47, 165
Baird's sandpiper, 27, 76, 86
Baird's sparrow, 169, 170
Bald eagle, 68, 70, 103, 121, 123, 182

Banding, 4, 14, 25-28, 33, 37, 38-39
Band-tailed pigeon, 35
Bank swallow, 181
Bar-headed goose, 101
Barn owl, 123, 126
Barn swallow, 128, 155
Barred owl, 55, 100
Barrow's goldeneye, 55, 68
Bay-breasted warbler, 38-39, 62, 152
Bay of Fundy, 60, 67-68, 75
Beaver, 54
Bell's vireo, 14
Belted kingfisher, 93, 94, 100, 112, 135, 156, 160
Bewick's wren, 14-15, 150, 163
Big Pine Key, Fla., 92, 98
Big Sur National Park, 152
Biloxi, Miss., 111
Binoculars, 135
Bird counts, 13, 38, 52, 120
Birder's Guide to Florida, A, 96
Birder's Guide to the Rio Grande Valley of Texas, A, 126
Birding
  equipment, 135
  ethics, 5-6, 14
  record-keeping, 134
  techniques, 15, 86, 127
Birds of Newfoundland, The, 69
Bittern
  American, 172
  "Cory's," 48
  least, 30-31, 48
Black and white warbler, 98, 152
Black-backed wagtail, 146
Black-backed woodpecker, 62
Black-bellied plover, 27, 76, 84, 97, 101, 109, 144
Black-bellied whistling duck, 134
Black-billed magpie, 117, 121, 154, 158, 161, 162, 175
Blackbird
  Brewer's, 148, 151, 152, 154, 160, 164
  red-winged, 22-23, 44, 57, 112, 122, 164, 174
  rusty, 43, 62, 181
  yellow-headed, 160, 161, 174
Blackburnian warbler, 152
Black-capped chickadee, 44, 123, 124
Black-chinned hummingbird, 155
Black-crowned night heron, 29, 33, 52, 57, 144, 164
Black duck, American, 33, 34, 55, 110, 111
Black francolin, 101

Black guillemot, 61, 63, 69, 149
Black-headed grosbeak, *122*, 124
Black-legged kittiwake, 63-64, 70, 80
Black-necked stilt, 155, 164
Black phoebe, 141, 146, 156
Black rail, 96, 149
Black-shouldered kite, 147, 156
Black skimmer, 14, 85
Black swan, 101
Black-tailed godwit, 146
Black tern, 32, 40, 43, 48, 174
Black-throated blue warbler, *15*, 16, 96, 98, 152
Black-throated gray warbler, 14, 148
Black-throated green warbler, 98
Black-throated sparrow, 129, *131*, 139
Black turnstone, 152
Black vulture, 100, 103, 112, 123, 130
Bluebird
  eastern, 37, 87, 113
  mountain, 144, 175
Blue-gray gnatcatcher, 15, 113, 127, 135
Blue grosbeak, 16, 155
Blue grouse, 177
Blue Hole, Fla., 94
Blue jay, 16, 87, 124
Bluethroat, 181
Blue-winged teal, 33, 34, 44, 134, 172
Blue-winged warbler, 46-47
Boat-tailed grackle, 86, 100
Boca Chica, Tex., 126
Bohemian waxwing, 120, *120*, 181
Bolinas Bay, 149
Bonaparte's gull, 27, 78, 174
Bonaventure Island, 62-67
Book of Birds, The, 129, 131
Boreal chickadee, 14, 44, 62, 76, 181
Boreal owl, 182
Boston, Mass., 78, 82
Boundary Bay, B.C., 123
Brambling, 146
Brant, 35
Brewer's blackbird, 148, 151, 152, 154, 160, 164
Brewer's sparrow, 175
Bridgeport, Calif., 158, 160, 161
Bridled titmouse, 44
Brier Island, N.S., 73-77
British Columbia, 116-24
Broad-winged hawk, 7, 77, 112, 123
Brooks, Major Allan, 1, 42, 116,

119, 121, 129, 131
Brown creeper, 62, *62*, 159
Brown-crested flycatcher, 127
Brown-headed cowbird, 57, 164
Brown-headed nuthatch, 110
Brown pelican, 94, 112, *113*, 149, 150
Brownsville, Tex., 125, 126
Brown thrasher, 31, 103, 112, 161, 175
Brown towhee. *See* California towhee
Budgerigar, 101
Bufflehead, 24, 55, *55*, 68, 172
Bulbul, red-whiskered, 101
Buller's shearwater, 148
Bunting
  indigo, 15
  lark, 14, 147, 175
  lazuli, 152, 156
  McKay's, 181, 183
  painted, 100-01, 103, *111*
  snow, 42, 54, 68-69, 86, 117, 180, 184
Burleigh, Thomas D., 69
Burrowing owl, 164, 165, 169, 176
Bushtit, 149, 150, 155
Buteo, 123, 176
Butterfly
  blue morpho, 104
  monarch, 36, 77
  zebra, 104
Buzzard, 123

Cactus
  birds and, 142
  cholla, 141, 142
Cactus wren, 128, 139, 142
California, 136-165
California gull, 144, 151, 155, 160, 161, 174
California quail, 119, 120, 156, 161
California towhee, 148, 156, 163
Canada goose, 53, 55-56, 172
Canada warbler, 152
Canary-winged parakeet, 101
Canvasback, 21, 172
Canyon towhee, 148
Canyon wren, 119
Cape May warbler, 87, 152
Caprimulgids, 97
Caracara, crested, 128, *129*
Cardinal, northern, 79, 87, 112, 113, 127
Carolina chickadee, 87, 113
Carolina wren, 87
Caspian tern, 33, 85, 97, 109, 144
Cassin's finch, 120
Cassin's sparrow, 14, 130

Catbird, gray, 21, 103
Cattle egret, 33, 102, 103
Chachalaca, plain, 132-33, *133*
Chaparral, chamise, 162, 163
Chat, yellow-breasted, 103, 119
Checklists, 134
Chestnut-backed chickadee, 153
Chestnut-collared longspur, 170
Chestnut-sided warbler, 38, 152
Chickadee, 38, 44, 149
 black-capped, 44, 123, 124
 boreal, 14, 44, 62, 76, 181
 Carolina, 87, 113
 chestnut-backed, 153
 gray-headed, 44
 mountain, *116*, 124, 159
Chickaree, 159
Chick-will's-widow, 14, 40, 97, 129
Chihuahuan raven, 126
Chimney swift, 46, *46*, 57
Chukar partridge, 119, 177
Churchill, Man., 178, 182
Ciconiiformes, 100
Cinnamon teal, 14, 155, 172
Clapper rail, 89, *89*, 149
Clark's nutcracker, 120, 158
Classification of birds, 100
Clay-colored sparrow, 175
Cliff swallow, 128, 163, 181
Common crane, 146
Common cuckoo, 146
Common eider, 62, 69, 71, 182
Common goldeneye, 55, 172
Common ground dove, 128
Common loon, 52, 56, 84
Common merganser, 52, 122, 160, 172
Common moorhen, 134, 144
Common murre, 64, *65*, 69, 149
Common nighthawk, 43, 57
Common pauraque, 129
Common poorwill, 97
Common raven, 62, 71, 139
Common redpoll, 42, 180
Common snipe, 27, 43, 76, 172
Common tern, 33, 52, 78, 108, 109, 144, 174
Common yellowthroat, *41*, 98, 174
Condor, 100
Connecticut warbler, 87
Cooper's hawk, 42
Coot, American, 121, 144, 172
Cormorant, 106, 148
 double-crested, 29, 33, 56, 61, 78, 81, 93, 94, 122, 128, 131, *168*, 172
 great, 63, 78
 olivaceous, 132
 pelagic, 122
 red-faced, 183
Corner Marsh, Ajax, Ont., 37-45
Corvids, 95
Cory's shearwater, 67

Cowbird, 160
 brown-headed, 57, 164
Coyote Hills Regional Park, 147
Cranberry Marsh, Whitby, Ont., 45
Crane
 common, 146
 sandhill, 172, *173*
 whooping, 169
Creeper, 38
 brown, 62, *62*, 159
Crested caracara, 128, *129*
Crested myna, 121-22
Crossbill, white-winged, 62, 181
Crow, 48, 95
 American, 112, 121, 126, 150, 175
 Mexican, 126
 northwestern, 121, 123
Cuckoo
 common, 146
 Oriental, 146
 yellow-billed, 175
Curlew
 Eskimo, 169, 181, 183
 long-billed, 146, 149, 174
Curve-billed thrasher, 127
Cypress, Monterey, 151

Dark-eyed junco, 62, 118, 181
Dauphin Island, Ala., 109, 110
Deer
 key, 92-93
 mule, 124, 152, 156, *156*, 160
 white-tailed, 24, 29, 88, 112, 127
Delta, B.C., 122
Desert sparrow. *See* Black-throated sparrow
Dickcissel, 175
Digby, N.S., 60, 68
Dipper, American, *118*, 119
Dolphins, 81, 85, 148
Double-crested cormorant, 29, 33, 56, 61, 78, 81, 93, 94, 122, 128, 131, *168*, 172
Dove
 common ground, 128
 Inca, 128
 mourning, 22, 56, 112, 129
 white-tipped, 133
Dovekie, 62, 70, 95, 182
Dowitcher, 164
 long-billed, 149
 short-billed, 27, 76, 92, 97, 149, 174
Downy woodpecker, 87
Duck
 American black, 33, 34, 55, 110, 111
 black-bellied whistling, 134
 harlequin, 29, 52, 54, 69, 122
 mottled, 110, 111
 Muscovy, 96, 110

ring-necked, 21, 29, 88
 ruddy, 150, 172
 wood, 44
Dunlin, 27, 36, 84
Dusky thrush, 146
Dusky warbler, 145, 146, 147, 148

Eagle
 bald, 68, 70, 103, 121, 123, 182
 golden, 121, 176, 182
 Mexican. *See* Crested caracara
Eared grebe, 149, 171
Eastern bluebird, 37, 87, 113
Eastern kingbird, 93, 175
Eastern meadowlark, 100, 161, 175
Eastern phoebe, 87, 112, 141
Eastern screech-owl, 54
Eco Pond, Fla., 102, 103
Egret, 149
 cattle, 33, 102, 103
 great, 15, 89, 101, 128, 131, 134, 150, 164
 reddish, 93, 94, 95, *95*
 snowy, 89, 101, 128, 134, 150, 153, 164
Eider
 common, 62, 69, 71, 75, 182
 king, 29, 52, 54, 182, *182*
 spectacled, 182
 Steller's, 182
Emperor goose, 182, 183
Eskimo curlew, 169, 181, 183
Eurasian skylark, 146
Eurasian wigeon, 15, 45
European starling, 47, 54, 122
Evening grosbeak, 38, *51*, 62
Everglades, the, 99-106
Everglades National Park, Fla., 99

Falcon
 peregrine, 94, 147, 182
 prairie, *114*, 120, 176
Falcon State Recreation Area, 126
Far North, the, 178-84
Ferruginous hawk, 123, 169, 176
Field guides, 134
Field Guide to the Birds, 1
Field marks, 79
Finch
 brambling, 146
 Cassin's, 120
 house, 56, 101, 118, 139, 154
 Java, 101
 little bunting, 146
 rosy, 181
Finfoot, 99
Fisher, James, 104
Flamingo, 100, 101, 102
 greater, 101
Flashing Wings, 57
Flicker, 175
 northern, 119, 156
 "red-shafted," 119, 120, 121
 "yellow-shafted," 119

Florida, 92-106, 112
Florida Keys, 92, 93, 94
Flycatcher, 95
 alder, 181
 ash-throated, 156
 brown-crested, 127
 gray, *v*
 great crested, 29, 86
 least, 62
 olive-sided, 62, *184*
 scissor-tailed, 130
 sulphur-bellied, 35
 vermilion, 79
 yellow-bellied, 62
Folsom Peninsula, Calif., 162-63
Fork-tailed swift, 146
Forster's tern, 44-45, 85, 128, 174
Fox, red, 12
Fox sparrow, 120, 123, 151, 181
Francolin, black, 101
Franklin's gull, 174
Fraser River Valley, B.C., 123-24
Frigatebird, magnificent, 94, *97*
Frog, pig, 105
Fuertes, Louis Aggasiz, 1
Fulmar, 95
 northern, *70*, 71, *71*, 182
Fulvous whistling-duck, 14

Gadwall, 33, 55, 171, 172
Gannet, 100
 northern, 14, 53, *60*, 63-66, 71, 76, 79, 81
Gannet, The, 66
Garbage dumps, as birding locales, 48, 126
Garden, planting for birds, 47
Garganey, 146
Gaspé Peninsula, Que., 62
Geiger tree, 95
Georgia, 83-89
Gizzards, 174
Glaucous gull, 47
Gnatcatcher, blue-gray, 15, 113, 127, 135
Goatsuckers, 97
Godwit
 black-tailed, 146
 Hudsonian, 183
 marbled, 44, 146, 149, 152, 172
Golden-crowned kinglet, 57
Golden-crowned sparrow, 148
Golden eagle, 121, 176, 182
Goldeneye
 Barrow's, 55, 68, 122
 common, 55, 122, 172
Golden-fronted woodpecker, 125, 130, 132
Golden plover, 75
 greater (Eurasian), 75
 lesser (American), 15, 75, 76
 Pacific, 75
Goldfinch, 163
 American, 163

Lawrence's, 163
lesser, 156, 163
Goose
bar-headed, 101
Canada, 53, 55-56, 172
emperor, 182, 183
Ross', 183
snow, 174
white-fronted, 14, 174
Goshawk, northern, 42, 182
Grackle, 38, 57
boat-tailed, 86, 100, 112
great-tailed, 126, 133, 135
Grasshopper sparrow, 175
Gray catbird, 21, 103
Gray-cheeked thrush, 39, 62
Gray flycatcher, v
Gray hawk, 123
Gray-headed chickadee, 44, 181
Gray jay, 62, 65, 76, 181
Gray kingbird, 92
Gray partridge, 177
Gray phalarope. See Phalarope, red
Gray plover. See Plover, black-
bellied
Gray wagtail, 146
Great black-backed gull, 61, 63, 71,
73, 78
Great blue heron, 40, 57, 89, 94, 95,
101, 106, 112, 123, 128, 164, 172
Great cormorant, 63, 78
Great crested flycatcher, 29, 86
Great egret, 15, 89, 101, 128, 131,
134, 164
Greater (Eurasian) golden plover,
75
Greater flamingo, 101, 103
Greater prairie chicken, 169, 176,
177
Greater scaup, 53-55, 68, 84
Greater shearwater, 67
Greater yellowlegs, 21, 24, 27, 76,
146
Great gray owl, 182
Great horned owl, 41, 118, 182
Great kiskadee, vi, 135
Great-tailed grackle, 126, 133, 135
"Great white" heron, 95
Grebe, 174
eared, 149, 171
horned, 149, 171
least, 131
pied-billed, 32, 88-89, 97, 134,
144, 149, 171
red-necked, 42, 53, 53, 171
western, 122, 171, 149
Green-backed heron, 39, 57, 100,
164
Green jay, 131, 133, 134, 135
Green kingfisher, 134
Green-tailed towhee, 158, 159
Green-winged teal, 77, 123, 172
Grenadier Pond, Toronto, Ont., 55,
57

Groove-billed ani, 125, 129, 135
Grosbeak
black-headed, 122, 124
blue, 16, 155
evening, 38, 51, 62
pine, 181
rose-breasted, 16, 29, 35
Groundsel, 87
Ground squirrel
California, 148, 151, 153, 154,
161
golden-mantled, 159
Grouse
blue, 177
ruffed, 29, 117
sage, 177
sharp-tailed, 117, 177
Guillemot, 95
black, 61, 63, 69, 149
pigeon, 149
Gulfport, Miss., 108
Gull, 29, 39, 47, 48, 95, 182
Bonaparte's, 27, 78, 174
California, 144, 151, 155, 160,
161, 174
Franklin's, 174
glaucous, 47
great black-backed, 61, 63, 71,
73, 78
Heermann's, 145, 151
herring, 33, 49, 52, 63, 70, 78,
109, 121
Iceland, 47, 70
ivory, 182
laughing, 16, 82, 84, 97, 109,
128
lesser black-backed, 47
little, 45
mew, 122
ring-billed, 33, 49-52, 55-56,
78, 84, 109
Ross', 182
Sabine's, 149
slaty-backed, 146
Thayer's, 47
western, 150, 151
Gull-billed tern, 110, 143
Gull-control programs, 50, 52
Gull Island, Ont., 32-33
Gumbo Limbo Trail, Fla., 104
Gumbo-limbo tree, 104
Gyrfalcon, 1, 14, 52, 182

Hairy woodpecker, 120
Harlequin duck, 29, 52, 54, 69,
122
Harlingen, Tex., 125
Harp seal, 68-69
Harrier, northern, 42, 44, 77, 112,
123, 176, 182
Harris' hawk, 128
Harris' sparrow, 181, 183
Hawk, 42, 100, 174
broad-winged, 77, 77, 112, 123

Cooper's, 42
ferruginous, 123, 169, 176
gray, 123
Harris', 128
red-shouldered, 100, 123
red-tailed, 42, 55-56, 112, 117,
123, 143, 176, 182
rough-legged, 42, 52, 117, 122,
123, 176, 182
sharp-shinned, 16, 42, 76, 94,
112, 182
short-tailed, 123
Swainson's, 14, 76, 123, 131,
155, 176
zone-tailed, 123, 132
Hawk-owl, northern, 42, 182
Heermann's gull, 145, 151
Henslow's sparrow, 15
Hepatic tanager, 79
Hermit thrush, 38, 62, 163
Heron, 39, 40, 149
black-crowned night, 33, 52, 57,
144, 164
great blue, 40, 57, 89, 94, 95,
101, 106, 112, 123, 128, 164,
172
"great white," 95
green-backed, 39, 57, 100, 164
little blue, 89, 195
tricolored, 89, 92, 97, 101, 102,
134
"Wurdemann's," 94, 95
Herring gull, 33, 49, 52, 63, 70,
78, 109, 121
Highway 1, Fla., 95
Hill myna, 101
Hoary redpoll, 42, 180
Holt, Harold R., 126
Hooded merganser, 88
Hooded warbler, 110, 152
Horned grebe, 149, 171
Horned lark, 42, 178, 180
House finch, 56, 101, 118, 139,
159
House wren, 133, 135, 160,
175
Hudsonian godwit, 183
Hummingbird
Anna's, 165
black-chinned, 155
ruby-throated, 134
rufous, 14
Ibis, 40
scarlet, 101
white, 14, 89, 96, 97, 101, 104
Iceland gull, 47, 70
Identification of birds, 54, 128
Inca dove, 128
Indian Point Nature Trail, Ont.,
29-32
Indigo bunting, 15
Ivory gull, 182
Ivy, poison, 29-30

Jaeger, 53, 182, 184
long-tailed, 14
pormarine, 148
Java finch, 101
Jay, 95
blue, 16, 87, 124
gray, 62, 65, 76, 181
green, 131, 133, 134, 135
scrub, 148, 151, 154, 157
Steller's, 120, 124, 149, 152,
160, 161
Jekyll Island, Ga., 83-89
Jizz, 79
Joshua tree, 136, 138, 139, 143
Joshua Tree National Monument
Park, 136, 137
Junco, 57, 65
dark-eyed, 62, 65, 118, 181
"Oregon," 118
"slate-colored," 118

Kentucky warbler, 111, 152
Kestrel, 141
American, 37, 42, 56, 76, 93,
94, 100, 112, 123, 128, 176,
182
Key West Botanical Gardens, 96-97
Key West, Fla., 97
Killdeer, 27, 57, 85, 144, 155, 169,
172
Kingbird, 95
eastern, 93, 175
gray, 92
loggerhead, 93
western, 106, 156, 164, 175
King eider, 29, 52, 54, 182, 182
Kingfisher
belted, 93, 94, 100, 112, 135,
156, 160
green, 134
ringed, 134
Kinglet, 38
golden-crowned, 57
ruby-crowned, 76, 113, 181
King rail, 89
Kiskadee, 95
great, vi, 135
Kite
American swallow-tailed, 14
black-shouldered, 147, 156
Mississippi, 14, 108, 132
snail, 100
white-tailed. See Kite, black-
shouldered
Kittiwake
black-legged, 63-64, 69, 80
red-legged, 183
Knot, red, 27, 36, 76

Ladder-backed woodpecker, 139
Lake Ontario, 28, 53, 60
Lake St. Clair, 19
Landfill sites, as birding locales, 47
Lane, James, 96, 126

Lapland longspur, 42, 180
Larids, 95
Lark bunting, 14, 147, 175
Lark, horned, 42, *178*, 180
Lark sparrow, 156, 175
Laughing gull, 16, 82, 84, 97, 109, 128
Lazuli bunting, 152, 156
LBJs, 147
Leach's storm-petrel, 67
Least bittern, 30-31
Least flycatcher, 62
Least grebe, 131
Least sandpiper, 27, 85, 86, 155
Least tern, 108
LeConte's sparrow, 53, 174
Lent, Madeleine, 73-74, 77
Lent, Wickerson, 72-75
Leslie Street Spit, Toronto, Ont., 48-53, 56
Lesser (American) golden plover, 15, 75, 76
Lesser black-backed gull, 47
Lesser goldfinch, 156, 163
Lesser nighthawk, 14
Lesser prairie-chicken, 176, 177
Lesser scaup, 55, 172
Lesser yellowlegs, 27
Lewis' woodpecker, 14, 120
Life birds, 13
Life lists, 13
Limpkin, 99, 100
Lincoln's sparrow, 62, 75
Little blue heron, 89, 95
Little bunting, 146
Little gull, 45
Lizard
    anole, 92
    sagebrush, 159
Loggerhead kingbird, 93
Loggerhead shrike, 100, 141, 155, 169
Long-billed curlew, 146, 149, 174
Long-billed dowitcher, 149
Long-billed thrasher, 135, 161
Long-eared owl, 3, *3*, 43, 122
Long Point Bird Observatory, 19
Long Point, Ont., 17-24
Long Point Provincial Park, 19
Longspur
    chestnut-collared, 170
    Lapland, 42, 180
    McCown's, 170
    Smith's, 181
Long-tailed jaeger, 14
Loon, 29, 178
    Arctic, *180*
    common, 52, 56, 84
    red-throated, 15, 52, 76, 84
    yellow-billed, 184
Lydia's Audubon Shoppe, 108

McCown's longspur, 170
McKay's bunting, 181

MacKay, Charles Davison (Dave), 4
MacKay, Phyllis E., 3
MacKay's Woods, 38
Magnificent frigatebird, 94, *97*
Magnolia warbler, 128, 150, 152
Magpie, 95
    black-billed, 117, 121, 154, 158, 161, 162, 175
    yellow-billed, 154, *154*, 161
Mahogany Hammock Trail, Fla., 104
Mallard, 33, 53, 55-56, 110, 111, 122, 134, 155, 160, 164, 172
Manchineel, 105
Mandarin, 101
Mangrove swamps, 100
Marbled godwit, 44, 146, 149, 152, 172
Marsh wren, 32, 155, 174
Martin, purple, 57
Massachusetts, 78
Meadowlark, 112
    eastern, 100, 161, 175
    western, 161, 164, 175
Mealy parrot, 23
Merganser, 29, 54
    common, 52, 122, 160, 172
    hooded, 88
    red-breasted, 52, 84, 122
Merlin, 35, 36, 77, 123, 176, 182
Mew gull, 122
Mexican Birds: First Impressions, 6
Mexican crow, 126
Mexican eagle. *See* Crested caracara
Miami Zoo, 101
Middendorf's warbler, 146
Migrants, nocturnal, 19, 20
Mississippi, 108-09, 111-12
Mississippi kite, 14, 108, 132
Mockingbird
    northern, 37, 76, 87, *90*, 100, 108, 112, 127, 140, 154, 161
Mojave Desert, 136, 138, 139, 142
Mongolian plover, 35, 146
Monk parakeet, 101
Monterey Peninsula, Calif., 151
Moorhen, 102, 164
    common, 32, 134, 144
Moth, yucca, 138
Mottled duck, 110, 111
Mountain bluebird, 144, 175
Mountain chickadee, *116*, 124, 159
Mountain plover, 169, 170, 172
Mourning dove, 22, 56, 112, 129
Mowat, Farley, 71
Muir Woods National Monument, 149
Murre, 62, 95
    common, 64, 66, 69, 149
    thick-billed, 14, 69, 182, 184
Murrelets, 62, 95
Muscicapidae, 146

Muscovy duck, 96, 101
Mute swan, 23, 55
Myna
    crested, 121-22
    hill, 101
Myrtle warbler. *See* Warbler, yellow-rumped
Myrtle, wax, 87

Names of birds, 87, 88, 95
Nashville warbler, 87
National Audubon Society's Sabal Palm Grove Sanctuary, 126
National Key Deer Refuge, Fla., 92
Nelson, Bryan, 66
Nest sites
    artificial, 52
    competition for, 63
Nets, mist, 25-26
New Brunswick, 67-68
Newfoundland, 69-72
New Orleans, La., 107
Nighthawk, 39, 97
    Antillean, 98
    common, 43, 57
    lesser, 14
Night heron, black-crowned, 33, 52, 57
Nightjars, 97
Northern cardinal, 79, 87, 112, 113, 127
Northern flicker, 119, 156
Northern fulmar, 70, *71*, 71, 182
Northern gannet, 14, 53, *60*, 63-66, 71, 76, 79, 81
Northern goshawk, 42, 182
Northern harrier, 42, 44, 77, 112, 123, 176, 182
Northern hawk-owl, 42, 182
Northern mockingbird, 37, 76, 87, *90*, 100, 108, 112, 140, 154, 161
Northern oriole, 14, 35
Northern parula warbler, 98, 103, 152
Northern pintail, 33, 150, *171*, 172
Northern raven, 180
Northern rough-winged swallow, 128
Northern shoveler, 55, 134, 172
Northern shrike, 42-43, 53, 120, 181
Northern waterthrush, 76, 181
Northern wheatear, 180
North Point, P.E.I., 68
Northwestern crow, 121, 123
Nova Scotia, 73-77
Nutcracker, 95
    Clark's, 120, 158
Nuthatch
    brown-headed, 110
    pygmy, 110
    red-breasted, 123, 124, 159
    white-breasted, 159
Nuttall's woodpecker, 155

Oak, Virginia live, 88, 112
Ocotilla, 142
Okanagan Lake, 120
Okanagan Valley, B.C., 116
Oldsquaw, 24, 53-55, 68, 184
Oliveceous cormorant, 132
Olive-sided flycatcher, 62, *184*
Olive tree pipit, 148
Ontario, 12-57
Ontario Bird Banders' Association, 19
Orange-crowned warbler, 146, 181
Orchard oriole, 15
"Oregon," junco, 118
Oriental cuckoo, 146
Oriole
    northern, 15, 35
    orchard, 15
    spot-breasted, 101
Oshawa, Ont., 45
Osprey, 94, 128, 182
Ovenbird, 20, 29, 38, 98
Owen Point, Ont., 29, 32-33
Owl, 174, 175
    barn, 123, 126
    barred, 55, 100
    boreal, 182
    burrowing, 164, 165, 169, 176
    great gray, 182
    great horned, 41, 118, 182
    long-eared, 3, *3*, 43, 122
    saw-whet, *10*, 52-53
    short-eared, 42, 52, 122, 176, 182
    snowy, 42, 54, 117, 176, 182
Oystercatcher, American, 85

Pacific golden plover, 75
Packrat, 141
Padre Island, Tex., 126
Painted bunting, 100-01, 103, *111*
Palm
    fan, 126
    sabal, 126
Palm warbler, 98, 152
Parakeet
    canary-winged, 101
    monk, 101
    rose-ringed, 101
Parrot
    mealy, 23
    red-crowned, 101
    yellow-headed Amazon, 101
Partridge
    gray, 177
    red-legged, 101
Passenger pigeon, 48
Pectoral sandpiper, 27
Peeps, 86
Pelagic cormorant, 122
Pelecaniformes, 100
Pelee. *See* Point Pelee
Pelican, 100, 148
    American white, 44, 112, 149, 172

brown, 94, 112, *113*, 149, 150
Pellets, 175
Penticton, B.C., 118, 119, 120
Percé Rock, Que., 62
Peregrine falcon, 94, 147, 182
Petchora pipit, 148
Peters, Harold S., 69
Peterson, Roger Tory, 2, 50-51, 69, 104, 125
Petrel, 95
Pewee, western wood, 156, 159
Phainopepla, 1, *136*, 138
Phalarope
  gray. *See* Phalarope, red
  red, 68, 81, *81*, 82, 148
  red-necked, 82, 148
  Wilson's, 41, 82, 172
Pheasant, ring-necked, 47, 177
Philadelphia vireo, 183
Phoebe, 95
  black, 141, 146, 156
  eastern, 87, 112, 141
  Say's, 140, 146, 150, *150*, 175, 181
Pied-billed grebe, 32, 88-89, 97, 134, 144, 149, 164
Pigeon
  band-tailed, 35
  passenger, 48
  white-crowned, 95, 96, 97, 105
Pigeon guillemot, 149
Pileated woodpecker, 29, 41, 86, 113, 120
Pine
  digger, 157, 162
  Monterey, 151
  ponderosa (yellow), 119, 121, 157
Pine grosbeak, 21, 62, 65, 181
Pineland Trail, Fla., 106
Pine warbler, 87
Pink-footed shearwater, 148
Pintail, northern, 33, 150, *171*, 172
Pinto Basin, 142
Piping plover, 85, 172
Pipit
  olive tree, 148
  petchora, 148
  red-throated, 148, 181
  Sprague's, 147, 175
  water, 148, 180
Pishing, 158
Plain chachalaca, 132-33, *133*
Plain titmouse, 150, 155
Plover
  black-bellied, 27, 76, 84, 97, 101, 109, 144
  golden, 75
  gray. *See* Plover, black-bellied
  greater golden, 75
  lesser golden, 15, 75, 76
  Mongolian, 35, 146
  mountain, 169, 170, 172
  Pacific golden, 75
  piping, 85, 169, 172

semipalmated, *33*, 85, 97
Point Lobos State Reserve, 153
Point Pelee National Park, 13
Point Pelee, Ont., 12-16, 40
Poisoning, of birds, 174
Poison ivy, 29-30
Pomacea snails, 100
Poorwill, common, 97
Pormarine jaeger, 148
Prairie-chicken
  greater, 169, 176, 177
  lesser, 176, 177
Prairie dog, 164
Prairie falcon, *114*, 120, 176
Prairies, the, 168-77
Prairie warbler, 87, 96, 103
Presqu'ile Provincial Park, Ont., 25-36
Pribilof Islands, 146
Prince Edward Island, 68-69
Procellarids, 95
Prothonotary warbler, 1, 15, *107*, 109, 152
Ptarmigan, 178, 184
  rock, 182
  willow, *166*
Puffin, 62, 64, 67, 69-70, 95
  Atlantic, 67, 69-70
Purple martin, 57
Purple sandpiper, 29, 36, 43, 54
Pygmy nuthatch, 110
Pyrrhuloxia, 127, 129

Quail
  California, 119, 120, 156, 161
  scaled, 127
Quebec, 60-67

Rabbit, marsh, 111
Raccoon, 52, 104
Rail
  black, 96, 149
  clapper, 89, *89*, 149
  king, 89
  sora, 172
  Virginia, 89, 172
  yellow, 96, 172
Raptors, finding, 42, 43
Rarities, finding, 16
Rat, desert wood, 141, 142
Raven, 48, 95, 140, 179
  Chihuahuan, 126
  common, 62, 71, 139
  northern, 180
  white-necked. *See* Raven, chihuahuan
Razorbill, 64, 66, 69, 95
Razor-billed auk. *See* Razorbill
Red-bellied woodpecker, 14, 86, 88, 100, 108, 112, 113
Red-breasted merganser, 52, 84, 122
Red-breasted nuthatch, 123, 124, 159

Red-breasted sapsucker, 159, *161*
Red-crowned parrot, 101
Reddish egret, 93, 94, 95, *95*
Red-eyed vireo, 20, 29, 88, 103, 183
Red-faced cormorant, 183
Redhead, 29, 35, 55, 172
Red-headed woodpecker, 15, 35, 54, 130
Red knot, 27, 36, 76
Red-legged kittiwake, 183
Red-legged partridge, 101
Red-necked grebe, 42, 53, *53*
Red-necked phalarope, 82, 148
Red osier dogwood, 24, 31, 37
Red phalarope, 68, 81, *81*, 82, 149
Redpoll
  common, 42, 180
  hoary, 42, 180
"Red-shafted" flicker, 119, 120, 121
Red-shouldered hawk, 100, 123
Redstart, American, 98
Red-tailed hawk, 42, 55-56, 82, 112, 117, 123, 143, 176, 182
Red-throated loon, 15, 52, 76, 84
Red-throated pipit, 148, 181
Red-whiskered bulbul, 101
Red-winged blackbird, 22-23, 44, 57, 112, 164, 174
Redwing, tricolored, 164
Reid-Henry, D.M., 2
Rickwood State Park, Ala., 113
Ring-billed gull, 33, 49-52, 55-56, 78, 84, 109
Ringed kingfisher, 134
Ringed turtle dove, 101
Ring-necked duck, 21, 29, 88
Ring-necked pheasant, 47, 177
Rio Grande River, 127, 130, 132
Roadrunner, 130, 144
Robin, American, 44, 87, 123, 154, 181
Rock ptarmigan, 182
Rock wren, 137, 138, 175
Rondeau Provincial Park, 13, 14
Roseate spoonbill, 101
Rose-breasted grosbeak, 16, 29, 35
Rose-ringed parakeet, 101
Ross' goose, 183
Ross' gull, 182
Rosy finch, 181
Rough-legged hawk, 42, 52, 117, 122, 123, 176, 182
Royal tern, 85, 97, 109
Ruby-crowned kinglet, 76, 113, 181
Ruby-throated hummingbird, 134
Ruddy duck, 150, 172
Ruddy turnstone, 27, 36, 76, 84, 97, 109
Ruff, 1
Ruffed grouse, 29, 117
Rufous hummingbird, 14

Rufous-sided towhee, 87, 112, 123, 163
Rusty blackbird, 43, 62, 181

Sabal Palm Grove Sanctuary, 126
Sabine's gull, 149
Sacramento, Calif., 154
Sagebrush lizard, 159
Sage grouse, 177
Sage sparrow, 143
Sage thrasher, 14, *161*, 175
Saint John, N.B., 60, 67
St. Lawrence River, 60
Salton Sea, 143, 144
Sanderling, 18, 27, 36, 76, 84-85, 109, 152
San Francisco Bay, 147, 149, 154
San Francisco, Calif., 150
Sandhill crane, 172, *173*
Sandpiper
  Baird's, 27, 76, 86
  least, 27, 85, 86, 155
  pectoral, 27
  purple, 29, 36, 43, 54
  semipalmated, 26, *27*, 76, 85, 86, 174
  solitary, 172
  spotted, 27, 47, 172
  stilt, 27, 150
  upland, 40, 174
  western, 85, 86, 146, 150, 155, 174
  white-rumped, 27, 86
Sandpiper Island, 32, 34
Sandspur, 87
Sandwich tern, 85, 97
Santa Ana National Wildlife Refuge, 132-35
Santa Rosa Island, Fla., 112
Sapsucker
  red-breasted, 159, *161*
  Williamson's, 159
  yellow-bellied, 159
Sasquatch Provincial Park, 124
Savannah sparrow, 38, 180
Saw-whet owl, *10*, 52-53
Say's phoebe, 140, 146, 150, *150*, 175, 181
Scaled quail, 127
Scarlet ibis, 101
Scarlet tanager, 15, 29, 35, 79, 183
Scaup, 29, 122
  greater, 53-55, 68, 84
  lesser, 55, 172
Scissor-tailed flycatcher, 130
Scollard, Norm, 56
Scoter, 35, 54, 122
  white-winged, 29, 52
Screech-owl, eastern, 54
Scrub jay, 148, 151, 154, 157
Seabirds, 61-62. *See also names of individual species*
Sea eagle, Steller's, 146
Seagull, 80

Sea oats, 87, 109
Sea of Slaughter, 71
Seaside sparrow, 107
Semipalmated plover, *33*, 85, 97
Semipalmated sandpiper, 26, *27*,
  76, 85, 86
Sewage settling ponds, as birding
  locales, 47, 48
Sharp-shinned hawk, 16, 42, 76,
  94, 112, 182
Sharp-tailed grouse, 117, 177
Sharp-tailed sparrow, 53
Shearwater, 68, 71, 95
  black-vented, 148
  Buller's, 148
  Cory's, 67
  greater, 67
  pink-footed, 148
  sooty, 67, *78*, 79, 81
Shorebird, 40
Short-billed dowitcher, 27, 76, 92,
  97, 149, 174
Short-eared owl, 42, 52, 122, 176,
  182
Short-tailed hawk, 123
Shortt, Terence M., 2, 180
Shoveler, northern, 55, 134, 172
Shrike, 42
  loggerhead, 100, 141, 155, 169
  northern, 42-43, 52, 120, 181
Siberian tit. *See* Gray-headed
  chickadee
Sibley, John, 100
Sierra Mountains, 156-57
Silent Spring, 2
Skimmer, black, 14, 35-36
Skylark, Eurasian, 146
"Slate-colored" junko, 118
Slaty-backed gull, 146
Smith's longspur, 181
Snail kite, 100
Snake, garter, 31-32, 44
Snake Bight Trail, Fla., 100
Snipe, common, 27, 43, 76, 172
Snow bunting, 42, 52, 54, 68-69,
  86, 117, 180, 184
Snow goose, 174
Snowy egret, 89, 101, 128, 134,
  153, 164
Snowy owl, 42, 54, 117, 182
Solitaire, Townsend's, 14, 120
Solitary sandpiper, 172
Solitary vireo, 183
Song sparrow, *18*, 20, 21, 31, 38,
  57, 112, 118, 123, 149, 158,
  160, 175
Sonoran Desert, 142
Sooty shearwater, 67, *78*, 79, 81
Sora rail, 172
Sparrow
  American tree, 180
  Baird's, 169, 170
  black-throated, 129, *131*, 139
  Brewer's, 175

Cassin's, 14, 130
clay-colored, 175
desert. *See* Sparrow, black-
  throated
fox, 120, 123, 151, 181
golden-crowned, 148
grasshopper, 175
Harris', 181, 183
Henslow's, 15
lark, 156, 175
LeConte's, 53, 174
Lincoln's, 62, 75
sage, 143
Savannah, 38, 175, 180
seaside, 107
sharp-tailed, 53, 175
song, *18*, 20, 21, 31, 38, 57,
  112, 118, 123, 149, 158, 160,
  175
vesper, 175
white-crowned, 38, 123, 136,
  137, 180
white-throated, 20, *21*, 23, 38,
  87, 112, 179
Spectacled eider, 182
Spoonbill, roseate, 101
Spot-breasted oriole, 101
Spotted sandpiper, 27, 47
Sprague's pipit, 147, 175
Squirrel
  fox, 133
  gray, 86, 154
Staging area, 24
Starling, European, 47, 54, 122
Steller's eider, 182
Steller's jay, 120, 124, 149, 152,
  160, 161
Steller's sea eagle, 146
Stellwagen Bank, 79-81
Stilt, 149
  black-necked, 164
Stinkbug, 18
Stints, 86
Stork, 40, 100
  wood, 89, 106, 132
Sulphur-bellied flycatcher, 35
Summerland, B.C., 120
Summer tanager, *12*, 15, 79, 111
Sun-grebe. *See* Finfoot
Sutton, George, M., 1-2, 6
Swainson's hawk, 14, 76, 123, 131,
  155, 176
Swainson's thrush, 38-39, 62
Swallow, 46, 93, 175
  Bahama, 98
  bank, 181
  barn, 128, 155
  cliff, 163, 181
  northern rough-winged, 128
  tree, 89, 112, 160, 181
  violet-green, 124
Swan
  black, 101
  mute, 23, 55

trumpeter, 23
tundra, *17*, 20, 21, 23-24
whistling. *See* Swan, tundra
Swift
  chimney, 46, *46*, 57
  fork-tailed, 146
  white-throated, 119, 156

Tameness in birds, 96
Tanager
  hepatic, 79
  scarlet, 15, 29, 35, 79, 183
  summer, 15, 79, 111
  western, 152, 156, 183
Teal, 44
  blue-winged, *33*, 44, 134, 172
  cinnamon, 14, 133, 168, 172
  green-winged, 77, 123, 172
Telescopes, 135
Tennessee warbler, 87, 152
Tern, 29, 39, 95, 182
  Aleutian, 183
  Arctic, 148
  black, 32, 40, 43, 48, 174
  Caspian, *33*, 85, 97, 109, 144
  common, *33*, 52, *78*, 108, 109,
    144, 174
  Forster's, 44-45, 85, 128, 174
  gull-billed, 110, 143
  least, 108
  royal, 85, 97, 109
  sandwich, 85, 97
  white-winged, 146
Texas, 125-35
Thayer's gull, 47
Thick-billed murre, 14, 69, 182,
  184
Thick-billed vireo, 98
Thickson's Woods, Ont., 45
Thistle, star, 163
Thrasher
  brown, 31, 103, 112, 161, 175
  curve-billed, 127
  long-billed, 135, 161
  sage, 14, 161, 175
Thrush
  dusky, 146
  gray-cheeked, 39, 62
  hermit, 38, 62, 163
  Swainson's, 38-39, 62
  varied, 118, 119, 181
  wood, 29, 57
Titmouse
  bridled, 44
  plain, 150, 155
  tufted, 15, 87, 108, 112, 113
Tit, Siberian, 181
Topography, of birds, 8-9
Toronto Islands, 53-54
Toronto, Ont., 46-57
Towhee
  brown. *See* Towhee, California
  California, 148, 156, 163
  canyon, 148

green-tailed, 158, *159*
rufous-sided, 87, 112, 123, 163
Townsend's solitaire, 14, 120
Townsend's vole, 122
Townsend's warbler, 148
Tree swallow, 89, 112, 160, 181
Tricolored heron, 89, 92, 97, 101,
  102, 134
Tricolored redwing, 164
Trumpeter swan, 23
Tufted titmouse, 15, 87, 108, 112,
  113
Tufts, Robbie, 73
Tundra swan, *17*, 20-21, 23-24
Turkey Point, Ont., 19, 23
Turkey vulture, 46, 100, 103, 112,
  123, 128, 130, 168, 176
Turnstone
  black, 152
  ruddy, 27, 36, 76, 84, 97, 109
Turtle dove, ringed, 101
Twentynine Palms, Calif., 136, 137
Twin Lakes, Calif., 158, 161
Tyrannids, 95
Tyrannulet, 95

Upland sandpiper, 40, 174
Utah Trail, Calif., 137

Vancouver, B.C., 121-22, 123
Varied thrush, 118, 119, 181
Vaseux Lake, 119
Vermilion flycatcher, 79
Vesper sparrow, 175
Violet-green swallow, 124
Vireo, 47
  Bell's, 14
  Philadelphia, 183
  red-eyed, 20, 29, 103, 183
  solitary, 183
  thick-billed, 98
  warbling, 88, 183
  white-eyed, 16, 86-87, 103,
    111, 112, 113
  yellow-throated, 183
Virginia rail, 89, 172
Virginia's warbler, 14
Vole, Townsend's, 122-23
Vulture, 100, 169
  black, 100, 103, 112, 123, 128,
    130, 168, 176
  turkey, 46, 100, 103, 112, 123,
    128, 130, 168, 176

Wader, 40
Wagtail
  black-backed, 146
  gray, 146
  white, 181
  yellow, 181
Warbler, 47, 87
  arctic, 181
  bay-breasted, 38-39, 62, 152
  black and white, 98, 152

Also available from
Key Porter Books
and National Book Network, Inc.

FLIGHT OF THE FALCON
by Michael Tennesen

This beautiful book, which is illustrated
with 120 color photographs and 38 line
drawings, examines the fascinating
history of falcons around the world and
conservation efforts to save them.

144 pages, hardcover,
$29.95 in Canada,
$24.95 in the United States
ISBN 1-55013-285-7

blackburnian, 152
blackpoll, 39, 181
black-throated blue, *15*, 16, 96, 98, 152
black-throated gray, 14, 148
black-throated green, 98
blue-winged, 46-47
Canada, 152
Cape May, 87, 152
chestnut-sided, 38, 152
Connecticut, 87
dusky, 145, 146, 147, 148
hooded, 110, 152
Kentucky, 111, 152
magnolia, 128, 150
Middendorf's, 146
myrtle. *See* Warbler, yellow-rumped
Nashville, 87
northern parula, 98, 103, 152
orange-crowned, 146, 181
palm, 98, 152
pine, 87
prairie, 87, 98, 103
prothonotary, 1, 15, *107*, 109, 152
Tennessee, 89, 152
Townsend's, 148
Virginia's, 14
Wilson's, 39, 158, 181
worm-eating, 152
yellow, 14, 38, 76, 160, 181
yellow-rumped, 76, *76*, 86-87, 113, 181
yellow-throated, 87, 98, 107
Warbling vireo, 88, 183
Water pipit, 148, 180
Waterthrush, northern, 76, 181
Waveland, Miss., 108
Wax myrtle, 87
Waxwing, bohemian, 120, *120*

Western Field Ornithologists, 145, 148, 149
Western grebe, 122, 149
Western gull, 150, 151
Western kingbird, 106, 156, 164, 175
Western meadowlark, 161, 164, 175
Western sandpiper, 85, 86, 146, 150, 155, 174
Western tanager, 152, 156, 183
Western wood-pewee, 156, 159
Westport, N.S., 76
Whale
  beluga, 60, 184
  humpback, 80-82
Whale bird. *See* Phalarope, red
Wheatear, northern, 180
Whimbrel, 35, 152
Whip-poor-will, 3, 29, *37*, 40, 97, 129
Whistling-duck, fulvous, 14
Whistling swan. *See* Swan, tundra
Whitby, Ont., 3, 45
White-breasted nuthatch, 159
White-crowned pigeon, 95, 96, 97, 105
White-crowned sparrow, 38, 123, 136, 137, 180
White-eyed vireo, 16, 87-88, 103, 111, 112, 113
White-faced ibises, 164, 172
White-fronted goose, 14, 174
White-headed woodpecker, 119
White ibis, 14, 89, 96, 97, 101, *104*
White-necked raven. *See* Raven, Chihuahuan
White pelican, American, 45
White-rumped sandpiper, 27, 86
White-tailed hawk, 123

White-tailed kite. *See* Black-shouldered kite
White-throated sparrow, 20, *21*, 23, 38, 87, 112, 179
White-throated swift, 119, 159
White-tipped dove, 133
White wagtail, 181
White-winged crossbill, 62, 181
White-winged scoter, 29, 52
White-winged tern, 146
Whooping crane, 169
Wigeon, 122, 172
  Eurasian, 15, 45
Wild America, 104
Wild turkey, 177
Willet, 84, 97, 101, 109, 149, 150, 152, 172
Williamson's sapsucker, 159
Willow ptarmigan, *166*
Wilson's phalarope, 41, 82, 172
Wilson's warbler, 39, 158, 181
Witless Bay, Nfld., 69-72
Woodcock, American, 24, 29, 35, 40, 43
Wood duck, 44
Woodpecker
  acorn, 130, 156, 157, 163
  black-backed, 62
  downy, 87
  golden-fronted, 125, 130, 132
  hairy, 120
  ladder-backed, 139
  Lewis', 14, 120
  Nuttall's, 155
  pileated, 29, 41, 86, 113, 120
  red-bellied, 14, 86, 88, 100, 112, 113
  red-headed, 15, 35, 54, 130
  white-headed, 119
Wood-pewee, 95
  western, 156, 159

Wood stork, *83*, 89, 106, 132
Wood thrush, 29, 57
Worm-eating warbler, 152
Wren
  Bewick's, 14-15, 150, 163
  cactus, 128, 139, 142
  canyon, 119
  Carolina, 87
  house, 133, 135, 160, 175
  marsh, 32, 155, 174
  rock, 137, 138, 175
Wrentit, 151, *151*, 156, 161, 162
"Wurdemann's" heron, 94, 95

Yellow-bellied flycatcher, 62
Yellow-bellied sapsucker, 159
Yellow-billed cuckoo, 175
Yellow-billed loon, 184
Yellow-billed magpie, 154, *154*, 161
Yellow-breasted chat, 103, 119
Yellow-headed Amazon parrot, 101
Yellow-headed blackbird, 160, 161, 174
Yellowlegs, 164
  greater, 21, 24, 27, 76, 146, 172
  lesser, 27, 172
Yellow rail, 96, 172
Yellow-rumped warbler, 76, *76*, 86-87, 113, 181
"Yellow-shafted" flicker, 119
Yellowthroat, common, *41*, 98, 174
Yellow-throated vireo, 183
Yellow-throated warbler, 87, 98, 107
Yellow wagtail, 181
Yellow warbler, 15, 38, 76, 160, 181
Yellow willow, 150
Yucca moth, 138

Zone-tailed hawk, 123, 132